RELIGION AND BROKEN SOLIDARITIES

CONTENDING MODERNITIES

Series editors: Ebrahim Moosa, Atalia Omer, and Scott Appleby

As a collaboration between the Contending Modernities initiative and the University of Notre Dame Press, the Contending Modernities series seeks, through publications engaging multiple disciplines, to generate new knowledge and greater understanding of the ways in which religious traditions and secular actors encounter and engage each other in the modern world. Books in this series may include monographs, co-authored volumes, and tightly themed edited collections.

The series will include works that frame such encounters through the lens of "modernity." The range of themes treated in the series might include war, peace, human rights, nationalism, refugees and migrants, development practice, pluralism, religious literacy, political theology, ethics, multi- and intercultural dynamics, sexual politics, gender justice, and postcolonial and decolonial studies.

RELIGION AND BROKEN SOLIDARITIES

Feminism, Race, and Transnationalism

Edited by

ATALIA OMER

and

JOSHUA LUPO

University of Notre Dame Press
Notre Dame, Indiana

University of Notre Dame Press
Notre Dame, Indiana 46556
undpress.nd.edu
Copyright © 2022 by the University of Notre Dame

Published in the United States of America

Library of Congress Control Number: 2022945957

ISBN: 978-0-268-20385-6 (Hardback)
ISBN: 978-0-268-20386-3 (Paperback)
ISBN: 978-0-268-20387-0 (WebPDF)
ISBN: 978-0-268-20384-9 (Epub)

CONTENTS

Introduction   1
ATALIA OMER AND JOSHUA LUPO

CHAPTER 1.   Broken Solidarities: Transnational Feminism,
Islam, and "the Master's House"   17
PERIN GÜREL

CHAPTER 2.   The Women's March: A Reflection on Feminist
Solidarity, Intersectional Critique, and Muslim
Women's Activism   51
JULIANE HAMMER

CHAPTER 3.   Transgressive Geography and Litmus Test
Solidarity   87
ATALIA OMER AND RUTH CARMI

CHAPTER 4.   "To Confound White Christians": Thinking
with Claude McKay about Race, Catholic
Enchantment, and Secularism   133
BRENNA MOORE

CHAPTER 5.   Seeing Solidarity   159
MELANI McALISTER

List of Contributors   169
Index   172

Introduction

ATALIA OMER AND JOSHUA LUPO

SETTING THE SCENE

This book reflects one of the many lines of questions and conversations generated by Contending Modernities' interdisciplinary working group focused on expanding inquiry into religion, modernity, and the secular. A few of us met initially in Chicago on June 5–6, 2018, and then again with some additional interlocutors at the University of Notre Dame the following year. Other voices were added along the way to expand the discussion, both geographically and conceptually. This concentrated effort to expand and open up theoretical avenues in the study of religion and modernity signals a turn in Contending Modernities' focus. In its earlier iterations, it focused on collecting empirical evidence to intervene in the study of global migration and cosmopolitanism in various urban centers in the global North. It also focused on illuminating new dimensions in the study of authority, community, and identity in sub-Saharan Africa and Indonesia. We approached these foci in deeply pluralistic and contextualist ways. As such, they brought to the foreground the traumatic experiences that followed from the colonialist intellectual, cultural, religious, and political ideologies of modernity. During these earlier stages, Contending Modernities also examined philosophical and theological accounts of modernity focused on issues in science and bioethics, as well as issues related to how we understand the human person. With our global network, diverse in its disciplinary approach, we now ask: To what degree can the massive scope of this research initiative and our accumulated findings—the labor of many researchers—also speak back to and enrich the sometimes tired and often self-replicating scholarly theoretical conversations on religion and modernity?

To reflect on this question, we invited a group of scholars to participate in a Theory Working Group. While many of these scholars were new to the Contending Modernities research initiative, some were old friends who were willing to pause for a moment to ask fresh questions about the findings generated by their previous research. One of our charges was to think in intersectional ways about "religion" as a modern category of analysis whose very disarticulation from global patterns of racialization and domination constitutes a colonial and myopic conceptual maneuver, one that distracts us from investigating its social and political expressions. This volume, in particular, shows the limits of analyzing "religion" in abstraction from specific nationalist discourses—which are made up of both semiotic and symbolic constraints—and the importance of analyzing religion's constitutive relation to social stratification and racialization as they produce and are reproduced by nationalist discourse. When one "abstracts" religion from these latter contexts, religion's role in demobilizing or mobilizing transnational solidarities focused on a social justice transformative agenda is obscured. Such an intersectional analysis is important for demonstrating the fallacy of the "clash of civilizations" rhetoric as well as ethically troubling forms of transnational coalition building, such as the one that coalesced around the US-led global "war on terror." While the approach taken by the contributors to this volume is no doubt critical, the aim is nonetheless to open up emancipatory possibilities via critique.

The Absent but Present

Religion and Broken Solidarities, one of three volumes that emerged from the working group, traces how modernity's political infrastructures and discourses have contributed to histories of sometimes ephemeral, fragmentary, and often unrealized solidarities. The book highlights especially the role or lack of a role of religious discourse in those ephemeral, fragmentary, and unrealized moments. If another volume in this series, *Religion, Populism, and Modernity: Confronting White Christian Nationalism and Racism* (forthcoming) traces the co-constitutive nature of religion, nationalism, and race, this volume traces how varying groups and individuals have tried and have struggled to move beyond them. The contributors also identify where national boundaries operate myopically to block people's capacity to see how their struggles are interlinked. For example, as Perin Gürel demonstrates in her analysis of an episode of what she calls a "broken" South-South transnational solidarity between Muslim women in Turkey and Iran, it is those structures and ideological discursive formations associated with secular modernity (in this case liberal thought) and not "religion" (as some might expect) that often deflate and demobilize transnational solidarity. The "west," even though physically absent, is still the ideological culprit (via political liberalism) preventing enhanced and productive Muslim-Muslim transnational (feminist) links. In relation to her case study, Gürel writes, "Muslim women's transnational political activism was curtailed by the very rationale of liberal thought and its attendant constructions, including choice, democracy, and human rights." Gürel scrutinizes the highly publicized case of Merve Kavakçi, an elected representative of a reformist Islamist party in Turkey, who, in 1999, was attacked by members of the laïc establishment for wearing a head covering in Parliament. Even when faced with this overt secularist denial and repression of her religious piety, Kavakçi, however, refused visible and tangible expressions of solidarity from Iranian Muslim women. Gürel, therefore, concludes that the culprits of this missed opportunity to form transnational Muslim-Muslim solidarity are the specific configurations and histories of state control of religion and religious agency—including the agency of Muslim women—which in turn have been shaped by secular and religious political settlements. Orientalist tropes depicting the wearing of the headscarf as a supposedly slippery slope that would turn Istanbul into Tehran circulated and filled Turkey's public discourse and led Kavakçi to refuse the calls of support from Iranian women.

Gürel shows that even in the absence of White feminists—and their colonialist and paternalistic concerns with benevolence—their secular hegemonic vision of how progress and emancipation should look is still present, lurking in the background. By dissecting the misfires of South-South solidarity, she also illuminates the missing dimensions necessary for transnational feminist theories to overcome the obstacles to North-South

solidarity. In particular, Gürel highlights how the very discursive formations of the west, which in addition to being present in the European
Court of Human Rights' support of the Turkish ban on veiling, are also
visible in the modernist and secularist structures that shape the political
and social contexts in which the Turkish representative declined the
"Iranian sisters'" call to solidarity. The focus on broken or unrealized
transnational Turkish-Iranian solidarity brings into sharp relief, therefore,
the role of the institutions and social mechanisms of the nation-state in
shaping and reconfiguring modern religion. Religion here is understood
as being co-constituted along national lines. Absent is an essentialist and/
or universalist approach to theorizing religion as apolitical, both of which
have historically been implicated in colonialist practices. While such an
approach is on the wane in the academic study of religion, its influence
can still be seen in political discourse, especially in the international
humanitarian sphere.[1] Gürel's chapter reminds us again why such an
approach must be abandoned if we are to understand the complexity of
instances of fragmented solidarity, as well as the lessons they offer for
building emancipatory political coalitions in the future. At stake in the
missed opportunity Gürel describes is not only the issue of the women's
different nationalities but also their national locations, which point to
distinct political arrangements of religion and female religious agency
and expression. In other words, the women's common Muslimness did
not enhance their feminist "sisterhood." For Gürel, the modern nation-
state, as an elastic site of contentions embedded in a broader international
matrix of power and ideological domination, inhibited the possibility of
transnational solidarity where it would otherwise have been possible and
perhaps fruitful and empowering. By pointing to these limits, Gürel helps
us imagine empowering possibilities beyond them. Melani McAlister's
concluding meditation in this volume on justice-oriented and inclusive
solidarity as a form of seeing through the boundaries that separate us from
one another captures why we need to interrogate religion's modernist legacy,
especially when it comes to its role in constructing and buttressing com-
munal and political walls. This is no easy task, as McAlister admits, for
these boundaries are held together by attachments that make it challenging
to see one another as interconnected. And yet by engaging in critique, we
make possible new attachments that allow us to build relationships differently, more capaciously perhaps, than before.

SYMBOLIC MINEFIELDS

In a different location, Israel—a society that describes itself through an orientalist trope as a "villa in the jungle"—Atalia Omer and Ruth Carmi examine the margins where Mizrahi, Ethiopian, and other non-normative Israelis reside. Women and other people inhabiting these margins are so embedded in a Jewish supremacist and ethnocratic nationalist discourse that, like the Turkish representative Gürel analyzes, they are unable to participate in and realize an intersectional vision of emancipation that transcends national boundaries. In this context, what is more challenging is the fact that even within Israeli society intersectional visions of solidarity are difficult to articulate. Omer and Carmi show that solidarity activism is beholden to binary metaphorical constructions of Israel as the representation of White settler colonialism and Palestine as the representation of (and/or a metaphor for) the liberation of all oppressed people. As a result, any openings for South-South solidarity between marginalized communities in the broader geographies of anticolonial resistance and the slums and peripheries of "White" Israel are made impossible. At the same time, because their entry into Israel's civic society and thus into political belonging is structured by mechanisms of stratification, socialization, and Eurocentricity, Arab Jews are incentivized to underscore their Jewish identity over and against their Arab or broadly Middle Eastern roots. This self-alienation is part of a political ethos that is underpinned by Eurocentric assumptions, and it is an expression of political identity shaped by a modernist ethos. This case thus presses on us once again the relevance of analyzing religion and modernity in reference to unrealized solidarities. This time the "rule" of such a failure is exemplified in locations where individual activists disrupt the operative forces of Euro-Jewish supremacy as it is inscribed in the project of Israelism.

While Gürel illuminates how nationalism and the politics of liberalism manifest in the state's control of expressions of religiosity, and consequently preclude South-South solidarity formation among Iranian and Turkish women, Omer and Carmi analyze how nationalism has precluded South-South solidarity between Mizrahi feminists and other "Third World" struggles (including the Palestinian one). The possibility of Mizrahi-Palestinian solidarity has only been imagined through a fragmentary prism by a few feminists and activists working at the margins of Israeli society who are able to see through the cracks in the walls of division and imagine alternative futures. In both instances—an unimaginable coalition of marginalized Israelis and "Third World" transnational struggles and an unrealized solidarity between Iranian and Turkish women—what comes to the foreground is the role of national ideology in erecting barriers to forming solidarity movements. In the case of Israel, the causes of the inability of international activists who stand in solidarity with Palestinians to imagine solidarity with marginalized Jews whose marginalization can be traced to the same Euro-Zionist hegemonic system (the "master's house") are obvious. This is because, on the one hand, the cause of Palestine has a long history in Black internationalism and other transnational social justice movement spaces and, on the other, Zionism is associated with the forces of (settler) colonialism. Conversely, and through a binary lens, the cause of Israel, regardless of the internal variations on Israeli identity embodied by non-normative Israelis, is assimilated in the minds of Palestinian activists into the White settler colonial and "civilizational" enemy against which global and intersectional social justice organizing should mobilize. Non-normative Israeli Jews seem stuck inside the cage that Euro-Zionism has constructed for them. Within the symbolic, semiotic, and discursive maps of solidarity, there is no room for nuance. Participation in social justice movement circles requires a certain kind of "purity test" that often metaphorically connects to support for a "free Palestine." Ironically, the refusal to form alliances and express solidarity with marginalized Black and Brown communities in Israel reveals how Europe or the "master's house" continues to dominate ideologically, even with regard to how activists and scholars imagine solidarity. In Israel, Europe persists as an ideology via its legacies of political liberalism, orientalism, antisemitism, and exclusionary nationalisms. It is perhaps unsurprising that it is a state whose conditions of formation germinated in Europe and were enabled by its colonial, fascistic, and antisemitic legacies.[2] Even among those activists who imagine themselves as "radical," it seems, solidarity is still understood from within a colonial framework.[3] They are unable to see beyond the walls that divide them from their potential allies. Such seeing, as McAlister demonstrates, is key if such walls are to be demolished and out of the rubble realizable forms of co-resistance and solidarity are to be built.

As previously noted, the case of Iran-Turkey also points to the absence/presence of Europe. Once again, the absence of Europe, as in the Turkish discourse surrounding the veil, is illusionary. It thus likewise shows that what is needed are more concrete and historical understandings of particular settings and the respective negotiations of women's rights vis-à-vis political and ideological frameworks. What is less necessary in these cases are abstract and metaphorical tools. From Turkish *laïcité* to the Iranian Velayat-e Faqih, the bodies of women are policed, and their policing is an expression of modes of imagining national belonging and nonbelonging. Beyond the important focus on the dynamics of nationalism and their contestations of the boundaries of religious and political belongings, both these cases also demonstrate the importance of inquiry into the origins of nationalist discourses. For, as we have seen, whether it is interreligious, intrareligious, or ethnic solidarity that is sought, nationalist discourse is likely to play an important role in limiting or promoting its success. Further scrutiny would invite an archaeological account of the enduring colonial legacies that have underpinned the development of modern Israel, Turkey, and Iran. Such an account would allow us to better understand how nationalist discourse functions in these contexts.

If Gürel and Omer and Carmi highlight the discursive force of western modernity/coloniality in the Middle East, Juliane Hammer takes us back to the heart of the empire and its politics of diversity, intersectionality, and multiculturalism. Her focus is on the emboldened and augmenting phenomenon of exclusionary and chauvinistic White (Christian) nationalism and the constraints this nationalism placed on the intersectional scope of the 2017 Women's March. The Women's March in Washington, DC, was the largest protest ever in the US and took place in the aftermath of the 2016 election to the presidency of Donald Trump, who ran on a platform that promised and then implemented hateful policies against multiple vulnerable communities. Hammer highlights not only the methodological nationalism of feminist mobilization that took place in light of Trump's coming to power but also the discursive and semiotic lines that prohibited a deepening of the intersectional impulse that produced the unprecedented event of the march. The story she tells, therefore, is also a story about one instance of a fragmentary yet unrealized solidarity. Hence, it is a story worth scrutinizing so as to be able to more clearly identify and articulate semiotic and discursive obstacles that stand in the way of a sustained, rather than ephemeral and fragmentary, broad coalitional social movement focused on social justice and emancipatory politics. Hammer's story is not a story of failure but of hopeful struggle toward emancipatory and coalitional pathways.

Hammer's contribution, in particular, exposes the uneasy place of religion and specifically Islam within intersectional mobilizations across race, class, and gender axes. She uniquely highlights where feminist intersectional theory can expand and unsettle modernist/secularist narratives of progress concerning women's self-determination and emancipation from the shackles of religious traditions. Intersectional theory is not without its own shortcomings, however. As Hammer shows, intersectional feminist thought also has drawbacks when it comes to identifying religion's potential emancipatory features. She traces how Linda Sarsour's Muslimness in particular could not be domesticated into the ideology of the White "feminist" critics of the Women's March and the movement that followed. From the orientalist and racialized account of visibly Muslim women such as Sarsour to the association of Tamika Mallory with the Nation of Islam and the explicitly antisemitic rhetoric attributed to Louis Farrakhan, Hammer surmises that the "religion problem" of intersectionality is a problem with a marked religion, namely, Islam. She demonstrates with ample evidence that Christian religiosity—so long as it generates spiritual ambience and motivation (and occasionally protest repertoire, or tools to mobilize) for social justice causes has not received the same vicious criticism and been subject to the kind of patronizing discourse that Muslim religiosity has. Intersectionality, and with it emancipatory political discourse, has indeed an uneasy relation with religion that may expose the traces of a Marxist critique of religion as a form of false consciousness and also of a Foucauldian-inspired power reductionist account of both oppression and liberation.

Rather than label it a failed instance of solidarity, Hammer's analysis of the controversy and contentions that rattled the leadership of the Women's March over real, perceived, and weaponized antisemitism offers an opportunity to expand and reexamine the meaning and scope of intersectional solidarity. Accordingly, she wants to ask why the Women's March, an event that took place at a specific moment in time, did not realize itself in a more fully and robustly sustained emancipatory movement. The outcome of the US presidential election of 2016 galvanized at least initially an apparently intersectional coalescing of oppositional voices. What controversies within the movement reveal, however, is the degree to which religion is not yet another variable to add on to an "intersection" already populated by race, gender, class, and so on, but how it too is raced, gendered, nationalized, and classed. Disentangling religion and religiosity from an analysis of race, class, gender, sex, and so forth constitutes one of the ongoing maneuvers of modernist discourse, a discourse that seeks to neatly divide members of different "races," classes, and religious orientations in order to manage and suppress any challenge to the status quo. This sequestering constrains potentially emancipatory possibilities. Not only does "religion" appear as an obstacle for solidarity, but so does nationalism, if we understand the latter to be always constituted and reproduced through selective retrievals of ethnoreligious and cultural conceptions of belonging. Religion also manifests itself differently in different occurrences of unrealized solidarity. Hammer's analysis traces the case of the Women's March, which was initially very effective but lost some of its power because of the symbolic force of accusations of antisemitism. Such accusations are part of a discursive landscape that equates Israeli with Jewish identity and further binarizes Jews and Arabs while assimilating Palestinians into this latter category of belonging. Here we can see precisely how, in spite of their different geographic locations, Omer and Carmi's case study connects with Hammer's. As in Omer and Carmi's account, in this case belligerent forms of nationalism, specifically Jewish Israeli nationalism, block the imaginations of those who might otherwise stand in solidarity with one another.

Not only does a person's or group's actual belonging to Israel prevent the possibility of forming alliances between Jewish Israeli marginalized communities and others engaged in struggle. In addition, Israel and Palestine, or the Palestinian struggle, also become symbolic tools to demobilize the formation of intersectional solidarity in the United States. If it is not through weaponizing antisemitism (or accusing people of antisemitism to dismiss their criticism of Israel or their aspirations for the freedom of Palestinians), then it is through the silencing and demobilization that happens when accusations of pinkwashing are made. This semiotic and symbolic landscape is fraught and demands interrogation. Demobilization resulting from concrete or symbolic roadblocks is not inevitable, and thus identifying how it operates clarifies emancipatory pathways for building coalitions that are more robust. Hammer, accordingly, underscores that "intersectional solidarity and feminist critique are simultaneously challenged by the focus on antisemitism and that the specter of Israel, Zionism, and Judaism and their relationship to each other is often (a deeply feared) elephant in the room of solidarity and critique." Indeed, Israel/Palestine has become a take it or break it card where analyzing nuances and creating spaces for strategic political maneuvering and un/learning are not easily allowed or facilitated. For example, one Jewish Israeli Ethiopian activist told Omer that when invited to speak to various Black organizing circles in the United States, she was asked if she supported BDS (Boycott, Divestment, and Sanctions) campaigns directed against Israeli policies, a point she felt uncomfortable about and understood as a conversation stopper before a conversation had even begun. Her leadership in a struggle against police brutality targeting Ethiopian Israeli Jews—a struggle with clear intersectional links to military brutality against Palestinians and Black Americans' resistance to police brutality (and the militarization of police forces)—is accepted as an entry ticket to a transnational conversation only so long as she brackets her rootedness in a Jewish nationalist discourse and piety. Beyond the automatic excommunication of potential allies from Israeli peripheries, the discursive minefield of the politics of antisemitism in the United States comes through in the story of the Women's March that Hammer tells. In Sarsour's case, her very being as a Palestinian American who openly connects the fight against White supremacy in the United States to the fight against Israeli oppression of Palestinians leads to accusations of antisemitism. This is because in this context—where the Working Definition of antisemitism produced by the International Holocaust Remembrance Alliance is often employed—all criticisms of Israel are considered antisemitic and thus illegitimate. The accusation of antisemitism leveled against Mallory, however, is more difficult to tackle because of her links to the Nation of Islam and episodes where she amplified the voice of some explicitly antisemitic leaders. That the Women's March movement's capacity to act intersectionally found itself in such explosive discursive terrain points to the need to centralize an analysis of religion and modernity. It is imperative to trace how modern constructions of religion play out in nationalist and internationalist discourses, as well as in the symbolic politics that shape and demobilize the ability of antiracist and feminist solidarities to consolidate and gain momentum.

Hammer's discussion of the internal disputes and controversies that the leadership of the Women's March generated as they underwent a process of routinizing their initial charisma into a "sustainable" organization, as in Omer and Carmi's analysis, reveals the semiotic and discursive obstacles that Palestine/Israel imposes on global social justice activism and coalition-building efforts. Such obstacles, unfortunately, have more to do with the agenda of those weaponizing each cause than with the actual people inhabiting Palestine/Israel and their aspirations and realities. Hence, reading Hammer's analysis together with Omer and Carmi's discussion of the blocked possibilities for South-South solidarity between Mizrahi and Ethiopian Jewish Israelis and other marginalized communities around the world demonstrates not only nationalist obstacles for solidarity mobilization but also discursive traps, such as the weaponization of antisemitism, that repeatedly silence, police, and demobilize the possibilities of broad and cross-cutting coalition building.

SEEING WITH CLARITY

Writing about an entirely different historical moment in the early to mid-twentieth century, Brenna Moore highlights an international community of Black Catholic writers, artists, and other activists whose friendship and solidarity with one another transcended their national locations and traveled across the Francophone world. Even though their solidarity was exemplary, she shows, it remained ephemeral and did not translate into a transformative social movement. Nonetheless, the capacity to transcend national boundaries resonates with the sites of transgressive geography that Omer and Carmi identify in their profiling of a few Jewish Israeli cultural loci where activists are reimagining their identities' relation to space and region. Like Gürel's case study, the historical moment about which Moore is writing offers a glimpse into what may enable or disempower Muslim-Muslim or Catholic-Catholic transnational solidarity. In the one case, what demobilized the opening for a transnational moment of solidarity was the politics of secularism in Turkey. In Moore's case, what undergirded the moment of Black Catholic internationalism was a cross-cutting analysis of race and racialization. Here was an ability of people populating a countercultural space to see with clarity the anatomy of modernity and its logic of division and (de)valuation. Often nationalist discourses, as McAlister also notes, obscure such analytic clarity. Indeed, the boundaries of the "nation," which are constituted by subjective lines that are distinct from geopolitical borders, often constitute the outer limits of the visible field of solidarity. Moore's analysis suggests that what enabled this boundary-breaking clarity of vision and the countercultural critique of modernity was an enchanted religiosity (Catholicity) rather than a secularist teleology of disenchantment. This intervention challenges and puts into sharp relief intersectionality's religion problem, or what we might also identify as the persistence of the Marxist critique of religion as a form of false consciousness in many analytical frameworks committed to solidarity. Moore's study shows the coexistence of nonfeminist religiosity and antiracism in one anti-imperialist site of counter-culturality.

If Hammer focuses on a context where Sarsour's Muslim Palestinian identity marked her as a target ultimately responsible for fragmenting soli- darity, Moore's story is one in which solidarity was always more ephemeral than fragmented. Thus far we have examined one case of fragmentary solidarity where Muslim women supposedly threatened the stability of an intersectional coalition otherwise focused on fighting the threats of an expli- citly White nationalist regime. We also examined another case of unrealized solidarity that showed that what was at stake was not only the claim that there is such a thing as Muslim feminism and feminist or female Muslim agency but also the demand for an in-depth and historically nonreductive analysis of Muslim feminisms and Muslim agency within these particular women's nationalist discursive specificity. This helped us see the misfire of South-South solidarity among Muslim women. The moment of ephemeral solidarity captured by Moore shows how Francophone Black Catholicism constituted the core for a small international network of actors influenced by Marxist critical thinking and anti-imperialist currents in the early to mid-twentieth century. The success of these actors, even if small, springs from their analysis of race in tandem with an enchanted Catholic piety. They drew on this piety in their penetrating critique of modernity. "For this small, transnational counter-culture of writers, activists, and artists," Moore writes, "Roman Catholicism was key in their efforts to forge interracial and international affiliations that could counter the rise of nationalism, European imperialism, and White bigotry."

While the other forms of unrealized (Gürel), unimaginable (Omer and Carmi), and fragmentary but potentially emancipatory (Hammer) solidari- ties engaged in our book illuminate the symbolic, discursive, and political operation of nationalism, the Black Catholic counterculture Moore describes consolidated precisely because its key interlocutors saw through the anatomy of these divisions. They practiced this form of seeing in their critique of modernity and secularity. Their cross-cutting analysis of race and racial- ization, however, did not necessarily also include a feminist and gendered analysis. Instead it relied on mystical appeals to Catholic enchantment that did not question authorized gendered hierarchies.

This counterculture of Black Catholics, who were participating in what Josef Sorett calls the "Afro-Catholic moment,"[4] Moore explains, stands in stark contrast to Catholicism's history of enshrining and reifying racialized and colonial differences. Of course, their location within a counterculture may be what is important here. An intersectional conception of solidarity seeks to mobilize political action of "power with" among different groups so that they can act transformatively in the sociopolitical and cultural spheres and subvert the dynamics of "power over." This is a different position to take from one that would remain in a countercultural location where critique amounts to mystical virtuosity. This virtuosity is not easily accessible and translatable into broad-based social movement coalition work. Moore highlights the case of this counterculture associated with the Harlem Renaissance as an example of mystical enchantment. The case conveys a particular account of Black Catholic experiences that constitute the ground from which anti-imperial and antiracist critique emerges. This is notably rather different from an approach that would draw on some disenchanted "secular" set of principles and values. Moore's account of enchantment therefore sheds light once again on intersectionality's religion problem, one that Hammer also highlights in her account of the Women's March and the key personalities that were initially at its helm.

MEDITATIONS ON UNREALIZED, UNIMAGINABLE, FRAGMENTARY, AND EPHEMERAL SOLIDARITIES

By no means a comprehensive account of the theoretical and empirical complexity of social, political, cultural, and religious solidarity, these meditations are an attempt to expose sites where the imaginative pathways for transnational and intersectional solidarities get interrupted by secularist, nationalist, semiotic, and discursive roadblocks and checkpoints. Such obstacles reveal modernity's persistent colonization of political and religious imaginations. While each chapter does not tackle the question of modernity directly, modernity is a central background framework for the volume as a whole. As such, each chapter helps us reimagine how to confront the problems wrought by modernity. The chapters combined invite a more capacious account of religious and feminist agency. They also make space for accounts of the religious, political, and ideological constructions in which intersectional solidarity movements mobilize. We show that such sites tell stories not only about ideological and symbolic roadblocks and misfires but also about what could have been but never materialized at the level of cross-cutting sociopolitical movements. We also show how such instances reflect back on our theoretical understanding of religion and modernity. The case studies, each in different ways, expose "religion" as a historically contextualized site of analysis that cannot be extracted from its embodied manifestations. To this extent, we underscore the need to think about religion intersectionally, and to think intersectionally with religion. Each case reveals its own colonial history, exploitative dynamics, and experiences of marginality. Each case also refuses reductive accounts of such experiences.

Our diverse historical and contemporary case studies from Iran and Turkey, Palestine/Israel, the Women's March of 2017, and the Harlem Renaissance point to the transnationalist critique of racialization and solidarity as pivotal for the analysis of modernity's political, social, cultural and religious formations, including their intersections and divergences. Of course, the concept of solidarity itself is ethically neutral. It can denote a coalition of violent and White supremacist interests just as much as a coalition of marginal communities seeking to transform their conditions of oppression and marginality. In this volume, however, we are interested in exploring potential intersectional coalitions and networks of solidarity intent on enhancing emancipatory aspirations and social justice objectives. We also underscore that the inability of South-South and intersectional solidarities to form robustly in the North constitutes different modernist plotlines. Here are stories of religion and ideology (secularist, theocratic, and multiculturalist) that reveal a persistent feminist suspicion of religious traditions and their clear historical underpinnings in heteropatriarchal norms and institutions.

Given the centrality of intersectional analysis to this volume, we would be remiss if we did not identify our own positionalities in this introduction's conclusion. Lupo is a heterosexual, cisgender, White male, who was raised in the United Methodist Church but is no longer practicing. Omer is an Ashkenazi, cisgender, Israeli Jewish scholar working in an American Catholic university. Both authors write with an ethical and political commitment to human rights–oriented forms of solidarity and resistance to matrices of oppression. They both aim to do so in a way that takes critical genealogical approaches to the study of religion as necessary but not sufficient for such reimagining.

As Gürel points out in her contribution, a focus on broken solidarities is not particularly novel within feminist scholarship, which has long challenged vague, paternalistic, and universalizing appeals to "sisterhood" as a foundation of solidarity across borders and identity boundaries. This scholarly intervention underpins Third World and African American intersectional interventions that expose and reject abstract claims to universal women's experiences that ignore or myopically conceal their colonial subjectivity, racialized bodies, and class marginality. To this important intervention, we add a focus on nationalist discourses, including various manifestations of secularist political formations as well as semiotic underpinnings such as the operation of antisemitism, Israel, and Palestine in international and transnational channels of solidarity. By bringing these distinct yet interrelated case studies of unimaginable, fragmentary, ephemeral, and unrealized forms of solidarity into conversation, our hope is to reveal not only the critical possibilities that show themselves when we think nation, race, and gender together but also the emancipatory possibilities that might be imagined beyond them.

NOTES

1. For a relevant engagement with these themes, see, e.g., Cecelia Lynch, *Wrestling with God: Ethical Precarity in Christianity and International Relations* (Cambridge: Cambridge University Press, 2020); Atalia Omer, *Decolonizing Religion and Peacebuilding* (forthcoming).

2. See also Atalia Omer, "Decentering Europe: Thinking Beyond 'Parting Ways' and Jewish-Arab Nostalgia," *Journal of Middle Eastern Politics and Policy* (Spring 2021): 72–78.

3. See Santiago Slabodsky, "Not Every Radical Philosophy Is Decolonial," Contending Modernities, June 4, 2020, https://contendingmodernities.nd.edu/decoloniality/not-every-radical-philosophy-is-decolonial/.

4. Joseph Sorett, *Spirit in the Dark: A Religious History of Racial Aesthetics* (Oxford: Oxford University Press, 2016), 85.

CHAPTER 1

Broken Solidarities

Transnational Feminism, Islam, and "the Master's House"

PERIN GÜREL

ABSTRACT

A central focus of transnational feminist scholarship has been the critical investigation of failures of solidarity across differences of race, religion, and nation in order to fix future praxis. Much of this work assumes a psychological/strategic "foil" model, demonstrating how subjects lacking belonging in nationalist, White supremacist patriarchies often claim their membership rights by othering subjects whose intersectional positioning makes them even more marginal to the nation-state. While most of this research focuses on breaking points in solidarity between White and non-White and western and Third World feminists, this essay examines a moment of missed solidarity that took place between Turkish and Iranian Muslim women activists who sought to expand Muslim women's participation in the political sphere and reform repressive clothing codes in the late 1990s. The research shows how discursive and structural blocks at the individual, national, and international levels overlapped to foreclose solidarity in this case, despite the similarities in the activists' goals. In this instance, the ruling Turkish govern-ment, which upheld a form of secularism (laïcism) that promoted a state-approved version of Sunni Islam, was supported by western institutions, such as the European Court of Human Rights, which presumed an essential opposition between Islam, democracy, and women's rights. This essay contributes to the literature on religion, modernity, and feminist solidarity by discussing how when devout Muslim women mobilize the liberal rhetoric of "choice" and "rights," their political agency is often constrained by the inherent exclusions and contradictions of liberalism. Responding to recent critiques of the dominant anti-imperialist bend in transnational feminist scholarship, the chapter argues for a multilevel analysis, following intersecting lines of power upward toward the most powerful entities and individuals in any conflict.

In 1981, the queer Black feminist poet and scholar Audre Lorde gave her important speech, "The Master's Tools Will Not Dismantle the Master's House," warning against the use of racism and other oppressive ideologies, such as classism and heterosexism, in the mainstream feminist movement. Published in 1984 in her vital collection of essays, *Sister/Outsider*, the text powerfully transformed many academic fields and political struggles.[1] Femi-nists examining the transnational manifestations of gender injustice, for example, have taken Lorde's dictum as a central principle, criticizing the imperialist uses of feminism in an era of endless wars on "terror." Commonly referred to as transnational feminists, these scholars have presented us with a host of characters who embody the drama of broken solidarities across lines of race, religion, and nation: White women "saving" Brown women from Brown men, White dancers "saving" Middle Eastern dance from Middle Eastern patriarchy, "feminist" drone operators, empowered "security moms," and tough female CIA agents.[2] Postcolonial queer studies has also given us critical concepts, such as "homonationalism" and "pinkwashing," that demonstrate how nonheterosexual subjects can be participants and symbolic agents in imperial ventures as well.[3] These cases have nuanced the close connection transnational feminist scholars identified between nationalism, "compulsory heterosexuality," and "rigidly dichotomized gender roles" in the wake of 9/11.[4] They have also demonstrated how groups facing marginalization due to at least one structure under heterosexist, patriarchal, capitalist imperialism may choose to highlight a foil (usually a racialized subject) as beyond the pale of the nation/civilization in order to claim cultural citizenship in a body politic from which they risk exclusion. Yet is it just a historical coincidence that the subject who is so often "othered" in this way by western liberal feminisms and LGBT movements happens to be Muslim?

"Transnational feminism" denotes both reality and aspiration. Studying movements and advocacy across nation-state boundaries, we seek a specific type of praxis: powerful and impactful solidarities that transcend the nation. However, since most transnational feminist research focuses on breaking points in solidarity between Third World and western feminists, it is difficult to distinguish the roles religion, the nation-state, and competing versions of modernity can play in bilateral Muslim-majority contexts.[5] In this essay, after reviewing how transnational feminist scholarship has historically approached the issue of cross-national solidarity, I turn to a case of unrealized solidarity between Turkish and Iranian Islamic women's activists at the turn of the twentieth century. I demonstrate how, in this instance, the type of transnational feminist Islamic solidarity Iranian activists sought was precluded not just by the Turkish Muslim woman activist they approached and the laïcist Turkish state but also by the vision of liberal secular modernity promulgated by western entities such as the European Court of Human Rights (ECHR) and the Clinton administration. I argue that, once the critique is carried to this level, an individualist psychological/strategic "foil" model fails to explain the problem of transnational feminist solidarity where Muslim women are concerned. Instead, solidarity was made impossible because devout Muslim women's transnational political activism was curtailed by the very rationale of liberal thought and its attendant constructions, including choice, democracy, and human rights.

Over two decades ago, the American philosopher Richard Rorty famously argued that religion functions as a "conversation-stopper" in public political discussions.[6] Rorty's argument focused on divisions within Christianity and did not engage with the issue of gendered religious practices. Yet Muslim women's public practices of piety often operate to not simply "stop" the conversation, but "break" it, folding the logic of liberalism onto itself, highlighting its contradictions and built-in exclusions. Given these facts, this essay argues for continuing to place exponential emphasis on western imperialism in its interlinked discursive, economic, and martial manifestations in transnational feminist scholarship and activism, despite recent arguments that this approach privileges one line of critique at the expense of others more germane to understanding gendered violence and oppression in Muslim-majority contexts.[7] Feminist anti-imperialism, however, must be structural and follow the lines of power to their highest point rather than focus inordinately on individual, low-power actors who may willingly or unwittingly further imperialist discourses. Otherwise, in our necessary dedication to critiquing aspiring allies who use "the master's tools" in attempts to "dismantle the master's house," as Audre Lorde warned, we might risk leaving "the master's house" undertheorized. Examining the role Islam, and specifically devout Muslim women's political agency, can play in highlighting the structural faults of that house must be an essential part of the transnational feminist project.

Transnational Feminism as a Critique of Broken Solidarities

A normative commitment to solidarity underlines feminism as "a movement to end sexist oppression."[8] Historians of feminism thus appear to keep time in a self-flagellating fashion by counting the breaking of "waves" and the splintering of "feminisms," marked by feminists' failures to form solidarity in the face of the complexities of identity, strategy, and context. Transnational feminism emerged out of one such break. As Jennifer C. Nash demonstrates in *Black Feminism Reimagined*, in the 1980s and 1990s the search for a corrective to a liberal White western feminism that privileged "sex" over other social formations led to the simultaneous rise of two analytics that have been read as separate (and sometimes even competing) frames: "intersectionality" and "transnational feminism."[9] However, feminists taking these approaches articulated shared concerns between western-based feminists of color and Third World feminists at a time when the White-dominated second-wave feminist movement had begun theorizing a worldwide patriarchy and advocating for a "global sisterhood" to counter it. According to the global sisterhood model, differences in women's experience of oppression overall paralleled each other: women everywhere were assaulted by "patriarchy," which simply took on different forms and intensities. Instead of this simplified vision, many non-White and nonwestern feminist scholars and activists advocated for a feminist struggle mobilized around the realities of women's differential social and economic positioning and sought to counter oppression along multiple axes of power.

Coined by Black feminist legal scholar Kimberlé Crenshaw, "intersectionality" emerged out of critical race theory to mobilize advocacy that was attentive to the unique oppressions generated by overlapping and co-constituting structures (especially, but not exclusively, race, gender, and class).[10] With somewhat different disciplinary commitments, transnational feminism formed at the intersection of postcolonial and poststructuralist feminist scholarship and came of age through a series of landmark edited volumes focused on women in the global South.[11] Since their earliest conceptualization, both analytics had a shared emphasis on highlighting and countering "interlocking oppressions."[12] Early theorists and practitioners did not always distinguish between the two movements. Members of the groundbreaking Combahee River Collective, for example, identified as "Third World Women," using a term of political solidarity that later came to be associated with transnational feminism alone.[13]

For its founding theorists, Third World (and later transnational) feminism necessitated a struggle on at least two fronts: the need to highlight the differential impact of racialized political, economic, and cultural imperialisms on women across the global South and in the diaspora; and the need to counter patronizing representations of Third World women. Thus, transnational feminism emerged out of "*feminist* critiques of the western model of sisterhood in the global context."[14] "The Women's Agenda" prioritized by western feminists in tandem with the declaration of the first UN Decade of Women (1975–85) had dismissed Third World Women's materialist, anti-imperialist critiques of patriarchy as too "political." A 1976 open letter from Nawal El Saadawi from Egypt, Fatima Mernissi from Morocco, and Mallica Varajton from Thailand forcefully articulated this divide.[15] In her 1979 "Open Letter to Mary Daly," Audre Lorde spoke out against the erasure of archetypes of "noneuropean female strength and power" in White-dominated radical feminism.[16] Five years later, Chandra Talpade Mohanty examined how the "women in development" approach had turned non-White, nonwestern women into a trope for "oppression" that highlighted the supposed liberation of the White western female self.[17] A few other milestones remain helpful in marking transnational feminism's roots in epistemologies of decoloniza-tion: Gloria Anzaldúa's *Borderlands/La Frontera*, Uma Narayan's revision of feminist standpoint theory, and Amrita Basu's critique of *Sisterhood Is Global*.[18] This commitment to highlighting how gender intersects with other social structures was institutionalized during the 1995 international women's conference in Beijing, as US-based women of color and women's activists from the global South forged coalitions and crafted resolutions on the need to address "multiple discriminations."[19] In the new century, scholars have expanded the terms of the critique to consider sexuality and sexual identities more robustly, emphasizing the transnational formation of modern LGBTQI identities and critiquing the liberal politics of international rights advocacy.[20]

In its contemporary form, transnational feminist scholarship interrogates the impact of the global capitalist political economy, imperialist wars, and extremist religious movements from an intersectional feminist perspective. Analyzing "transnationalism from above" and "transnationalism from below," it investigates the connection between "local organizing and global economic restructuring."[21] Its main goals have been to highlight and empower Third World women and queer activists in response to international and global challenges by forming transnational networks and allowing for knowledge sharing across national divides. In addition, "transnational feminist cultural studies" transcends a focus on feminist organizing to problematize the nation-state and nationalism as constructions aligned with modern styles of patriarchal racism. Academics taking this approach foreground issues of representation alongside the "scattered hegemonies" produced under global capitalism and practices of imperialism.[22]

Transnational feminist scholarship regarding Muslim-majority contexts has taken various forms that reflect these multivalent concerns. Scholars have shown how the tropes of "the oppressed Muslim woman," "the veil," and the need to "reform" Islam have been used to bolster western imperial ventures. They have also examined the history and activities of Muslim women's transnational networks, such as Musawah and Sisters in Islam, and studied how women's activists across the so-called Muslim world have employed Islamic jurisprudence (*fiqh*) in efforts to combat injustice and violence.[23] Indeed, a large part of transnational feminist scholarship focusing on Muslim-majority contexts involves the investigation (and sometimes the advancement) of religiously grounded feminist discourses. As with Womanist scholarship and Third World liberation theologies, Muslim scholars and activists working from within Islamic arguments have pushed against the assumed secularism of feminism.[24] Going beyond considering religious identity as another highway to consider when analyzing overlapping oppressions, they have examined how Islamic belief and practice (*dīn*) can offer new ways of conceptualizing subjectivity, agency, knowledge production, and justice.[25]

Islamically grounded feminist critiques and movements have also met with criticism and resistance. Some feminists from Muslim backgrounds have argued that referencing Islamic sources might work in the short term but ultimately risks entrenching patriarchal authority and erasing the diversity of local feminisms.[26] Others have critiqued western interest in and demand for "Islamic feminism" and the orientalist overemphasis on Muslim women's supposed piety.[27] Indeed, soon after 9/11, finding a visibly devout (read: headscarf-wearing) Muslim woman to speak to Muslim women's issues turned into an obsession for internationally focused nongovernmental organizations (NGOs) and for progressive western organizations.

At the same time, there have been attempts to appropriate and absorb devout Muslim women's activism within liberal western feminism. Julie Elisabeth Pruzan-Jørgensen, in a 2012 study prepared for the Danish Institute for International Studies, for example, suggests approaching Islamic women's movements as potential allies for "traditional liberal/secular women's activism" as long as "common interests" can be identified. On the other hand, Isobel Coleman has proposed a secular teleology, musing whether, given enough time, "Islamic feminism, like other reform movements that preceded it, may well end up unapologetically secular."[28] Whether critical, appropriative, or barely tolerant, these approaches refuse to fully engage with the productive challenges Islamically grounded arguments could make to normative conceptions of the nation-state, secular modernity, and human rights.

Although most often called on to add a touch of "diversity" to hegemonic liberal feminism, forms of Islamic feminism—if properly engaged—can reveal the breaking points of liberalism itself. An interaction between Turkish and Iranian Islamic women's activists at the turn of the twenty-first century offers one helpful case study of the radical challenge liberal conceptions of secular modernity has posed to transnational feminist solidarity and vice versa. As I explain in depth below, breaking points in solidarity occurred at the individual, national, transnational, and international levels. Yet in examining broken solidarities, one locates another breaking point: the point at which liberal articulations of democracy and human rights folded onto themselves as the ECHR used these arguments to uphold the

Turkish ban on headscarves, dismissing a Muslim woman plaintiff's argument utilizing these very same concepts. My analysis of this breaking point
contributes to scholarship on how nation-states employ religion in their
secular modernization projects and on the imbrications of international
human rights discourses with western imperialism and Christianity. It also
urges continued attention to scales of power in transnational feminist critique, placing greater critical emphasis on loci of greater political, economic,
military, and discursive power.

Solidarity Refused: Reforming the Clothing Laws in Turkey and Iran

A comparative and transnational analysis of the imbrications of the local
and the global is necessary for adequately contextualizing the political
positioning of Muslim women activists in late twentieth-century Turkey
and Iran. Turkey and Iran's parallel and intersecting histories regarding
the coevolution of dominant perceptions of womanhood alongside shifting
forms of nationalism and religion offer fertile grounds for an analysis based
on what Mohanty has termed "the *comparative feminist studies/feminist
solidarity* model."[29] According to Mohanty, this type of study traces the
impact of world-shaping global processes, avoids cultural relativism while
examining local differences, and emphasizes "the interweaving of the histories" of different communities under asymmetrical relations of power.[30]
At the end of World War I, Turkey and Iran emerged as nation-states
born of unraveling empires and were guided by authoritarian leaders
with military backgrounds who shared a similar vision of centralization,
secularization, and modernization.[31] Turkey's Mustafa Kemal Atatürk and
Iran's Reza Shah were responding to problems related to precarious national
sovereignty: political and economic imperialism, internal fragmentation,
and a general need to counter perceptions of civilizational inferiority.
They also tackled these problems in similar ways, launching programs of
authoritarian modernization.

The programs that Atatürk and Reza Shah followed hinged on European-
inspired legal reforms, an ethnonationalism that privileged the pre-Islamic
past (imagined as more authentically "Turkish" or "Persian"), and attempts
at state centralization through increased control over religious power

structures. In Turkey, where the Ottoman state had long employed the Sunni clergy, Atatürk followed and expanded on this precedent. After abolishing the Caliphate in 1924 and striking the precept in the constitution that had declared Islam the religion of the state, the Kemalist cadres settled on a version of laïcism that promoted an official Sunni Islam subservient to state goals.[32] They founded the Ministry of Religion (*Diyanet*) and brought religious leaders under state rule as salaried employees. In addition, being Muslim was, from the beginning, cast as a defining feature of Turkishness.[33] The Turkish utilization of a particular version of Sunni Islam as a tool of the state and for national identity building operated alongside an assault on nongovernmental religious networks, such as Sufi shrines, and the policing of the religious attire of men outside of places of worship. These aspects of the Kemalists revolution raised concerns in neighboring Iran, where high-ranking religious scholars (*'ulamā*) and traditional merchants protested the push toward a republic taking place simultaneously under Reza Shah.[34] In response to these movements and British pressure, the Shah backed away from instituting a secularizing republic. Instead, his regime reduced the political power of the *'ulamā* through judicial, educational, and economic reforms.[35]

As Houchang Chehabi has convincingly argued, Atatürk and Reza Shah instituted clothing reform for both men and women in the service of nation building and with an eye toward international image building.[36] Responding to the gendered aspects of western orientalist critique, secularizing measures targeted women as symbols of modernity, marking the state's authority to fashion its citizens' public presentation. Both leaders advanced a form of "state feminism."[37] Scholars debate the connections between the women's rights developments established in the service of nation building and the independent feminist movements that preceded them.[38] Either way, the legalistic and cultural measures Atatürk and Reza Shah instituted influenced the symbolic role policy makers assigned to women long after these leaders' demise.

Under Atatürk, Turkish women achieved expanded educational and career opportunities and gained the right to vote and be elected for office. The new civil code abolished polygamy and granted women equal rights to divorce and inheritance. While the early Kemalists did not implement a nationwide ban on head covering, a public relations campaign led by Atatürk, his wife, and his party discouraged veiling.[39] The image of the modern

Turkish woman the state promoted left little place for public displays of piety in the civic sphere. In Iran, Reza Shah initiated measures expanding women's education and ending gender segregation in public places. After a highly publicized 1934 visit to Turkey, Reza Shah increased the speed of reform, focusing on clothing reform and gender desegregation to an even greater extent. In addition to laws relating to men's headdresses, the decree on *kashf-i hijāb* (lit., "unveiling") outlawed the traditional outdoor cover known as *chādur* and other forms of women's veiling in public spaces.[40] These parallel symbolic burdens placed on the public visibility of Turkish and Iranian women would repeatedly surface in struggles over national identity and the character of each regime as the century progressed.

In midcentury, both Iran and Turkey saw the rise and suppression of democratic movements. The Iranian National Front movement, led by Prime Minister Mossadegh, was squashed by a British- and US-led coup in 1953. Starting in 1960, Turkey, for its part, experienced repeated military coups whenever the ruling Kemalist generals decided the laïcist vision of modern Turkey established by Atatürk had come under too much strain. The 1979 revolution in Iran was followed by, and possibly helped prompt, a 1980 coup in Turkey.[41] As Iran transitioned into a new system based on Ayatollah Khomeini's theorization of "the rule of jurists," Kenan Evren, the Turkish general who had led Turkey's 1980 coup, advocated a new "Islamic-Turkish synthesis." Evren and the junta emphasized the role of Islam in the formation of Turkish identity as a counterbalance to militant leftism. In keeping with the laïcist assertion of the modern nation-state's right to determine the parameters of civic religiosity, the very generals who highlighted Islam as an essential aspect of Turkishness also initiated Turkey's first official nationwide ban on headscarves at government institutions.[42]

Throughout the 1980s, as the regimes of Turkey and Iran solidified new configurations of state and religion, they also experienced pushback and opposition, especially regarding issues related to women. During the Iran-Iraq War, with vast numbers of men engaged in combat, the need for reforms to the strict interpretations of Islamic law on family matters became obvious. As a result, the 1980s and 1990s saw multiple reforms that expanded women's rights in education, careers, and the domestic sphere. The Iranian women's press led the way in constructing what some have called an "Islamic feminism," whereby theological arguments were utilized to expand women's opportunities.[43] The development of a loose coalition of Islamist and secular intellectuals, activists, and aligned clergy working to change the prevailing system fueled the 1997 election of the reformist candidate, Mohammad Khatami.[44]

In Turkey, a newly energized feminist movement with laïcist commitments challenged Kemalist paternalism and sexual puritanism in the 1980s.[45] At the same time, Muslim women activists demanded visibility and respect in the public sphere on different terms and regularly found themselves at odds with laïcist feminists.[46] In 1997, the same year the reformists in Iran captured the presidency under Khatami, the Islamist party Refah (Welfare) received the most votes in the Turkish national election. Thus, as the 1990s progressed, Muslim reformist movements flourished in electoral politics in both countries and challenged how the established regime organized its approach to religion and women.

Restrictions on women's clothing became central to the debate over the regime and the alignment of state-religion relations in both countries. Because women's unveiling had operated as such an important symbol of the Pahlavi political will, after the revolution in Iran, women's reveiling became an essential marker of a "return" to authenticity.[47] Following an initial mass protest, however, the political opposition to forced veiling was squashed, and the subject became a taboo issue, even for the reformist press.[48] Throughout the 1980s and 1990s, Iranian women's resistance to clothing laws functioned in an "apolitical," individualist manner, visible in uncoordinated, subversive practices of self-styling. Dress codes were far from the most central issue for those working on improving women's lives in the country.

In Turkey, on the other hand, the headscarf issue rose to the center of national politics after the 1980 ban. Along with protests supporting preacher–prayer leader (imam-hatip) schools, protests against the headscarf ban constituted the public face of Islamist activism in the 1980s and 1990s. In 1989, the elected government relaxed its position on veiling by delegating the issue to university administrators.[49] This decree eased the way for some women but not others, and the crisis continued.

On February 28, 1997, the Turkish military shut down Refah and banned its leaders from participating in politics by issuing a memorandum. Often called a "postmodern" coup, the directive initiated a new crackdown on sectors of society believed to be a threat to the prevailing system of laïcism.[50] Under instructions from the junta, the new government began enforcing the headscarf ban in universities and state institutions with new zeal, punishing lax administrators. In April 1999, the tension increased when two women wearing headscarves were elected to the Turkish Parliament. When the representative for the right-wing nationalist party MHP agreed to remove her headscarf before entering the Parliament, all eyes turned to Merve Kavakçı, the thirty-one-year-old representative for Fazilet, the reformist Islamist party that had replaced the banned Refah. On May 2, 1999, Merve Kavakçı entered the Turkish Parliament wearing a navy-blue pantsuit and a headscarf. She was booed and prevented from taking her oath as the representatives of the laïcist parties blocked her way to the podium.[51] The left-leaning prime minister, Bülent Ecevit, rose to the podium to condemn Kavakçı, exclaiming, "Please show this lady her place" (*haddini bildirin*).[52] Center-right president Süleyman Demirel responded to the crisis with a televised speech condemning Kavakçı as a "provocateur," hinting at foreign connections.[53]

Transnational connections developed almost immediately around the Kavakçı affair. Even as Turkish laïcists attempted to cast Kavakçı as beyond the pale of Turkishness and associate her with various Middle Eastern terrorist organizations, she became a cause celebré in many Muslim-majority countries, including Palestine, Yemen, and the neighboring Islamic Republic of Iran.[54] Already in a "symbolic cold war" with Turkey's postcoup regime, conservative Iranian news outlets used the Kavakçı affair to condemn Turkish laïcism, publishing multiple articles, opinion pieces, and editorial cartoons about the headscarf crisis every single day.[55] "In the one-way street of laïcism, religion does not have the right to intervene in politics," observed an editorial in the semiofficial *Kiyhān* newspaper wryly, "however, politics can intervene in all religious affairs."[56] The conservative woman MP Nayyirih Akhavān-Bīṭaraf—a key figure in pushing back against the gains made under Islamic feminism in the 1990s—delivered a speech supporting Kavakçı in the Iranian Parliament in the name of all-female representatives.[57] Protests in support of Kavakçı took place at various universities; the event at Tehran University was headlined by another conservative woman MP, Dr. Marżīyih Vahīd Dastjirdī.[58]

Turkish laïcists used these Iranian state-linked expressions of support to argue Kavakçı was collaborating with outside forces to turn Turkey into "another Iran." Ecevit argued the protests marked yet another example of Iran attempting to "export its ideology."[59] "Here are her friends!," exclaimed a headline in the daily *Sabah*, using a photo of Iranian women in dark *chādurs* carrying Kavakçı's image alongside posters of Ayatollah Khamenei to make the same argument.[60] However, some of the most vocal forms of support from Iran came from Islamic feminists whose politics conflicted with the Supreme Leader and regime hard-liners. Faezeh Hashemi Rafsanjani, daughter of the previous president, Rafsanjani, and a women's activist then serving as a reformist MP, wrote Kavakçı an open letter expressing solidarity and asking her to not think of herself as alone in her struggle.[61] Dr. Zahra Rahnavard, the first woman to head an Iranian university, led a protest of women university students and made a speech in support of Kavakçı, referring to her as "sister."[62] While neither Kavakçı nor Rafsanjani nor Rahnavard explicitly identified as feminists, they were all working to "expand women's opportunities"—a key focus of feminist activism and scholarship in Muslim-majority contexts.[63] Kavakçı, however, refused all Iranian offers of solidarity and sisterhood wholesale, stating, "There's nothing to be gained from support which comes from a state that curbs freedoms."[64]

Unlike in Iran, where secular and Islamic women's activists had developed arenas of cooperation, Turkey's most influential feminists were adamantly in favor of the prevailing system of laïcism and categorically objected to women's veiling. KA.DER, the prominent Turkish feminist organization founded to help women political candidates, not only refused to support Kavakçı but also released a statement asking the ban on headscarves in Parliament to be stated more explicitly in the official rules.[65] KA.DER representatives also minimized Kavakçı's agency, calling her a "pawn" of (male) Islamist politicians working behind the scenes.[66] Although Kavakçı condemned KA.DER's lack of solidarity with her plight, her own dismissal of Rafsanjani and Rahnavard smacks of a similar denial of agency and nuance, erasing her Iranian supporters' differences with the prevailing regime of their country.[67]

What abstract concept would have allowed these women reformists to "recognize" each other as sisters? What structural blocks foreclosed transnational Islamic feminist solidarity? The nation-state emerges as an obvious breaking point in this story, having an impact on multiple factors. First, the internal instability of the nation-state structure, marked by the hyphen between "nation" and "state," fueled the nationalists' anxieties that were at play in Turkey. As Benedict Anderson has pointed out, the hyphen signifies the imperfect overlap between the nation as an "imagined community" of individuals supposedly sharing ethnic, cultural, and religious traits and the state as the internationally recognized political entity claiming the right to represent and rule this community. The crises caused by the imperfect overlap of these two constructions are apparent in the Turkish laïcist outcry over Kavakçı's headscarf, in Kavakçı's retort to the laïcists, and in her rejection of Iranian women's outreach.[68] The laïcists who held the reins of power promoted an overlap between the nation, the regime, and the state in condemning Kavakçı as an agent provocateur. This was apparent when Prime Minister Bülent Ecevit stated that the parliament "is no place to threaten the state" (*devlet*).[69] As a retort, Kavakçı identified a disconnect between the prevailing regime and the people's will and, therefore, between the state and the nation. Pointing out that she campaigned and was democratically elected while wearing a headscarf, she argued that she was sent by the nation (*millet*) to serve in its name.[70] In this formulation, the laïcist regime was guilty of severing the nation from the state by not allowing democratic representation in Parliament.

Her Iranian supporters mimicked Kavakçı's reasoning about the wishes of the people of Turkey and even used sympathetic Turkish nationalist language, as when Rahnavard stated in her outreach to Kavakçı, "You are victorious, and the nation that has produced you and chosen you will last forever."[71] Yet, in Kavakçı's response to this outreach, we once again find a presumed overlap between the nation, the state, and the regime, in which all Iranian support emanates from "a state that curbs freedoms." Certainly, Kavakçı's Turkish detractors, in associating her with the Iranian system of government, had made it very difficult for her to accept any type of positive outreach from that country. However, her published response further erased nuance. In a homogenizing move, her wording collapsed any difference between Iranian reformists and hard-liners, between the people and the regime. The rejection transferred the negative stereotypes foisted on her by her Turkish detractors across the nation-state boundary.

Although I believe it was not the nation-state's sturdiness but its vulnerability as an imperfect construction that primarily contributed to the failure of transnational solidarity, nation-state boundaries also played a role in circumscribing the discursive field. In addition to having contrasting histories of secularist/Islamist feminist interactions as outlined above, domestic political reformists in Turkey and Iran often mobilized different discursive frameworks. In her fieldwork based in the first decade of the twenty-first century, Mona Tajali has demonstrated how Iranian reformist women's arguments for the expansion of women's opportunities referenced sacred sources such as the Qur'an, in contrast to the statements of Turkish Islamist women, who often used the "secular" language of human rights.[72] Indeed, Kavakçı herself exclusively used a liberal, human rights framing in arguing for her right to serve while wearing a headscarf, citing the US Civil Rights movement as precedent and inspiration.[73]

Prominent Iranian observers have suggested that these different rhetorical frames contributed to the failed outreach. Writing in the reformist newspaper *Nishāt*, the progressive cleric Ḥasan Yūsifī Ishkivarī blamed Rafsanjani and Rahnavard for reaching out to Kavakçı with reference to their shared Muslim identity and not on the basis of a universalist discourse of human rights. Calling Kavakçı's rejection an "important message" and a lesson for the Muslim women of Iran, Ishkivarī argued, "In today's world, on a global or national level, religious beliefs, and moral values can only be defended through a single logic, and that logic is freedom and democracy and human rights."[74] In her writings, the prominent Iranian feminist Nayereh Tohidi echoes this assessment, suggesting that the lack of a solid commitment to freedom and democracy served as a critical determinant for the failure of Iranian Islamic feminist outreach abroad.[75] It is essential to take these liberal Iranian critiques seriously. Would a more substantial non-Islamic "human rights" framing in the Iranian outreach have helped build transnational solidarity? Are universalist declarations of human rights the way out of the othering that always seems to follow on the heels of religious/racial/national demarcation, or is "human rights" itself a category bound up with related assumptions about the proper subject of rights? I take these questions up below by way of the "master's house."

MUSLIM WOMEN'S RIGHTS IN TRANSNATIONAL PERSPECTIVE

While liberal Iranian observers have blamed the Islamic tones of the outreach to Kavakçı, following the transnational feminist "foil" model of failed solidarity that currently prevails in western-dominated academia would lead us to critique Kavakçı herself. Here she was refusing the offer of transnational solidarity, buying into and furthering the very nationalist and civilizational discourses mobilized against her. In fact, this is precisely where Robert Olson ends the story: "The dilemma of both women [Kavakçı and

Rafsanjani] was that they did not support each other or the democratizing forces they represented."[76] Yet, despite the note of wistfulness, there is a sense of completion, a rhetorical neatness in such a history. We might feel Foucault smiling down on us: here indeed is "power at its capillaries," a dominant discourse traveling and humming like a well-oiled machine.[77]

Going a small step up the power ladder would mean noting that the male leaders of Kavakçı's party, fearing for their political futures, did not come to her defense. Turkey's current president, Recep Tayyip Erdoğan, then a past mayor of Istanbul and a rising political star, remained silent about the crisis. Abdullah Gül, who would become president in 2007, even suggested Kavakçı change her style of headscarf to minimize the perceived offense to laïcism.[78] Yet, at the time, Fazilet was a party under investigation and barely a year away from being shut down and banned. As a result, its leaders had little maneuvering room to take defiant stances on hot-button issues.

Even more powerful than Fazilet's leaders were the primary wielders of political rhetoric in Turkey (President Süleyman Demirel, Prime Minister Bülent Ecevit, the generals, the legislative branch, and the media cartels). They used a multipronged strategy combining nationalist, universalist, and *religious* language, foreclosing avenues for transnational solidarity. The laïcist media described Kavakçı's style of a tightly pinned headscarf as a foreign export and, therefore, as a political symbol demanding an Iran-style Islamist regime incompatible with women's rights, as opposed to an "authentic" and "innocent" Turkish-Islamic form of head covering.[79] President Demirel condemned her actions as *fitne* (sedition), mobilizing this Qur'anic term politically to defend laïcism, long before the Islamic Republic of Iran popularized its use against the leading figures of the Green movement.[80] Such use of religious language in defense of a system of secularism helped construct Kavakçı's headscarved appearance in the Turkish Parliament as simultaneously constituting a political-religious assault on Kemalism and failing on Turkish Islamic grounds. By this formulation, the democratically elected MP was beyond the pale of the state, the nation, the regime, and Islam. Simply put, Kavakçı could not have vocally accepted the support of any Iranians, including reformist Iranian women, without validating concerns regarding her plans for turning Turkey into "another Iran."

Yet, the story cannot end here either. A step farther up the power ladder would have us looking at the European Union (EU), which Turkey was attempting to join at the time. A veiled woman representative would have clashed with the "western" image of the country the Turkish elite wanted to draw to join the club. However, here it appears as if the Turkish elite misunderstood what the EU wanted from Turkey: a series of real human rights reforms and not crackdowns on devout women's public practices of piety. Indeed, in an interview, Merve Kavakçı herself referenced a BBC news piece that had found Turkey's headscarf law incompatible with its application for membership in the EU.[81] Certainly, restricting Muslim women's rights was not a criterion of EU membership, right? Yes and no. What the Kavakçı affair and the headscarf ban ultimately revealed was the hidden subtext of articulated EU criteria. The EU did criticize Turkey on human rights grounds, particularly in connection with the extensive antiterror campaign it had been executing in the southeast. However, no such objection appeared regarding the headscarf ban. On the contrary, the headscarf crisis hinted that EU decision makers were resistant to Islam and used human rights rhetoric as a pretext of denial. When headscarf-wearing women who had suffered educational and career-based discrimination, including Kavakçı, sued the Turkish state at the ECHR, they not only ran into nationalist accusations that they were "traitors" embarrassing their country in the international sphere but also revealed breaking points in European human rights rhetoric.

The ECHR's role in the nation-state formation is itself germane to this discussion: founded after World War II to protect citizens' rights against the states to which they belong, the court can be read as a threat to national and cultural sovereignty, especially when the country under investigation appears peripheral to Europe. Turkey is perhaps the iconic borderland to Europeanness—sometimes conceived as a "bridge" between Europe and Asia and at other times constructed as the alien other. However, in *Sahin* v. *Turkey*, concerning a medical student who was denied the right to take her final exams because of her headscarf, the ECHR ruled against the right to wear the headscarf in state institutions, agreeing with the Turkish state.[82] In 2007, a chamber of seven ECHR judges also heard Kavakçı's case alongside those of other Fazilet party members. The court dismissed Kavakçı's claims that her rights to "freedom of thought, conscience, and religion" had been violated and chose not to consider her case concerning the principles of "anti-discrimination." The only one of her grievances it validated was the "right to free elections"; on this principle, the court ruled that the Turkish state had not been wrong per se but had taken disproportionate measures. Going further, the court cast laïcism as the necessary ingredient to Turkish democracy and claimed the ruling regime's actions—against both Kavakçı and the party she represented—were motivated by appropriate concerns.

> ECHR notes that the temporary restrictions made to the complainant's political rights are ultimately intended to protect the secular character of the Turkish political regime. Considering the importance of that principle to Turkish democracy, ECHR believes the measure pursued legitimate aims regarding the preservation of the prevailing order and the protection of the rights and liberties of others.[83]

By what alchemy did this reference to laïcism convert undemocratic measures curtailing women's rights to education and political participation into "the protection of the rights and liberties of others"? What made laïcism so essential to Turkish democracy? Islam provides a conceptual breaking point here. Saba Mahmood has demonstrated how the principles of "public order" and rhetorical distinctions between belief and outward manifestations of faith have been used to uphold majoritarian norms in cases involving issues of "religious freedom." However, the Turkish headscarf ban was not the concern of a minority, given the fact that Turkey boasted an approximately 99 percent Muslim population, and the headscarf was quite widespread in its various local manifestations. Moreover, it is essential to note that not all devout Turkish Muslims in the public and political spheres were penalized in the same way. Turkish laïcism and the western support for it punished Muslim women especially, even as it claimed to be freeing them specifically. In response to Muslim women's public piety (read as both a claim on the state and a claim on the conscience of others), democracy, women's rights, and even the discourse of individual "choice"—so essential to modern liberalism—could be suspended in the name of these exact concepts. These rhetorical conversions are even more striking because Kavakçı herself never once deviated from the liberal language of individual choice, democracy, and civil rights while making her appeal.

As a stumbling block for transnational feminism, the nation is inseparable from the unequal world system and the civilizational assumptions that undergird it, even when examining South-South contexts. As noted, Kemalists forged modern Turkish nationalism in conjunction with (not in opposition to) Islam; however, the regime's application of western-inflected concepts, such as secularism and modernity, left little space for devout

Muslim women's public and political presence. With the headscarf ban, Turkish laïcists, who held the organs of the state at the end of the twentieth century, were defending their right to determine the gendered parameters of the religion-state interaction. The ECHR, in turn, upheld the non-Islamic and patriarchal construction of "modern" civilization in the name of "public order and civil peace."[84] In the court of international law, these two endeavors overlapped to stack the deck against headscarf-wearing Muslim women.

It is surprising that progressive Iranian commentators have been quick to blame reformist Iranian women's excess of Islamic language for the lost solidarity. This has meant assigning near-omniscience to Kavakçı, implying she made the decision consciously after reviewing the outreach rhetoric in detail and finding it unsatisfactory on universalist grounds when there is no evidence she was either familiar with or interested in the operations of the Iranian women's movement. At the same time, the critics seem to expect the impossible from Rafsanjani and Rahnavard, who had developed their mixed tactics in a local political context that tolerated only certain types of critique. Finally, the argument that the Islamic framework was too estranged from universal human rights language to connect to Kavakçı's struggles falsely imagines "human rights" as a unique space free of religion. Instead, the history of the development of human rights discourses and the normative secularism mobilized by dominant western institutions such as the ECHR is imbricated with both hegemonic Christianity and racial, colonialist perspectives.[85] As noted, laïcist Turkish nationalism itself did not involve the "separation" of religion and state. At its most perceptive, Iranian Islamic feminist discourse on the Turkish headscarf crisis came close to revealing these imbrications even as its proponents mobilized for Kavakçı's political rights.

Different Iranian actors commenting on the Turkish headscarf crisis had differing goals. Whereas conservatives were content to score ideological points over Turkish laïcism, devout reformist women simultaneously offered solidarity to Kavakçı, promoted a social justice-oriented vision of Islamic politics, and called out western human rights talk for its imperialist exclusions. Iranian Islamic feminists' supposed inability to speak "human rights" is belied by the primary documents demonstrating a complex transnational imaginary mobilizing multiple intersecting frames of reference. Far from being buried in a parochial Islamism, these declarations evinced a keen awareness of the global context of prevailing human rights discourses.

Faezeh Hashemi Rafsanjani's open letter is a good example of the nuanced, multilevel perspective Iranian Islamic feminists brought to bear on the crisis. Highlighting the silence of committed defenders of human rights on the violation of Turkish Muslim women's rights under the headscarf ban, Rafsanjani noted, "Unfortunately, human rights are being used again as a tool for the continuation of Western imperialist oppression." Then she continued, "Individuals who cannot tolerate Muslim women's advancement and rising consciousness are working to ensure that their presence in the political and social spheres does not progress beyond superficial and symbolic maneuvers."[86]

This reference could not have been to Turkey alone, which sought to ban precisely the "symbols" of Muslim women's public presence. Instead, the discerning reader familiar with Iranian political double-speak would have read these as comments about Iranian regime hard-liners as well, who sought to keep the presence of women like her at a superficial level. Iranian reformists thus built on the Kavakçı affair to mobilize for a change in the local political imagination, even as they launched transnational critiques of the Turkish state and western entities.[87] These formulations anticipated the open debates about the Iranian Parliament's dress codes that would take place with the election of the reformist-dominated sixth Parliament the following year.[88] However, it would be unfair to read Rafsanjani's words simply as underhanded "resistance" to the dominant national forces; they also affirm Islam's role in the public sphere and train their most direct critique on "Western imperialist oppression."

The declaration of the Organization of Islamic University Students, quoted in the women's magazine *Zan-i Rūz* similarly affirmed Kavakçı's choice based on *dīn* (religion), even as it called out human rights organizations in a universalist language. "It is astounding that monitors of human rights are ignoring this obvious violation of the rights of a Muslim person," declared the group with discernible sarcasm. "Have global organizations for the defense of women's rights eliminated the rights of Muslim women and those with headscarves from the foreground of their feminist lexicon?"[89] The 1990s were indeed a time when President Clinton and the neoliberal Democratic cadres, in association with liberal feminist organizations, had elevated concern for Muslim women's rights to a foreign policy priority.[90] Yet here were devout Muslim women in Turkey being denied "the right to have rights" during a so-called golden age of US-Turkey relations.[91] The European Union's stonewalling and the silence of the Clinton administration suggest that at the exact point western policy elites felt entitled to save "Muslim Women" from violations of their rights, they imagined these violations and rights in a limited, Islamophobic, and sexist framework.

The Kavakçı incident thus supports well-established theorizations regarding the built-in exclusions of liberalism—the foundation of modern human rights discourse—and its connections to racism, sexism, and colonialism.[92] However, my goal is not to offer a general theory regarding how "human rights" relate to "religion" (or even to "Islam") or to declare "human rights" off-limits for transnational feminists now and forever. I agree with Margaret A. McLaren that noting the imbrications of human rights discourses with imperialism is an important step toward including rights claims as strategies within a multilayered framework for social justice.[93] Therefore, the goal of this analysis has been to highlight how, in a specific geopolitical context, the "universal" human rights framework was *made* unusable for specific historically situated individuals mobilizing for gender justice within and across nation-state boundaries. It is the mandate of transnational feminist cultural studies to examine such discursive flows and blocks and identify the structures that foreclose justice and solidarity. Of course, each level of this story is vital in revealing the intersections of modernity, nation, and religion and the international operations of power in a specific historical context. Yet the direction of discursive flows marks the dominance of secular western categories, and only with the international mandate of the ECHR did these constructions become binding across nation-state lines. Thus, any analysis that does not carry this story of broken feminist solidarities to the door of the ECHR would leave "the master's house" wholly untouched in its attempt to critique a Muslim woman's use of "the master's tools."

BEYOND THE FOIL:
POWER AND TRANSNATIONAL FEMINIST CRITIQUE

In November 2020, the Iranian anti-veiling activist Nasībih Shamsāyī who was seeking refuge in Turkey at the risk of deportation back to Iran made news in Turkish and international media.[94] Studies of Turkish and Iranian women's rights movements, however, remain comparative, with little or no reference to moments of bilateral contact and friction.[95] Of course, even transnational feminist analysis comes without guarantees. As early as 2001, Inderpal Grewal and Caren Kaplan, two key theorizers of transnational feminism, noted how the word "transnational" risked losing its "political valence" as it became popularized.[96] Revising her discipline-shaking essay, "Under Western Eyes," years later, Mohanty warned against the ease with which postcolonial feminist theorizing can slip into relativism, given its emphasis on difference.[97] Transnational feminist praxis, therefore, requires that we ask along with Alexander and Mohanty, "When is the transnational a normativizing gesture—and when does it perform a radical, decolonizing function?"[98] Critics of transnational feminism have focused mainly on the NGO-ization of activism, the sidelining of local struggles in favor of issues that resonate for global funders, and the US-centered assumptions undergirding its operations in academia.[99] Dulling the radical edges of transnational feminism, however, does not just happen when feminists uncritically adopt "the master's tools"; it occurs any time the outcome of scholarship is a foregone conclusion, that is, every time we rehearse the same deflating story of "Third World Women's victimization" due to broken solidarities and stop our analysis with blaming individual (often women) actors.[100]

In a thought-provoking essay, Rochelle Terman has critiqued the feminist "privileging" of anti-imperialist critique at the expense of other factors affecting Muslim women's lives. However, as Terman also acknowledges, western discourses and policies penetrate the local and the national in the postcolonial world, whereas the reverse is simply not true. In addition, as the endless War on Terror has shown, the stakes of ascendant western discourses are simply too high, and those stakes are born primarily by communities who are already experiencing intersecting oppressions. The problem is not emphasizing one line of domination (in this case, imperialism) more than others but to the exclusion of others. Transnational feminist critique must foreground anti-imperialism because of imperialism's immense power to affect lives on the ground through multiple, intersecting forms of violence: military, political, economic, and cultural. However, I agree with Terman that identifying low-power actors, who may wittingly or unwittingly further racist, nationalist, and imperialist discourses, cannot be the end goal of transnational feminist critique. There are serious political limits to the "foil" model of analysis. In other words, while we might find an exploration of "power at its capillaries" helpful to understanding a case, we must emphasize the most extensive loci of power.

The story of failed solidarity traced above could not end with the Iranian Islamic feminists as Iranian liberals have suggested; nor do I believe it should end with Kavakçı's use of liberal and nationalist rhetoric to refuse the Iranian outreach. Taking our critical inquiry as far as we can toward the highest loci of power fits the mandate of transnational feminism to examine the intersections of the local and the global.[101] It is also crucial to recharging the politics of our scholarship and retargeting "the master's house." Transnational feminists largely agree on the importance of structural critique. Asking who has the power to control the structures and disseminate and turn into law their preferred discourses opens up emancipatory possibilities that might otherwise go unnoticed or untheorized. Rafsanjani's multilayered critique in response to the Turkish headscarf ban, which placed greater emphasis on "western imperialism," even as it urged readers to rethink Iranian laws and critiqued Turkish laïcism, is a productive example of this approach.

NOTES

1. Audre Lorde, "The Master's Tools Will Never Dismantle the Master's House," in *Sister/Outsider: Essays and Speeches* (Berkeley, CA: Crossing, 2007), 110–14.

2. Lila Abu-Lughod, "Do Muslim Women Need Saving? Reflections on Cultural Relativism and Its Others," *American Anthropologist* 104, no. 3 (2002): 783–90; Sunaina Maira, "Belly Dancing: Arab-Face, Orientalist Feminism, and U.S. Empire," *American Quarterly* 60, no. 2 (2008): 317–45; Gargi Bhattacharyya, *Dangerous Brown Men: Exploiting Sex, Violence and Feminism in the War on Terror* (London: Zed Books, 2008); Inderpal Grewal, "'Security Moms' and 'Security Feminists': Securitizing Family and State," in *Saving the Security State: Exceptional Citizens in Twenty-First-Century America* (Durham, NC: Duke University Press, 2017), 118–43; Sarah Rahimi, "Female Drone Operators Are Not a Feminist Victory," *Muftah*, January 25, 2016, http://muftah.org/female-drone-operators-are-not-a-feminist-victory/; Moustafa Bayoumi, "Chaos and Procedure," in *This Muslim American Life: Dispatches from the War on Terror* (New York: New York University Press), 217–39.

3. Lisa Duggan, *The Twilight of Equality? Neoliberalism, Cultural Politics, and the Attack on Democracy* (Boston: Beacon Press, 2003); Jasbir K. Puar, *Terrorist Assemblages: Homonationalism in Queer Times* (Durham, NC: Duke University Press, 2007); David L. Eng, *The Feeling of Kinship: Queer Liberalism and the Racialization of Intimacy* (Durham, NC: Duke University Press, 2010).

4. Paula Bacchetta, Tina Campt, Inderpal Grewal, Caren Kaplan, Minoo Moallem, and Jennifer Terry, "Transnational Feminist Practices against War," *Meridians: Feminism, Race, Transnationalism* 2, no. 2 (2002): 302–8 (302).

5. Vera Mackie, "Shifting the Axis: Feminism and the National Imaginary," in *State/Nation/Transnation: Perspectives on Transnationalism in the Asia-Pacific*, ed.

Katie Willis and Brenda S. A. Yeoh (London: Routledge, 2004), 238–56 (240); Omaima Abou-Bakr, "Islamic Feminism? What's in a Name? Preliminary Reflections," *Middle East Women's Studies Review* 15–16 (2001): 1–2.

6. Richard Rorty, "Religion as Conversation-Stopper," *Common Knowledge* 3, no. 1 (1994): 1–6; and "Religion in the Public Square: A Reconsideration," *Journal of Religious Ethics* 31, no. 1 (2003): 141–49.

7. Rochelle Terman, "Islamophobia, Feminism and the Politics of Critique," *Theory, Culture & Society* 33, no. 2 (2016): 77–102.

8. bell hooks, *Feminist Theory: From Margin to Center*, 3rd ed. (New York: Routledge, 2014), 18.

9. See Jennifer Nash, *Black Feminism Reimagined: After Intersectionality* (Durham, NC: Duke University Press, 2018), 81–111, on the various origin stories told about the coining of "intersectionality" and previous theorizations of overlapping oppressions. See also Maylei Blackwell, "Translenguas: Mapping the Possibilities and Challenges of Transnational Women's Organizing across Geographies of Difference," in *Translocalities/Translocalidades: Feminist Politics of Translation in the Latin/a Américas*, ed. Sonia E. Alvarez, Claudia de Lima Costa, Verónica Feliu, Rebecca J. Hester, Norma Klahn, Millie Thayer, and Cruz Caridad Bueno (Durham, NC: Duke University Press, 2014), 299–320; Rachel Lee, "Notes from the (Non) Field: Teaching and Theorizing Women of Color," *Meridians* 1, no. 1 (2000): 85–109.

10. See Kimberlé Crenshaw, "Demarginalizing the Intersection of Race and Sex: A Black Feminist Critique of Antidiscrimination Doctrine, Feminist Theory, and Antiracist Politics," *University of Chicago Legal Forum* 1, no. 1 (1989): 139–67; and "Mapping the Margins: Intersectionality, Identity Politics, and Violence against Women of Color," *Stanford Law Review* 43, no. 6 (1994): 1241–99.

11. Chandra Talpade Mohanty, Ann Russo, and Lourdes Torres, eds., *Third World Women and the Politics of Feminism* (Bloomington: Indiana University Press, 1991); Inderpal Grewal and Caren Kaplan, eds., *Scattered Hegemonies: Postmodernity and Transnational Feminist Practices* (Minneapolis: University of Minnesota Press, 1994); Amrita Basu, ed., *Challenge of Local Feminisms: Women's Movements in Global Perspective* (Boulder, CO: Westview Press, 1995); M. Jacqui Alexander and Chandra Mohanty, eds., *Feminist Genealogies, Colonial Legacies, Democratic Futures* (New York: Routledge, 1997); Ella Shohat, ed., *Talking Visions: Multicultural Feminism in a Transnational Age* (New York: MIT Press, 1998).

12. For "interlocking oppressions," see Patricia Hill Collins, "Intersectionality's Definitional Dilemmas," *Annual Review of Sociology* 41, no. 1 (2015): 1–20; and "matrix of domination," in Patricia Hill Collins, *Black Feminist Thought*, 2nd ed. (New York: Routledge, 2000), 299.

13. Keeanga-Yamahtta Taylor, ed., *How We Get Free: Black Feminism and the Combahee River Collective* (Chicago: Haymarket Books, 2017); see also Chandra Talpade Mohanty, "Cartographies of Struggle: Third World Women and

the Politics of Feminism," in Mohanty, Russo, and Torres, *Third World Women and the Politics of Feminism*, 1–47 (2).

14. Grewal and Kaplan, *Scattered Hegemonies*, 4; emphasis in original.

15. Cynthia Cockburn, "The Women's Movement: Boundary Crossing on Terrains of Conflict," in *Global Social Movements*, ed. Robin Cohen and Shirin M. Rai (London: Athlone Press, 2000), 46–61.

16. Audre Lorde, "An Open Letter to Mary Daly" (1979), in Lorde, *Sister/Outsider*, 66–71.

17. Chandra Talpade Mohanty, "Under Western Eyes: Feminist Scholarship and Colonial Discourses," *boundary 2* 12, no. 3 (Spring-Autumn 1984): 333–58.

18. Gloria E. Anzaldúa, *Borderlands/La Frontera: The New Mestiza* (San Francisco, CA: Aunt Lute, 1987); Amrita Basu, ed., *Challenge of Local Feminisms: Women's Movements in Global Perspective* (Boulder, CO: Westview Press, 1995); Uma Narayan, "The Project of Feminist Epistemology: Perspectives from a Nonwestern Feminist," in *Gender/Body/Knowledge: Feminist Reconstructions of Being and Knowing*, ed. Alison M. Jaggar and Susan Bordo (New York: Rutgers University Press, 1989), 256–69.

19. Esther Ngan-Ling Chow, "Making Waves, Moving Mountains: Reflections on Bejing '95 and Beyond," *Signs: Journal of Women in Culture and Society* 22 (1996): 185–92 (189). See also Amrita Basu, "Globalization of the Local/Localization of the Global: Mapping Transnational Women's Movements," *Meridians: Feminism, Race, Transnationalism* 1, no. 1 (2000): 29–67.

20. Duggan, *The Twilight of Equality?*; Joseph Massad, *Desiring Arabs* (Chicago: University of Chicago Press, 2007); Puar, *Terrorist Assemblages*.

21. Sarah Mahler, "Research Agenda for Transnationalism," in *Transnationalism from Below*, ed. Michael Peter Smith and Luis Eduardo Guarnizo (New Brunswick, NJ: Transaction Publishers, 1998), 66–67; Nancy A. Naples, "Changing the Terms: Community Activism, Globalization, and the Dilemmas of Transnational Feminist Praxis," in *Women's Activism and Globalization: Linking Local Struggles and Transnational Politics*, ed. Nancy A. Naples and Manisha Desai (New York: Routledge, 2002), 3–14 (3). See also M. Jacqui Alexander and Chandra Mohanty, "Introduction: Genealogies, Legacies, Movements," in *Feminist Genealogies*, xiii–xli; Mary Hawkesworth, *Globalization and Feminist Activism* (Lanham, MD: Rowman and Littlefield, 2006); Peggy Antrobus, *The Global Women's Movement: Issues and Strategies for the New Century* (New York: Zed Books, 2004); Rawwida Baksh-Soodeen and Wendy Harcourt, eds., *The Oxford Handbook of Transnational Feminist Movements* (New York: Oxford University Press, 2015).

22. Grewal and Kaplan, *Scattered Hegemonies*; and "Transnational Feminist Cultural Studies: Beyond the Marxism/Poststructuralism/Feminism Divides," *Positions: East Asia Cultures Critique* 2, no. 2 (1994): 430–45.

23. E.g., Abu-Lughod, "Do Muslim Women Need Saving?"; Saba Mahmood, "Secularism, Hermeneutics, and Empire: The Politics of Islamic Reformation," *Public Culture* 18, no. 2 (2006): 323–47; Nima Naghibi, *Rethinking Global Sisterhood: Western Feminism and Iran* (Minneapolis: University of Minnesota

Press, 2007); Saba Mahmood, "Feminism, Democracy, and Empire: Islam and the War on Terror," in *Women's Studies on the Edge*, ed. Joan Scott (Durham, NC: Duke University Press, 2008), 81–114; Mackie, "Shifting the Axis"; Valentine Moghadam, "Islamic Feminism and Its Discontents: Towards a Resolution of the Debate," *Signs: Journal of Women in Culture and Society* 27, no. 4 (2002): 1135–71; Asma Barlas, *Believing Women in Islam: Unreading Patriarchal Interpretations of the Qur'an* (Austin: University of Texas Press, 2002); Margot Badran, "Between Secular and Islamic Feminism/s: Reflections on the Middle East and Beyond," *Journal of Middle East Women's Studies* 1, no. 1 (2005): 6–26; Ziba Mir-Hosseini, "Muslim Women's Quest for Equality: Between Islamic Law and Feminism," *Critical Inquiry* 32, no. 4 (2006): 629–45; Meena Sharify-Funk, *Encountering the Transnational: Women, Islam and the Politics of Interpretation* (Burlington, VT: Ashgate, 2008); Ziba Mir-Hosseini, Lena Larsen, Christian Moe, and Kari Vogt, eds., *Gender and Equality in Muslim Family Law: Justice and Ethics in the Islamic Legal Tradition* (London: I. B. Tauris, 2013); Mulki Al-Sharmani, "Islamic Feminism: Transnational and National Reflections," *Approaching Religion* 4, no. 2 (2014): 83–94.

24. Alice Walker, *In Search of Our Mothers' Gardens: Womanist Prose* (New York: Harcourt, Brace & Jovanovich, 1983); Elina Vuola, "Religion, Intersectionality, and Epistemic Habits of Academic Feminism: Perspectives from Global Feminist Theology," *Feminist Encounters: A Journal of Critical Studies in Culture and Politics* 1, no. 1 (2017): 1–15 (4).

25. Amina Wadud, *Qur'an and Woman: Rereading the Sacred Text from a Woman's Perspective* (Oxford: Oxford University Press, 1996); Leila Ahmed, *Women and Gender in Islam* (New Haven, CT: Yale University Press, 1992); Fatima Mernissi, *The Veil and the Male Elite: A Feminist Interpretation of Women's Rights in Islam* (London: Addison-Wesley, 1991); Asma Barlas, *Believing Women in Islam*. For a contextualized critique of this body of scholarship, see Aysha A. Hidayatullah, *Feminist Edges of the Qur'an* (Oxford: Oxford University Press, 2014).

26. Moghadam, "Islamic Feminism and Its Discontents"; Hania Sholkamy, "Islam and Feminism," *Contestations* 1, www.contestations.net/issues/issue-1/religion-and-gender-justice/.

27. Haideh Moghissi, *Feminism and Islamic Fundamentalism: The Limits of Postmodern Analysis* (London: Zed Books, 1999), esp. ch. 7.

28. Julie Elisabeth Pruzan-Jørgensen, "Islamic Women's Activism in the Arab World: Potentials and Challenges for External Actors," DIIS REPORT 2012:02, https://www.diis.dk/files/media/publications/import/extra/rp2012-02-islamic-womens-activism_web_1.pdf; Isobel Coleman, "Women, Islam and the Push for Reform in the Muslim World," reprinted in *Mother Pelican: A Journal of Sustainable Human Development* 7, no. 4 (2011), www.pelicanweb.org/solisustv07n04page8.html.

29. Mohanty, "Under Western Eyes Revisited," 523–24; emphasis in original.

30. Ibid., 522.

31. Touraj Atabaki and Erik Jan Zürcher, *Men of Order: Authoritarian Modernization under Atatürk and Reza Shah* (London: I. B. Tauris, 2004).

32. Ümit Cizre Sakallıoğlu, "Parameters and Strategies of Islam-State Interaction in Republican Turkey," *International Journal of Middle East Studies* 28, no. 2 (1996): 231–51.

33. Soner Cagaptay, *Islam, Secularism, and Nationalism in Modern Turkey: Who Is a Turk?* (London: Routledge, 2006).

34. Touraj Atabaki, "The Caliphate, the Clerics, and Republicanism in Turkey and Iran: Some Comparative Remarks," in Atabaki and Zürcher, *Men of Order*, 44–61.

35. Mohammad H. Faghfoory, "The Impact of Modernization on the Ulama in Iran, 1925–1941," *Iranian Studies* 26, no. 3–4 (1993): 277–312; Nikki R. Keddie, *Modern Iran: Roots and Results of Revolution* (New Haven, CT: Yale University Press, 2006), 102–3.

36. Houchang Chehabi, "Dress Codes for Men in Turkey and Iran," in Atabaki and Zürcher, *Men of Order*, 209–37.

37. Hamideh Sedghi, *Women and Politics in Iran: Veiling, Unveiling, and Reveiling* (New York: Cambridge University Press, 2007), 3.

38. Camron Michael Amin, "Propaganda and Remembrance: Gender, Education, and 'The Women's Awakening' of 1936," *Iranian Studies* 32, no. 3 (1999): 351–86; Serpil Çakır, "Feminism and Feminist History-Writing in Turkey: The Discovery of Ottoman Feminism," *Aspasia* 1 (2007): 61–83; Afsanah Najmabadi, "Authority and Agency: Revisiting Women's Activism during Reza Shah's Period," in *The State and the Subaltern: Modernization, Society and the State in Turkey and Iran*, ed. Touraj Atabaki (London: I. B. Tauris, 2007), 159–77.

39. Nilüfer Göle, *The Forbidden Modern: Civilization and Veiling* (Ann Arbor: University of Michigan Press, 1997); Murat Aksoy, *Başörtüsü-Türban: Batılılaşma-Modernleşme, Laiklik ve Örtünme* (Istanbul: Kitap Yayınevi, 2005); Cihan Aktaş, *Türbanın Yeniden İcadı* (Istanbul: Kapı, 2006); "Mme. Kemal's Clothes Are Pledge of Reform: Her Riding Breeches Indicate Her Intention of Sweeping Away the Harem Conventions," *New York Times,* March 15, 1923, 2; Enis Dinç, *Atatürk on Screen: Documentary Film and the Making of a Leader* (London: I. B. Tauris, 2020), 76–77.

40. Houchang E. Chehabi, "Staging the Emperor's New Clothes: Dress Codes and Nation Building under Reza Shah," *Iranian Studies* 26 (Summer–Fall 1993): 209–21; Afsaneh Najmabadi, "(Un)Veiling Feminism," *Social Text* 18, no. 3 (2000): 29–45; Jasamin Rostam-Kolayi, "Expanding Agendas for the 'New' Iranian Woman: Family Law, Work, and Unveiling," in *The Making of Modern Iran: State and Society under Riza Shah, 1921-1941*, ed. Stephanie Cronin (New York: Routledge, 2003), 157–81.

41. Süleyman Elik, *Iran-Turkey Relations, 1979–2011: Conceptualising*

the *Dynamics of Politics, Religion and Security in Middle-Power States* (New York: Routledge, 2012), 37.

42. Aktaş, *Türbanın Yeniden İcadı*, 82–89; Pınar Kemerli, "Religious Militarism and Islamist Conscientious Objection in Turkey," *International Journal of Middle East Studies* 47, no. 2 (2015): 281–301.

43. Haleh Afshar, *Islam and Feminisms: An Iranian Case Study* (Basingstoke: Macmillan, 1998). See also Ziba Mir-Hosseini, "Stretching the Limits: A Feminist Reading of the Shari'a in Post Khomeini Iran," in *Feminism and Islam: Legal and Literary Perspectives*, ed. Mai Yamani (London: University of London, 1996), 285–319; Mir-Hosseini, "Divorce, Veiling, and Feminism in Post-Khomeini Iran," in *Women and Politics in the Third World*, ed. Haleh Afshar (London: Routledge, 1996), 284–320; Mir-Hosseini, *Islam and Gender: The Religious Debate in Contemporary Iran* (Princeton, NJ: Princeton University Press, 1999); Afsaneh Najmabadi, "Feminism in an Islamic Republic: Years of Hardship, Years of Growth," in *Islam, Gender, and Social Change*, ed. Yvonne Yazbeck Haddad and John L. Esposito (Oxford: Oxford University Press, 1998), 59–84; Mirjam Künkler, "In the Language of the Islamic Sacred Texts: The Tripartite Struggle for Advocating Women's Rights in the Iran of the 1990s," *Journal of Muslim Minority Affairs* 24, no. 2 (2004): 375–92; Fereshteh Ahmadi, "Islamic Feminism in Iran: Feminism in a New Islamic Context," *Journal of Feminist Studies in Religion* 22, no. 2 (2006): 33–53.

44. Nikki Keddie, "Women in Iran since 1979," *Social Research* 67, no. 2 (2000): 405–38 (411).

45. Sibel Erol, "Sexual Discourse in Turkish Fiction: Return of the Repressed Female Identity," *Edebiyat* 6, no. 2 (1995): 187–202.

46. Yesim Arat, *Rethinking Islam and Liberal Democracy: Islamist Women in Turkish Politics* (Albany: State University of New York Press, 2005); Alev Çınar, *Modernity, Islam, and Secularism in Turkey: Bodies, Places, and Time* (Minneapolis: University of Minnesota Press, 2005), 78–83.

47. Minoo Moallem, *Between Warrior Brother and Veiled Sister: Islamic Fundamentalism and the Politics of Patriarchy in Iran* (Berkeley: University of California Press, 2005), 81–82; Ziba Mir-Hosseini, *Islam and Gender: The Religious Debate in Contemporary Iran* (Princeton, NJ: Princeton University Press, 2000), 56.

48. Ziba Mir-Hosseini, "The Conservative-Reformist Conflict over Women's Rights in Iran," *International Journal of Politics, Culture, and Society* 16, no.1 (2002): 37–53 (41).

49. Elisabeth Özdalga, *The Veiling Issue, Official Secularism and Popular Islam in Modern Turkey* (Richmond: Curzon Press, 1998), 46.

50. Mirgün Cabas, *2001: Eski Türkiye'nin Son Yılı* (Istanbul: Can Yayınları, 2017), 17.

51. Richard Peres, *The Day Turkey Stood Still: Merve Kavakçı's Walk into the Turkish Parliament* (Reading, UK: Ithaca Press, 2012).

52. "Meclis Devlete Meydan Okunacak Yer Değildir," *Hürriyet*, May 3, 1999, first page.

53. "Demirel: Kavakçı Provokatör," *Milliyet*, May 2, 1999, 19.

54. Perin Gürel, "Good Headscarf, Bad Headscarf: Drawing the (Hair)lines of Turkishness," *Journal of the Ottoman and Turkish Studies Association* 5, no. 2 (2018): 171–93.

55. Süha Bölükbaşı, *Türkiye ve Yakınındaki Ortadoğu* (Ankara: Dış Politika Enstitüsü Yayınları, 1992), 101–6.

56. Yūnis Shukrkhāh, "Khīyābān-i yik taraf-i lāyīk-hā," *Kiyhān*, May 9, 1999, 3.

57. "Namāyandigān-i zan-i majlis, barkhurd-i duwlat-i Turkīyih bā namāyandih-yi muḥajjabih-yi pārlimān-i īn kishvar rā bi shiddat maḥkūm kardand," *Jumhūrī-yi Islāmī*, May 6, 1999, 12.

58. "Himāyat-i zanān-i Irānī az Marvih Kāvākchī," *Zan-i Rūz*, no. 3, May 10, 1999, 7.

59. "İran kendi ideolojisini ihraç için çalışıyor," *Hürriyet*, May 10, 1999, 24.

60. "İşte Dostları," *Sabah*, May 9, 1999, front page.

61. "Fāʾizih Hāshimī dar nāmih-yī khaṭāb bi namāyandih-yi bā-ḥijāb-i turkīyih iʿlām kard: "Mudāfiʿān-i ḥuqūq-i bashar dar barābar-i raftār-i ghiyr-i-insānī-yi lāyīk-hā sukūt kardih-and," *Iran*, May 12, 1999, 3.

62. "Shakhṣīyat-hā, sāzmān-hā va dafātir-i umūr-i zanān mukhālifat-i duwlat-i Turkīyih bā vurūd-i yik namāyandih-yi muḥajjabih rā maḥkūm kardand," *Īrān*, May 6, 1999, 4.

63. I take the language of "expanding opportunities" from Yeşim Arat, "Islamist Women and Feminist Concerns in Contemporary Turkey: Prospects for Women's Rights and Solidarity," *Frontiers: A Journal of Women Studies* 37, no. 3 (2016): 125–50 (126). Valentine Moghadam names both Hashemi Rafsanjani and Rahnavard as prominent Islamic feminists in her important article "Islamic Feminism and Its Discontents: Toward a Resolution of the Debate," *Signs: Journal of Women in Culture and Society* 27, no. 4 (2002): 1135–71 (n. 1). Sedghi, who rejects the notion of "Islamic feminism," calls both women "trespassers" who, regardless of their devoutness, share secular feminists' concern (*Women and Politics in Iran*, 267–70).

64. "Turkey's Veiled MP Defends Herself against Secularist Onslaught," *Mideast Mirror* 13, no. 96 (May 21, 1999), https://advance-lexis-com.proxy.library .nd.edu/api/document?collection=news&id=urn:contentItem:3WHT-P330-008M -N0RT-00000-00&context=1516831. See also Robert Olson, *Turkey-Iran Relations, 1979–2004: Revolution, Ideology, War, Coups and Geopolitics* (Costa Mesa, CA: Mazda, 2004), 50; "Kavakçı İran'ı reddetti," *Milliyet*, May 25, 1999, 17; Nayereh Tohidi, "Piyvand-i jahānī-yi junbish-i zanān-i Īrān," *guft-u-gū*, no. 38 (November 2003): 5–50 (32).

65. Ruhat Mengi, "KA.DER Niye Sessiz?," *Sabah*, May 14, 1999, 8.

66. Stephen Kinzer, "Musings on Freedom, by Wearer of Muslim Scarf," *New York Times*, May 12, 1999, A4; "Bir Hocanın Inadı," *Hürriyet*, May 2, 1999, 26.

67. For Kavakçı's criticism of KA.DER, see Merve Kavakçı Islam, *Headscarf Politics in Turkey: A Postcolonial Reading* (New York: Palgrave Macmillan, 2010), 112.

68. Benedict Anderson, introduction to *Mapping the Nation*, ed. Gopal Balakrishnan and Benedict Anderson (London: Verso, 1996), 1–16 (8).

69. "Burası Devlete Meydan Okunacak Yer Değildir," *Nokta*, May 9–15, 1999, front cover.

70. "Gönüllerin Vekili," *Yeni Şafak*, May 4, 1999.

71. "Shakhṣīyat-hā, sāzmān-hā va dafātir-i umūr-i zanān, mukhālifat-i duwlat-i Turkīyih bā vurūd-i yik namāyandih-yi muḥajjabih rā maḥkūm kardand," *Īrān*, May 6, 1999, 4.

72. Mona Tajali, "Islamic Women's Groups and the Quest for Political Representation in Turkey and Iran," *Middle East Journal* 69, no. 4 (2015): 563–81. Tajali's work examines the first decade of the twentieth century, but her observations hold for this earlier era as well, especially regarding Kavakçı's foregrounding of human rights language.

73. "Headscarved Turkish Deputy Calls Incident Breach of Human Rights," *Tehran Times*, May 4, 1999, www.tehrantimes.com/news/35445/Headscarved -Turkish-Deputy-Calls-Incident-Breach-of-Human-Rights; Kavakçı Islam, *Headscarf Politics in Turkey*, 123.

74. Ḥasan Yūsifī Ishkivarī, "Difāʿ az arzesh-hā bā manṭiq-i dimukrāsī," *Nishāṭ*, April 23, 1999.

75. Nayereh Tohidi, "Jinsīyat, mudirniyat va dimukrāsī," *Jins-i Duvvum* 3 (1378/1999): 10–23; and "Piyvand-i jahānī-yi," 32.

76. Robert Olson, "Turkey-Iran Relations, 1997 to 2000: The Kurdish and Islamist Questions," *Third World Quarterly* 21, no. 5 (October 2000): 871–90 (876).

77. Michel Foucault, "Two Lectures: Lecture Two," in *Power/Knowledge: Selected Interviews and Other Writings, 1972–1977* (New York: Pantheon, 1980), 92–108.

78. Peres, *The Day Turkey Stood Still*, 63.

79. For more on the religious discourse emanating from laïcist politicians and media during the crisis, see Gürel, "Good Headscarf, Bad Headscarf."

80. "Bu Hanım Ajandır," *Sabah*, May 3, 1999, 27.

81. "Turkey's Veiled MP Defends Herself."

82. See Angela Wu Howard, "Leveraging Legal Protection for Religious Liberty," in *The Future of Religious Freedom: Global Challenges,* ed. Allen D. Hertzke (Oxford: Oxford University Press, 2013), 67–83, www.oxford scholarship.com/view/10.1093/acprof:oso/9780199930890.001.0001/acprof -9780199930890-chapter-3; and Amélie Barras, "A Rights-Based Discourse to Contest the Boundaries of State Secularism? The Case of the Headscarf Bans in

France and Turkey," *Democratization* 16, no. 6 (2009): 1237–60. See also Sahin v. Turkey, App. No. 44774/98 (Eur. Ct. H.R. June 29, 2004), *aff'd*, App. No. 44774/98 (Eur. Ct. H.R. November 10, 2005); and Kavakçı v. Turkey, App. No. 71907/01 (Eur. Ct. H.R. April 5, 2007).

83. Author's translation from Turkish. See "Kavakci v. Turkey; Silay v. Turkey; Ilicak v. Turkey," *Human Rights Case Digest* 17, no. 4 (2006–7): 743–46 (745). *HeinOnline*, https://heinonline.org/HOL/P?h=hein.journals/hurcd17&i=729.

84. Nehal Bhuta, "Two Concepts of Religious Freedom in the European Court of Human Rights," *EUI Working Papers LAW*, no. 33 (2021): 10.

85. Samuel Moyn, *Christian Human Rights* (Philadelphia: University of Pennsylvania Press, 2005); Saba Mahmood, *Religious Difference in a Secular Age: A Minority Report* (Princeton, NJ: Princeton University Press, 2016); Elizabeth Shakman Hurd, *The Politics of Secularism in International Relations* (Princeton, NJ: Princeton University Press, 2007); Michael J. Perry, *Idea of Human Rights: Four Inquiries* (New York: Oxford University Press, 1998); Khaled Abou El Fadl, "The Human Rights Commitment in Modern Islam," in *The Human Rights and Responsibilities in the World Religions*, ed. Joseph Runzo and Nancy Martin (Oxford: Oneworld Publications, 2003), 301–64; Joseph Massad, *Islam in Liberalism* (Chicago: University of Chicago Press, 2016).

86. "Fāʾizih Hāshimī dar nāmih-yī khaṭāb bi namāyandih-yi bā-ḥijāb-i Turkīyih iʿlām kard: ʿmudāfiʿān-i ḥuqūq-i bashar dar barābar-i raftār-i ghiyr-i-insānī-yi lāyīk-hā sukūt kardih-and," *Īrān*, no. 1229, May 12, 1999, 3.

87. For another example of how print commentary on the Kavakçı affair was used as indirect criticism of the Iranian regime, see S. H. Pūrḥusaynī, "Ānchih nabāyad ittifāq mī-uftād: darbārih-yi Marvih Kāvākchī" *Ṣubh-i Imrūz*, Tehran, May 19, 1999.

88. "Marżīyih Dabbāgh: Agar namāyandih-yī bidūn-i chādur vārid-i majlis shavad kutak mīkhurad," *Āftāb-i Imrūz*, March 7, 2000, 1. See also Ziba Mir-Hosseini, "The Conservative-Reformist Conflict over Women's Rights in Iran," *International Journal of Politics, Culture, and Society* 16, no. 1 (2002): 37–53.

89. "Bayānīyih-yi Jāmiʿi-yi Islāmī-yi Dānishjūyān nisbat bi mumāniʿat-i namāyandih-yi bāhijāb dar Turkīyih," *Zan-i Rūz*, no. 1702 (May 5, 1999): 55.

90. Karen Garner, *Gender and Foreign Policy in the Clinton Administration* (Boulder, CO: Lynne Rienner, 2013); Kelly J. Shannon, *U.S. Foreign Policy and Muslim Women's Human Rights* (Philadelphia: University of Pennsylvania Press, 2018).

91. Arendt's famous formulation highlighting the connection between nation-state membership and human rights protection is particularly relevant here as the Turkish state eventually stripped Kavakçı of her citizenship, using a minor formality as an excuse. Hannah Arendt, *The Origins of Totalitarianism* (New York: Meridian Books, [1951] 1958), 455. See also Stephanie DeGooyer, Alastair Hunt, Lida Maxwell, and Samuel Moyn, eds. *The Right to Have Rights* (New York: Verso, 2020).

92. E.g., Immanuel Wallerstein, *After Liberalism* (New York: The New Press, 1995), chapter 8; Nikhil Aziz, "The Human Rights Debate in an Era of Globalization: Hegemony of the Discourse," in *Debating Human Rights: Critical Essays from the United States and Asia*, ed. Peter Ness (London: Routledge, 1999), 32–55; Gayatri Chakravorty Spivak, "Righting Wrongs," *South Atlantic Quarterly* 103, nos. 2–3 (2004): 523–81 (523); Lila Abu-Lughod, "Do Muslim Women Need Saving"; Walter Mignolo, *The Darker Side of Western Modernity: Global Futures, Decolonial Options* (Durham, NC: Duke University Press, 2011); Pascha Bueno-Hansen and Sylvanna M Falcón, "Indigenous/Campesina Embodied Knowledge, Human Rights Awards, and Lessons for Transnational Feminist Solidarity," in *Decolonizing Feminism: Transnational Feminism and Globalization*, ed. Margaret A. McLaren (London: Rowman and Littlefield International, 2017), 57–82; Justine Lecroix, Jean-Yves Pranchère, and Gabrielle Maas, *Human Rights on Trial: A Genealogy of the Critique of Human Rights* (Cambridge: Cambridge University Press, 2018), 206–28.

93. Margaret A. McLaren, "Decolonizing Rights: Transnational Feminism and 'Women's Rights as Human Rights,'" in McLaren, *Decolonizing Feminism*, 83–116.

94. "Parliamentary Subcommittee Must Convene for the Iranian Anti-Hijab Activist," *Bianet*, November 20, 2020, https://m.bianet.org/english/women/234766-parliamentary-subcommittee-must-convene-for-the-iranian-anti-hijab-activist.

95. See, e.g., Gi Yeon Koo and Ha Eun Han, "To Veil or Not to Veil: Turkish and Iranian Hijab Policies and the Struggle for Recognition," *Asian Journal of Women's Studies* 24, no. 1 (2018): 47–70; Tajali, "Islamic Women's Groups"; Deniz Durmuş, "Middle Eastern Feminisms: A Phenomenological Analysis of the Turkish and the Iranian Experience," *Comparative and Continental Philosophy* 10, no. 3 (2018): 221–37.

96. Inderpal Grewal and Caren Kaplan, "Global Identities: Theorizing Transnational Studies of Sexuality," *GLQ: A Journal of Lesbian and Gay Studies* 7, no. 4 (2001): 663–79 (664).

97. Chandra Talpade Mohanty, "'Under Western Eyes' Revisited: Feminist Solidarity through Anticapitalist Struggles, *Signs: Journal of Women in Culture and Society* 28, no. 2 (Winter 2003): 499–535; and "Transnational Feminist Crossings: On Neoliberalism and Radical Critique," *Signs: Journal of Women in Culture and Society* 38, no. 4 (2013): 967–91.

98. M. Jacqui Alexander and Chandra Talpade Mohanty, "Cartographies of Knowledge and Power: Transnational Feminism as Radical Praxis," in *Critical Transnational Feminist Praxis,* ed. Amanda Lock Swarr and Richa Nagar (Albany: State University of New York Press, 2010), 23–45 (24).

99. Gayatri Chakravorty Spivak, "Diasporas Old and New: Women in the Transnational World," *Textual Practice* 10, no. 2 (1996): 245–69; Sonia Alvares, "Advocating Feminism: The Latin American Feminist NGO 'Boom,'" *International*

Feminist Journal of Politics 1, no. 2 (1999):181–209; Sonia Alvares, "Translating the Global: Effects of Transnational Organizing on Local Feminist Discourses and Practices in Latin America," *Meridians: Feminism, Race, Transnationalism* 1, no. 1 (2000): 29–67; Basu, "Globalization of the Local," 76; Herr, "Reclaiming Third World Feminism"; Leela Fernandes, *Transnational Feminism in the United States: Knowledge, Ethics, Power* (New York: New York University Press, 2013).

100. Jasbir Puar, "'I Would Rather Be a Cyborg than a Goddess': Intersectionality, Assemblage, and Affective Politics," *Transversal* (2011), http://eipcp .net/transversal/0811/puar/en.

101. Alexander and Mohanty, "Introduction: Genealogies, Legacies, Movements," in *Feminist Geneaologies,* xix; Vrushali Patil, "From Patriarchy to Intersectionality: A Transnational Feminist Assessment of How Far We've Really Come," *Signs: Journal of Women in Culture and Society* 38, no. 4 (2013): 847–67.

CHAPTER 2

The Women's March

A Reflection on Feminist Solidarity, Intersectional Critique, and Muslim Women's Activism

JULIANE HAMMER

ABSTRACT

In this chapter, I reflect on the complex dynamics of intersectional feminist solidarity and critique. I consider how intersectional feminists have engaged in acts of solidarity; who engages in critique, when, and where; and what role religion might play in intersectional analysis and activism. I am especially interested in the question of where religion fits into intersectional frameworks and what might be particular about Islam as the religion under consideration. I explore these questions in the context of several specific historic moments related to the Women's March movement that began in late 2016 following the election of Donald Trump. I am especially interested in the roles, positions, and actions of two Muslim women activists, Linda Sarsour and Zahra Billoo, in the leadership team of the Women's March. I analyze Sarsour's and Billoo's self-representations and reflections as well as the ways in which their respective presence and leadership roles made them targets of anti-Muslim hostility. I also address the specter of their critiques of Zionism and Israeli

*policies on Palestinians as purported expressions of antisemitism.
The chapter highlights the centrality of the notion of solidarity for the
Women's March by refusing to take its meaning for granted. Instead
of deciding whether the Women's March is an example of failed or
unrealized solidarity, or alternatively celebrating it as the epitome
of feminist and intersectional solidarity, I consider the history of the
march as an opening to further reflection on solidarity, movement
and coalition building, and accountability.*

I love the word *solidarity*. Every time I see it in an email signature or a
statement, I feel a thrill. Solidarity is a feeling of connection with and between those who are oppressed. In my native Germany, I was introduced
to the concept of Solidarität at an early age in summer youth camps and in
the Weltfestspiele der Jugend und Studenten (World Festivals of Youth and
Students) that took place twice during my youth. My first foray into activism
was when I joined a German-Palestinian solidarity group in my late teens.
Solidarity's association with socialism and the political Left has made it
a term that for many years did not seem part of the vocabulary of many
activists, including those I have studied as part of several projects focused
on Muslim women's activism for gender justice as social justice. Lately, I
have been seeing it more often, both because Left activism during Trumpism
became more vocal and because it seems to have become more acceptable,
even in more centrist circles. The resurgence of the word *solidarity* itself is
a good enough reason to put it at the center of my analysis here.

In this chapter, I reflect on the complex dynamics of intersectional feminist solidarity and critique. I ask: How have intersectional feminists engaged
in acts of solidarity? How have they expressed solidarity with others in their
complex movements? Where are moments and openings that require critique?
Who gets to critique? And when does critique turn into deconstruction of the
kind that might make solidarity unrealized or even impossible? If intersectional analysis focuses on the intersection between oppressive hierarchies
based on gender, race, and class, where then might religion fit and what might
be particular about Islam as the religion to be considered? Can religion, and
specifically Islam, be explored beyond the oppressive/emancipatory binary?
I explore these questions in the context of several specific historic moments
related to the Women's March movement that began in late 2016 following
the election of Donald Trump. I am especially interested in the roles, positions, and actions of two Muslim women activists, Linda Sarsour and, later,

Zahra Billoo, in the leadership team of the Women's March and how their presence and participation was perceived, celebrated, and also criticized. I analyze Sarsour's and Billoo's self-representations and reflections as well as the ways in which their respective presence and leadership roles made them targets of anti-Muslim hostility. I am especially interested in the tension around their own feminist and intersectional politics and commitments, on the one hand, and the ways in which critical approaches to their work were framed as intersectional feminist critiques, on the other. I also address the specter of their critiques of Zionism and Israeli policies on Palestinians as purported expressions of antisemitism. Based on feminist scholarship on the Women's March, Sarsour's memoir, her and Billoo's media presence in interviews and on social media, and on media coverage of the events and debates under consideration, I tell a story of several pivotal moments in the history of the Women's March as an organization and in relation to these Muslim women activists. The chapter highlights the centrality of the notion of solidarity for the Women's March by refusing to take its meaning for granted. Instead of deciding whether the Women's March is an example of failed or unrealized solidarity, or alternatively celebrating it as the epitome of feminist and intersectional solidarity, I consider the history of the march as an opening to further reflect on solidarity, movement and coalition building, and accountability.

FEMINISM, INTERSECTIONALITY, AND RELIGION

My scholarly interest in intersectionality as a theoretical framework grew out of my engagement with feminist and gender theory combined with an increasing awareness that my work on American Muslims, gender and sexual norms, and anti-Muslim hostility really makes sense as a theoretical and activist intervention only when it acknowledges as foundational to US society, both historically and in the contemporary moment, the intersection of sexism and patriarchy with racism (and, less obviously, class-based exploitation). Intersectionality as a theory, an analytic, and as a tool for activism owes its existence to Black feminist scholars. While most often immediately associated with Kimberlé Crenshaw in the context of law, others, including Patricia Hill Collins, have contributed to its development, contestation, and critical reception.[1] Hill Collins, Anna Carastathis, Jennifer Nash, and others have noted the increasingly common use of intersectionality as a rhetorical stand-in for overlapping identities and thus a liberal notion of diversity that aims to acknowledge that various identity categories, foremost among them gender, race, and class, affect the ways in which human beings live their lives.[2] I see this appropriation of an analytic produced by Black feminist theorists, which was and is a radical critique of racial, class, and gender hierarchies and the resulting oppression of people on the lowest level of these intersecting hierarchies, as an intentional blunting of their instrument of critique as mere identity politics.[3]

As a feminist scholar of religion, in particular Islam, and as a Muslim feminist, I have also considered where religion might fall within intersectionality as an analytic. I am interested in two possibilities that go beyond simply adding religion to the intersection. The first is to introduce intersectionality theory into the study of religion in order to explore how oppressive gender, race, and class hierarchies affect religious practice, discourse, and experience in the past and the present without yet again falling back on intersecting identity categories. Here, studying Muslim women would entail recognizing that a hierarchy of (world) religions, itself a product of the colonial European enterprise that used Christianity to assert European superiority in yet another register, placed Muslims in an inferior category that justified the colonization and thus oppression of Muslim societies and communities. That work is already being done by scholars, including me.[4] The second possibility is more complicated as it considers how religion could be engaged, not as an additional identity category, thereby crowding the intersection, but as a force to reckon with in the struggle against oppression, exploitation, and injustice that is at the heart of intersectional feminism as a theory and as a movement.[5] I think here of a paradigm from anti–domestic violence work in which different categories, such as religion, culture, and family, can be identified as either a roadblock or a resource in the struggle against domestic abuse. Expanded to the topic at hand, Muslim women could (and do) mobilize Islamic ethical notions of justice as a resource to draw on in their activism for intersectional social justice projects.[6]

The caveat here is that Black feminist scholars in the United States share with many other feminists a deep reluctance to engage religion (discursively and institutionally) at the very least and outright rejection of such engagement at the most. This spectrum from ambivalence to rejection in feminist discourse, often described with the term "secular," is reflected clearly in the work of intersectionality theorists if in no other form than by the absence of religion from their works. It is not difficult to see why feminist activists and thinkers would be suspicious of religion: their experiences of patriarchal oppression and exploitation are historically linked to religious structures, discourses, and institutions that support(ed) and legitimate(d) patriarchy. The entanglement of religion in patriarchy clearly intersects with religion's (especially Christianity's) complicity in anti-Black racism and the enslavement of Africans and African Americans. From the prosperity gospel to Protestant support for euthanasia, there is also a direct link to the legitimation of class structures and class-based exploitation as divinely mandated and thus justified.

Consequently, religious feminists, namely, those who do embrace their religion as a source of inspiration for the struggles for justice while also challenging their own religious traditions and communities, have been met with suspicion, occasional ridicule, and rejection by secular feminists. The picture becomes even more complicated when we focus specifically on Muslim feminist activists and scholars, as responses to their work and conviction have been met with disapproval from at least two directions: patriarchal Muslim scholars, leaders, and communities;[7] and secular feminists. We can also trace a somewhat patronizing inclusion of Muslim feminists, in at first Christian and then Jewish-Christian feminist circles, in which they have been treated as relative latecomers who need to catch up.[8]

In what follows, I am taking seriously Linda Sarsour's and Zahra Billoo's expressions of faith (beyond their headscarves!), not to measure their sincerity, but to develop an analysis of how their Muslimness, alongside other aspects of their positionalities, matters in the interplay between activism, solidarity, and critique. I argue that the involvement of religious feminists in the movement building of the Women's March matters but/and that Muslim organizers have been put under a different kind of scrutiny from others, both on account of their Muslimness as their religious affiliation and through their racialization as Muslims.

FEMINISTS, ANTI-MUSLIM HOSTILITY, AND RACISM

There is a robust literature on anti-Muslim hostility (and Islamophobia)[9] that has become so theoretically sophisticated and diversified that it is no longer easy to offer a basic definition or statement.[10] I employ the following as a working definition of anti-Muslim hostility: a set of phenomena including hate crimes against Muslims, orientalist media and politicians' pronouncements about Islam, racist discrimination and attacks against Muslims, hate speech, and myriad forms of rhetorical and practical othering. These many expressions of anti-Muslim hostility are held together by the intentional production of Islamophobic rhetoric and media content, as well as by the systemic production of state policies, laws, and practices, including surveillance, criminalization, infiltration, and denial of citizenship. While the relationship between religion and race is complex, it is important to recognize the link between anti-Muslim hostility and racism, as they are both directed primarily at Black and Brown people. Also significant is the racialization of Muslims as non-White and thus foreign bodies in the social fabric of the United States, whose otherness is variously linked to skin color, culture, and/or religion, as has been demonstrated in a growing body of scholarship that has influenced my own work.[11] A last important dimension is the treatment of Muslimness as pseudoracial, imprinted on Muslims' bodies and beyond their control.

The focus on anti-Muslim hostility as entangled with racism, formulated in specific ways in the US context,[12] should not distract us from the ways in which anti-Muslim hostility is also always entangled with gender and sexuality. I have analyzed these gendered dimensions of anti-Muslim hostility in earlier work and want to draw together just a few strands of that work here to move my analysis forward and connect several theoretical pieces to each other. As I argued in an essay in 2013, Muslim women have been "center stage" in Islamophobic discourses because the trope of the oppressed Muslim woman in need of saving by White men (and increasingly women) has been around for several centuries. Scholars such as Leila Ahmed and Charlotte Weber have traced European (and especially British) feminists' complicity with and direct ideological support for the colonial project in Asia and Africa. American feminists followed them in the early twentieth century as the United States pursued its neocolonial interests in the Middle East and beyond.[13] Edward Said's idea of Orientalism, while not invested in a gendered analysis, can be extended to show how the study of Muslim and Middle Eastern societies as an academic subject for the consumption of colonial administrators included ideas about Muslim women and their oppression.

As Saba Mahmood and others have shown, American (mostly White) feminists continue to be important agents in anti-Muslim discursive production because they represent female and feminist authenticity.[14] In their support for military intervention in Afghanistan and Iraq they cast Muslim women as victims of Muslim men, Muslim societies, and Islam who are in need of saving, naturally by American and/or European intervention. There is no recognition, though, of the myriad ways in which Muslim women are victimized, harassed, discriminated against, threatened, and killed by people in the American society of which they are a part. It is this victimization of Muslim women that demonstrates the power of anti-Muslim hostility as a political discourse, which when turned into acts of violence especially targets women who wear a headscarf because they are most easily recognizable as Muslim women.[15]

Feminist entanglements with anti-Muslim hostility are but one dimension of the history of American feminisms. It was the interventions by Black feminists that moved the (always already plural) feminist movement into what has been described as its third wave. That wave brought the analytic of intersectionality—which calls for the analysis of the intersecting oppressive hierarchies of gender, race, and class and other oppressive systems—into full view.[16] Womanist scholars and activists included spirituality and religion as resources for their work.[17] Writings such as those from the Crunk Feminist Collective—which includes Brittney C. Cooper, Susana M. Morris, and Robin M. Boylorn—weave considerations of Black and queer feminist Christianity into reflections, dreams, and radical visions for Black futures.[18] Mujerista feminists included considerations of sexuality, religion, and immigration status and experiences in their work, thereby creating multidimensional representations and analyses at first of women and then of nonmale individuals.[19] Outspoken, even if marginalized, Christian and Jewish feminists, albeit predominantly White, contributed to a further opening up of feminist possibilities. Muslim women are Black, Brown, immigrants, negotiating sexual and gender norms, and subjected to anti-Muslim hostility, racism, and sexism in specific configurations. Contrary to the picture I presented above, however, they are also agents, scholars, and activists. Anti-Muslim hostility happens to them but is not their only defining feature or even their only impetus for activist and intellectual engagement.

Because of the colonial and racist entanglement of feminisms, Muslim women scholars and activists have positioned themselves vis-à -vis feminism on a spectrum ranging from identifying with the label to rejecting it as nonauthentic and counterproductive. Fatima Seedat has explored these positionings, thereby demonstrating that Muslim women participate actively not only in the reshaping of Islam but also in the reshaping of what feminism means.[20] Both Linda Sarsour and Zahra Billoo have identified as feminists and Muslims in their public representation.

That has also put them, as well as scholars who write about Muslim women and activism, in what Rochelle Terman calls the "double bind," which serves as the diagnosis of a problem that can be "cured" by responsible critique. Terman recognizes the weight of navigating the dual pressures of engaging in critique of imperialist and anti-Muslim modes of representing Muslim women, on the one hand, and patriarchal limitations from within Muslim contexts, on the other. She concludes, "In order to engage in the 'productive undoing' of the double bind, I propose we shift the paradigm of responsible critique from recruitability to one based on openness. A responsible critique is one that opens the widest analytic space in which a double critique can take place, qualifies the most voices, and allows for the greatest creativity in producing new political imaginaries."[21]

RELIGION, ISLAM, AND THE WOMEN'S MARCH

In the next step, I reflect on the ways in which several feminist scholarly articles published after the 2017 Women's March addressed (or did not address) religion in general and Islam in particular. Mindful of the entanglement of secular feminists in particular forms of anti-Muslim hostility, as well as the broader suspicion of religion as a source for social justice activism, I read these articles and book chapters for their treatment of religion, more specifically, the religious identities and expressions of the four-woman leadership team of the original Women's March. The conclusion, namely, that the publications considered here do not address religion at all or do address them in ways that erase the religious identities of the organizers, is juxtaposed to the image of the woman with the American flag hijab that became one of the most popular poster choices during the march.[22] This is not an exhaustive analysis of everything that has been published on the Women's March but a spot check, so to speak, of whether feminist scholars have addressed religion in their analysis.[23]

My first example is a chapter by Marie Berry and Erica Chenoweth titled, "Who Made the Women's March?"[24] The authors explore how the national co-chairs of the Women's March, Bob Bland, Tamika Mallory, Carmen Perez, and Linda Sarsour, managed to organize an event of this magnitude in just nine weeks. They also chronicle the various critiques of the movement and "how and why the Women's March evolved from a mostly white, elite, liberal feminist movement to a broader-based, intersectional march through various framing techniques and a process of coalition-building." I especially appreciate their image of the Women's March as a river and their research task as exploring its "organizational tributaries."[25] However, curiously, the words *religion, religious*, or *Christian* do not appear at all in the chapter. The word *Muslim* appears three times but never attached to Linda Sarsour or the possible participation of other Muslim women activists. Rather, in all three instances, we find Muslims listed among those attacked by the incoming Trump administration or as the focus of connected solidarity activities to support Muslim immigrants, that is, as the objects of Women's March activism but not the agents of it. The word *solidarity* appears ten times and is celebrated as organically connected to the narrative of the movement.

In their critical sociological study published in 2018, Sierra Brewer and Lauren Dundes explored the qualitative responses of twenty young African American women and their assessment of the Women's March's potential to transform US women's movements into racially inclusive ones through a framework of intersectional feminism.[26] The study includes a quote from Tamika Mallory but does not mention the other three national co-chairs by name. It also does not mention any of the words I had already searched for in the previous example: *religion, religious, Christian*, or *Muslim*.

In Rachel Presley and Alane Presswoods's powerful and autoethnographic analysis of representation at the Women's March, we find feminist thinkers including Gloria Anzaldúa, Audre Lorde, Leela Fernandes, and Sara Ahmed and a profound reflection on the politics of activism and the relationship between solidarity and intersectionality. I return to the solidarity aspect below but want to yet again first search for signs of reflection on the significance of religion. The word *Muslim* again appears three times, twice as part of a list of groups attacked by the Trump campaign and administration and once in relation to a Facebook group, Pantsuit Nation, that "emerged as a safe place for women of color, trans* people, immigrants, Muslims, and other historically marginalized individuals to share their stories of oppression and resistance."[27] No other mention is made of religion or the religious affiliation of the organizers.

In a communications study of the role of affect and emotion in relation to intersectionality, Jessica Gantt-Shafer, Cara Wallis, and Caitlin Miles argue that participants had different entry points to the march as the beginning of a movement, including gender, sexuality, ethnicity, and generation. They describe how inviting Sarsour, Perez, and Mallory to co-lead the march turned it into an intersectional movement as well, directly quoting Perez.[28] The word *Muslim* appears once in a list of marginalized identity categories. Despite their interest in affect, the study does not consider religion otherwise.

In yet another example, the feminist geographers Pamela Moss and Avril Maddrell focus on the Women's March in terms of the creation of spaces for inclusion and the acknowledgment of intersectional dynamics. Yet again, we see that religion is not even considered as a factor or motivator. The phrase "Muslim women" appears once in a list of women invited to participate in the march, and it comes as a direct quote from the invitation announcement.[29] In summary, each of the four pieces examined here does not engage religion as a category in any substantial way.

The point of this spot assessment is not to complain about these publications or their authors. Rather, it serves as an illustration of the point that religion remains a blind spot in much of feminist analysis, certainly on the Women's March.[30] That intuitive rather than intentional erasure can morph into more explicit expressions of antireligious feminist bias and, more problematically, anti-Muslim hostility in its liberal feminist forms. What falls victim to the latter is the possibility of Muslim feminist agency.[31] The Muslim woman with the flag hijab on Fairey's poster, albeit perhaps reduced to her hijab in some ways or made iconic by it, is at least acknowledged as religious and connected to Islam. The "we the people are greater than fear" text on the poster seems to tacitly acknowledge anti-Muslim hostility albeit defined as fear. I have already discussed above how some liberal feminist discourse has intentionally demonized Muslim women activists by withdrawing the, however patronizing, blanket of saving Muslim women from Islam and Muslim men. For intersectional solidarity to be inclusive will require consideration of religion where activists and participants in movements draw on them as sources of inspiration for their work.

The Women's March and Solidarity

Solidarity as a concept was so central to the Women's March that it is easy to take its meaning(s) for granted. It runs through the announcements of the organizers and appears frequently and organically in the academic literature on the march. In this section, I want to revisit the four publications above, and draw on a few additional ones, to demonstrate that the nature of solidarity is not self-evident but instead is itself subject to constant negotiation and interpretation. Solidarity is a sentiment, a value, a project, and a commitment.

Deborah Frizzell's photo essay and reflections from the day of the march present us with a promising title: "Positions in Solidarity." I am struck by the preposition *in* and how it allows for thinking solidarity as movement while the plural "positions" also opens up consideration of solidarity as multivalent and open to interpretation. Elsewhere in the essay, Frizzell compares the Women's March to the Occupy movement she also participated in: "As a participant in Occupy Wall Street, I was slightly bored milling around without direction. Where were the front lines? It was a completely different kind of action, more a show of solidarity and support than a protest. It was exciting to see that many people, shocking numbers of people, an endless stream of new posters and more hats. The overwhelming numbers stood for something meaningful. We spent the day reading posters and chatting with people, all excited to be there. It seemed that everyone felt they couldn't miss this moment in history."[32]

In their article, Diane H. Felmlee and colleagues explore the expression of sentiments on Twitter about the march, including hashtags and words in hashtags, which they code as positive or negative. Like Frizzell, they juxtapose solidarity (along with peace, love, unity, and democracy) to protest (and resistance), but they do so by also coding them as a positive/negative binary.[33] For Presley and Presswood, solidarity is multivalent as well: they define working "towards solidarity as its own political act." They also link protest and solidarity instead of juxtaposing them. As such, the exercise of protest and the plural performance of intersectional solidarity quite literally makes the body present in a viewable space of public appearance, to later again describe solidarity not as a sentiment or a given but as a goal: "The March's continual push toward intersectional solidarity attends well to the tangled identities of women on a mass scale, advocating for protest as a deterritorialized movement."[34]

Moss and Maddrell take us further in our exploration of solidarity and critique: "For some, the Women's March was an epiphany, a political awakening, a wondrous expression of interwoven resistance and solidarity. Yet in the days before and immediately after the March, criticism arising from feminist activists, bloggers, and scholars about the way in which intersectionality and inclusion were taken up by organizers, protesters and marchers eclipsed the glow of solidarity experienced by many participants."[35] They define solidarity as a set of practices, thus plural,[36] that attend to "solidarity ties" among marchers that can be broken by internal critique and see "hope in feminist solidarity within and across all genders."[37] Their essay is the introduction to a collection of essays in the immediate aftermath of the march. It states, "In the search for solidarity, tensions within groups and among individuals shaped the way in which resistance and protests were responded to and organized. The authors in this collection take up themes of intersectionality and inclusion/exclusion via politicizing the personal, contesting the state, and challenging simplistic notions of unity in solidarity."[38]

It is helpful to acknowledge that there is of course an important connection to be drawn between solidarity, movement building, and coalition building. Where solidarity emphasizes a project, a feeling, and a potentially abstract idea based on connection and affinity, coalition building acknowledges more directly the strategic steps necessary to movement building that include finding the smallest common denominator and building out from there. The notion of solidarity and the name of the Women's March signaled a focus on women, and with that, albeit unacknowledged, a focus on reproductive rights so central to the feminist project. Commentators and analysts of the march have suggested repeatedly that the emphasis on unity always masked (or veiled) deep tensions between organizers and marchers over other aspects of their identities, most prominently race. The celebration of women's solidarity then may have felt to some like an erasure of their connected and equally relevant social justice concerns.

In the second half of this chapter, I take the theoretical insights and configurations from the first half and apply them to three specific moments, so to speak, in which Linda Sarsour and then Zahra Billoo appeared as central figures in media representations and assessments of and debates about the Women's March. I trace how they represented themselves as Muslim women and feminists who also embrace and support causes such as Black Lives Matter, immigrant rights and protections, LGBTQIA recognition, and, not least, strong political support for Palestinians. I also track moments of critique from within the march movement and from allies, as well as from detractors of the march movement as a whole. Given that the Women's March constituted the largest single-day protest in history until then, according to Felmlee and colleagues, including 680 "sister marches" in other US locations as well as many more across the globe, it is difficult to draw boundaries between the march movement and what was "outside" it. Remember also the image of tributary streams (organizations) that came together to support the march, express intersectional solidarity, incorporate related political agenda items, and supply seasoned activists and organizers. Throughout my analysis, I keep a close eye on expressions of and references to Islam and religion, both from the protagonists and the people commenting on their work.

MUSLIM WOMEN ACTIVISTS AND THREE MOMENTS IN THE LIFE OF THE WOMEN'S MARCH

Organizing the Women's March: Late 2016 to January 2017

As the story is told, shortly after the election of Donald Trump as president in November 2016, a White woman by the name of Teresa Shook, who lived in Hawaii, created an event on Facebook, calling for a women's march in Washington, DC, and hundreds of people responded. Around the same time, another White woman, Bob Bland, called for a march along similar lines, and within less than two days, a movement was formed that included Bob Bland, Linda Sarsour, Tamika Mallory, and Carmen Perez as co-chairs of what would eventually become the Women's March. Sarsour, Mallory, and Perez, who had a shared history of community organizing, were brought on board after concerns were expressed about a women's movement being led by White women only. Teresa Shook supported the formation of the Women's March but did not take an active role in its leadership.[39]

In her speech at the March on January 18, 2017, Linda Sarsour identified as "unapologetically Muslim American, . . . Palestinian American, and from Brooklyn, New York." She denounced the new president as having won the election on the backs of "Muslims and Black people, and undocumented people, and Mexicans, and people with disabilities, and on the backs of women." A little later, she called on those attending to keep their "voices loud for Black women, for Native women, for undocumented women, for LGBTQIA communities, for people with disabilities."[40] Expressing solidarity with such groups who experience intersecting modes of oppression had already been one of the hallmarks of her public remarks and activism and a reflection of her intersectional movement for justice commitments. In a 2015 feature about Sarsour in the *New York Times*, Alan Feuer described her, in her engagement with New York Muslim communities: "The voice she brings to New York's Muslims, a diverse group of Arabs, Southeast Asians, Africans and African-Americans, is loud, strident and inflected with both street smarts and the tropes of 'intersectionality,' as the trending term has it. That means Ms. Sarsour has sought to speak not only for those who share her religion, but also for others—women, gays, prison inmates, victims of racial profiling—facing the problems that concern her."[41]

She had already had a history of activist work when the 2016 election changed the political climate. She was the director of the Arab American Association of New York, had organized and participated in Black Lives Matters protests since 2014, had played a significant part in the recognition of Islamic holidays as public-school holidays in New York City schools, and had helped organize resistance to the surveillance and intimidation of Muslim communities in New York by the New York Police Department (NYPD).

In her memoir, *We Are Not Here to Be Bystanders*, Sarsour describes her realization that she does not remember first meeting with either Tamika Mallory or Carmen Perez. They were in one another's activist orbit, and it felt like they had always been around, fighting for the same causes. Sarsour writes, "These two fierce and loving women were my touchstones even before I knew they were my sisters."[42] In early 2015, their friendship and co-organizing were galvanized by their joint organization of a march from New York City to Washington, DC, called "March2Justice." Halfway through the chapter "Nine Days in April," she pauses to detail one of the marchers' stopovers at a mosque in North Philadelphia. In reading the passage, I was struck by this description: "Sometime around 11 P.M., Carmen lit some sage and waved it over our group, and spoke prayers for our safety and success. She did this every evening before we retired and every morning before we set off."[43] Here is one of several places in which Sarsour describes Perez as a deeply religious person and accepts expressions of such rituals like the one described. It is worth noting that I have not come across any criticism of Perez as "too religious" or because of her religion not able to identify as a feminist, all accusations that have been leveled at Sarsour.

Later in the same chapter, Sarsour describes everyone being awakened the next morning by the call to prayer from the imam of the mosque.

She explained the meaning and watched as "everyone grew still and just listened, entranced by the sheer beauty of the imam's voice and the way it reverberated in the heart. Some people bowed their heads and said their own prayers, while others stared up at the ceiling or down at their hands in respectful silence."[44] She concludes the chapter: "For me, that was perhaps the most meaningful aspect of our night at the mosque in Philly—to be able to introduce fellow marchers to my Palestinian community and my faith."[45]

One particular feature of the attacks on Sarsour came from pundits who took issue with her self-identification as a feminist. In what follows I bring together two examples of such attacks and what could well be read as Sarsour's response to the latter.

In August 2015, Danusha Goska published an open letter to Sarsour in *FrontPage Magazine*. Goska, who holds a PhD from Indiana University, describes herself as a child of Polish Catholic immigrants, is the author of several books and a frequent writer, often reviews of books, for *FrontPage Magazine* and the *Jewish Voice*. Goska is intensely anti-Muslim and also rejects the Black Lives Matter movement and activist scholarship. *FrontPage Magazine* is one outlet of the David Horowitz Freedom Center, a right-wing think tank that also maintains the hate website Jihad Watch. The letter lists Sarsour's positions and the honors she has received and contains a quote in which Sarsour identified as a feminist because she is a Muslim. Goska then tells the story of Kayla Mueller, a young American woman who was a humanitarian worker in Syria when she was captured by the Islamic State (IS) in 2013. Mueller died in IS captivity in 2015. Goska takes issue with Sarsour's insistence that the sexual assault and enslavement of women by IS fighters and leaders has nothing to do with Islam. The purpose of the letter is to demonstrate that Sarsour is a hypocrite who lies about the true nature of Islam and that she has no right to call herself a feminist either. The tone of the letter is condescending and accusatory. Goska quotes from the Qur'an and cites scholarly authorities for her claims about Islam and slavery. In the end, she tells Sarsour that she could be saved if she recognized the true will of God and the prophets (Sarsour claims to believe in). She does not say how.[46]

In January 2017, *The Federalist*, a conservative online magazine founded in 2013, published an essay by Shireen Qudosi, who is described as a "Sufi Muslim of Afghan and South Asian ancestry, and writer on Islam." In it, Qudosi rails against the Women's March, liberal feminism, and the

Democratic Party's supposed embrace of Sarsour. She also hails President Trump as the quintessential representation of what has always moved America forward: productive controversy. The essay contains racist statements like this one: "An entire group of women, particularly women of color, have adopted the disability of self-victimization, even going so far as to ask 'white-women' participating in the march to observe and make space for women of color." Qudosi describes Sarsour in these words: "Venerated by leftists, Sarsour now rides the great beast of modern feminism much like the 'god-King' Xerxes in '300.' This weekend she and other heads of the Soros-connected movement protested against a democratically elected president. This is a Palestinian woman protesting about the democratic process in the freest country in the world."[47] Profiled and maligned on websites like Counterjihad, Jihad Watch, and many others, Sarsour is depicted as radical and extremist, naive and cunning, hypocritical and dangerous. She is apparently the nightmare of right-wing and neoconservative pundits and politicians.

Sarsour, for her part, was undeterred by the attacks and actively pushed back. In August 2017, she reiterated her commitments in a public Facebook statement in which she linked her feminism to her "unapologetic love for Palestine and the Palestinian people," her "opposition to military occupation, colonization and land grabbing," her hijab, and her love for and adherence to her Islamic faith, challenging those who cannot "fathom to see women of color lead, inspire and win," who have faith "in a system that brutalizes people of color," and whose feminism "puts our lives in more danger." The post ends by saying, "YOU can keep your feminism. We promise you, we don't want it."[48]

Her leadership in the Women's March expanded the spotlight on Sarsour and brought her to the attention of more people, both those who supported her and those who were out to attack and undermine her. Melissa Harris-Perry would later write that "Sarsour has been the most reliable target of public vitriol this year. Within days of the historic gathering in Washington, DC, right wing media began to characterize her as a sharia law implementing terrorist. Conservative college student groups have shared talking points used to question her credibility. They video her responses, post them online, sending subsequently more trolls in her direction. More importantly, the controversy reduces requests for speaking engagements, a key source of income for all movement organizers since Dr. King."[49]

Internal critiques are significantly more difficult to find, in part because one response to the "double bind" described above is an impulse to keep such critique internal, in a process that activists think of as "calling in rather than calling out." One interesting space for me to observe the unfolding of such critique is a public Facebook group called FITNA: Feminist Islamic Trouble Makers of North America. Since its inception in 2016, members have reposted Facebook statuses from Linda Sarsour but also links to pieces that are critical of her positions, for example, in a case of sexual harassment that allegedly occurred in an organization that Sarsour led. Similarly, members have voiced frustration with the ways in which Sarsour is alleged to take up the spotlight on Muslim women, which erases Black Muslim women from the broader picture. There have also been concerns about the stance Sarsour seemed to be taking in defense of the Palestinian store owner whose employee called the police on George Floyd in Minnesota, leading to Floyd's murder by police in 2020.[50]

Similarly, and also very differently, if we want to think of US Muslim communities as "her communities," as she has in her life of activism, then there is also a different and equally complicated tracing of internal critique that echoes on social media or will alternatively appear as an absence of sorts. I admit that I have been puzzled that Sarsour enjoys significant popularity in the (perhaps imagined) Muslim mainstream, despite her stances on political organizing and on LGBTQIA acceptance and the fact that she is a young woman activist rather than a male religious leader. Sarsour does not seem to worry about such acceptance, but she has it nonetheless, as demonstrated by the fact that she was invited to and spoke at the conventions of the Islamic Society of North America in 2016 and 2017.[51]

The above paragraphs drive home several of my broader arguments: Sarsour was attacked differently from Perez and Mallory (not to mention Bland) because she is visibly, and unapologetically, as she has said, Muslim. Perez, who identifies as Chicana, and Mallory who identifies as Black, as well as Sarsour as a Palestinian and thus Arab American, are all caught up in racist hierarchies that endanger their lives, deny them agency, and see them as a threat to entrenched systems of White supremacy and patriarchy. Debate over Sarsour also illustrates the difficulty of "calling in" in various community settings. For example, how would one go about asking Sarsour to recognize that taking up space as an organizer and a leader may displace others, especially Black women? Concepts such as solidarity and justice, both central to Sarsour's self-representation, are not self-evident but rather require negotiation and reflection, especially about power distribution and platform holding in activist spaces and progressive movements.

The co-chairs organized several other events over the course of 2017 and 2018, including the strike action "A Day Without a Woman" on March 8, 2017, International Women's Day, and a significantly smaller Women's March in January 2018.[52] Sarsour's book, while published in 2020, actually ends around the end of 2018, with brief reflections on the midterm elections and a local protest in New York against the murder of Saheed Vassell by police in April 2018.

The End of the First Leadership Team in 2019

That solidarity, like love, requires continuous nurturing, reflection, and consideration, became clear when in September 2019 news outlets began reporting that a major reshuffle of leadership had taken place at the organization that the Women's March had developed into over several years. Perhaps even further, the solidarity of and within the Women's March as a movement, while never uncontested, seemed to disintegrate in the face of persistent accusations of antisemitism. Solidarity could no longer be realized or maintained. The *Washington Post* ran an article that declared, "Women's March replaces three original leaders, after anti-Semitism accusations, with 16 board members." The article, by Marissa Lang, goes on to explain that Linda Sarsour, Bob Bland, and Tamika Mallory had all stepped down on July 15 but that the organization had not announced their departure earlier. The team of four co-chairs was to be replaced by a board of sixteen very diverse women, and Carmen Perez was slated to stay on as part of that board. One of the main reasons for the departure of Sarsour, Bland, and Mallory, as stated in the title of the article, was the persistent accusation of antisemitism, especially as it had been leveled at Sarsour and Mallory.[53] Other concerns revolved around infighting, financial mismanagement, and a lack of commitment to participation in the preelection struggle to vote Trump out of office.

Responses from Bland, Mallory, and Sarsour emphasized that they themselves had initiated the changes rather than, as the original headline of the article read, having been "ousted" from the Women's March leadership. The NBC announcement of their departure singled out antisemitism as the sole reason and included a joint statement by the three women released by the Women's March: "Our mission was to build a powerful institution that defied the status quo, centered the leadership of women of color and united diverse women around a set of principles that are intersectional, visionary and bold and we feel accomplished," also noting that all three would focus on other projects in their respective organizations.[54]

It is clear from these and many other news pieces in those few days in September 2019 that the labeling of Sarsour and Mallory in particular as antisemitic, or at the very least as not having distanced themselves from antisemitic people and remarks, was the main issue in their departure from the leadership of the Women's March. Bland seemed to have been put into a different category and supposedly left for different reasons. As a White woman, unmarked by religion, Bland did not face the entangled discrimination of Sarsour as Palestinian and Muslim and Mallory as a Black woman. The label of antisemitism in its contested connection with criticism of Israel and/or Zionism is central to my reflections here. Consequently, I attend to its analysis further in a separate section later in this chapter.[55] As a preview of that analysis I suggest here that intersectional solidarity and feminist critique are simultaneously challenged by the focus on antisemitism and that the specter of Israel, Zionism, and Judaism and their relationship to one another is often (a deeply feared) elephant in the room of solidarity and critique.

New Leadership and the Ouster of Zahra Billoo

The same news pieces that announced the "departures" of Sarsour, Mallory, and Bland from the leadership of the Women's March also included mention of the new sixteen-member board that was to elect the new leadership. I remember thinking that a sixteen-member collective was too large to lead the organization but that having so many members might also alleviate some of the issues connected to figureheads of organizations gaining recognition but then also holding significant decision-making power, as was the case for Mallory, Perez, Bland, and Sarsour. They consulted others, and there were additional people in leadership positions, but they also seemed to make many decisions alone and in an undemocratic fashion that posed problems, especially for a feminist organization. It is clear from academic and activist analysis that the organization was built around notions of solidarity and justice and thus an intersectional analysis of overlapping and systemic oppression of groups and communities other than women. The "feminist" platform was, from the very start, complicated by questions of the definition of women (are trans* women included?), as well as the recognition that not all women see their goals or even analysis and critique of patriarchy as aligned. For example, there was talk of antichoice women's organizations wanting to join, which turned out to be a bridge too far for the movement's leaders.

In the lead up to the Women's March in January 2019, debates about direction and inclusion were renewed when frustrated local organizers were denied the Women's March "brand" and a separate organization,[56] March On, broke away from the larger group over the allegations of antisemitism. As *The Guardian*'s Lucia Graves wrote in 2019:

> From its earliest days the Women's March has been fraught with racial tensions, with minority women concerned that white participants had ignored their needs. Some women feel the current fracas around antisemitism is just one more way for women to be divided from one another.
>
> That's why sponsors such as Planned Parenthood are sticking with the march, even as they "unequivocally reaffirm that there is no place for antisemitism, racism, homophobia, transphobia or any kind of bigotry in our communities."[57]

The creation of the sixteen-member board seemed to check more "diversity and inclusion"[58] boxes: "The 16 new board members are Samia Assed, Zahra Billoo, Charlene Carruthers, Mrinalini Chakraborty, Rabbi Tamara Cohen, Rev. T. Sheri Dickerson, Sarah Eagle Heart, Lucy Flores, Ginny Goldman, Ginna Green, Shawna Knipper, Isa Noyola, Kelley Robinson, Rinku Sen, Leslie Templeton and Lu-Shawn Thompson."[59] Among them were three Jewish women, a transgender woman, a former legislator, two religious leaders, and a member of the Oglala tribe of the Lakota Nation.

A *Salon* article on September 17, 2019, immediately singled out Zahra Billoo: "The 16-member board of the Women's March, which includes three Jewish women, has also included Zahra Billoo, a controversial figure who heads the San Francisco Bay Area chapter of the Council on American-Islamic Relations. According to the *Forward*, Billoo has posted tweets claiming that "apartheid Israel kills children as a hobby" and that "Zionism is a very real threat to our national security."[60] The tweets are cited third hand in this article rather than taken from Billoo's Twitter account directly. However, as discussed below, Billoo did not deny posting the tweets one of which embraces the notion of an apartheid system perpetuated by Israel, a designation that would later be confirmed by both the Israeli human rights organization B'Tselem and by Human Rights Watch.[61] That same tweet also traffics in the antisemitic trope of killing children "as a hobby."

Only two days later, the *San Francisco Chronicle* reported that the "Bay Area Muslim leader [was] booted off [the] Women's March board over Israel tweets." Billoo responded by describing the ouster as linked to her Muslim identity and secondarily to her position on Palestine.

> In a lengthy Twitter thread, Billoo, executive director of the Council on American-Islamic Relations' Bay Area chapter, said the decision followed an "Islamophobic smear campaign" largely led by "people who oppose me and my work challenging the occupation of Palestine, our country's perpetuation of unjust and endless wars, and law enforcement operations targeting the American Muslim community." . . . Billoo admitted Thursday on Twitter to writing "passionately," and said that while she might phrase some of her statements differently today, she stands by her words. "I told the truth as my community and I have lived it, through the FBI's targeting of my community, as I supported families who have lost loved ones because of U.S. military actions, and as I learned from the horrific experiences of Palestinian life," she said."[62]

The organization Stop Antisemitism called Billoo "the antisemite of the week."[63] Liz Jackson of Palestine Legal wrote that Billoo "embodies what it means to challenge all systems of violence—fighting the patriarchy, resisting Islamophobia, and supporting Jewish people like me in a time of rising bigotry against Jewish people and all vulnerable populations." Jackson distinguishes between being anti-Jewish, the accusation made against Billoo, and "naming Israel as an apartheid state that maintains a system of laws privileging the rights of Jewish people over Palestinians."[64]

Interestingly, there was and still is, as of the writing of this chapter, another Muslim woman who is a member of the board: Samia Assed, who has been involved with the Women's March from its inception in 2016. Assed, who is Palestinian American and an activist from New Mexico, also wears hijab and has identified as unapologetically Palestinian and Muslim. Even more confounding, she offered, in 2016, clear support for the Boycott,

Divestment, and Sanctions (BDS) movement when she celebrated the support of Black Lives Matter for the Palestinian cause and for BDS.

> "It is very courageous of Black Lives Matter to take this position at this time, when they are already facing heat from white supremacist movements, Donald Trump and the Democrats doing everything they can to delegitimize Black Lives Matter," Samia Assed, a Palestinian-American activist and president of the Coordinating Council of the Albuquerque Center for Peace and Justice, told AlterNet. "Palestinians have been vilified over and over, even though they are the victims. For the Movement for Black Lives to have this bold statement says that we will not stand for selective oppressions, we are going to stand with a human rights agenda no matter where it is."[65]

The Specter of Antisemitism versus Critiques of Zionism and Israel

Much has been written since 2016 about the issue of (alleged) antisemitism and the Women's March, mostly focusing on Linda Sarsour and Tamika Mallory. While I realize the folly of trying to capture the nuances of that debate (if it was then a nuanced debate), I want to pay attention specifically to Sarsour's and Mallory's self-positioning in response to the allegations.

While Linda Sarsour is Palestinian American and supports the Palestinian quest for self-determination, Tamika Mallory saw the label of antisemitism attached to her in the context of her support for Louis Farrakhan, leader of the Nation of Islam. Mallory had attended the Nation of Islam's Saviours' Day event in February 2018, at which Farrakhan made both antisemitic and anti-LGBTQIA statements. Mallory was accused of antisemitism by association because she refused to distance herself from Farrakhan and continued to amplify some of his statements through her social media platforms. In a January 2019 interview on *The View*, the host, Meghan McCain, confronted Mallory about her description of Farrakhan as "the Greatest of All Time (GOAT)," to which she responded that she did not call him that because of his antisemitic remarks but "because of what he's done in black communities." McCain also brought up allegations made by Vanessa Wruble about antisemitic and disparaging remarks about Jews in the early days of organizing the Women's March. *Tablet Magazine* had reported those allegations, and Wruble, after leaving the march, was the key organizer of the alternative March On in 2019. Mallory and Bland, who was also interviewed on *The View*, both rejected the accusations leveled in the *Tablet*. Bland said, "And I think it's important for us to understand, and I'll be very clear in this room, that the women's march unequivocally condemns anti-Semitism, bigotry."[66]

In a post to *NewsOne*, Tamika Mallory said that though she very much believes in and takes part in the struggle against LGBTQIA oppression, she would not disavow the Nation of Islam. "Where my people are is where I must also be. I go into difficult spaces," she writes.[67] In a long and nuanced reflection, "Why Tamika Mallory Won't Condemn Farrakhan," published in *The Atlantic* in March 2018, Adam Serwer attempted to explain her position. Serwer expands the frame from Mallory to other Black and civil rights leaders and analyzes Farrakhan's courting of controversy with his remarks as free advertising and "a hustle." He argues that "many black people come into contact with the Nation of Islam as a force in impoverished black communities—not simply as a champion of the black poor or working class, but of the black underclass: black people, especially men, who have been written off or abandoned by white society." This is where Mallory's struggle to distance herself from Farrakhan is rooted, as Serwer sees it.[68] Mallory had worked with the Nation of Islam on local antiviolence campaigns. When her son's father was murdered, Mallory would later write, "In that most difficult period of my life, it was the women of the Nation of Islam who supported me and I have always held them close to my heart for that reason." Serwer's analysis might also help us reconsider intersectional solidarity, not as a flattening of or equal inclusion of all marginalized groups in social justice activism, but as a broader network of affinity groups who can both focus on the oppression of their own people and recognize the systemic connection between their oppression and that of others. The Women's March may have held that potential for intersectional solidarity at some point and certainly lay rhetorical claim to it, but it also demonstrated the possibility of limits on how such solidarity can be actualized in a particular movement and moment in time.

The idea of political affinity groups linked by their recognition of systemic and interconnected oppression is reflected better in the central tenet of the Black Lives Matter (BLM) movement, namely, that Black Lives need to matter. This does not mean that other lives do not matter. Rather, it means that the focus has to be on those lives most under threat. Mallory's self-positioning demands such nuance in analysis. As has become clear, the broad platform of the Women's March, from the beginning, contained divergent and at times opposing affinity group interests engaged in various appeals to solidarity across group differences as well as clear critiques that were justice focused and referenced solidarity.

Linda Sarsour's activism around and commitment to Palestinians and her critique of Israel have garnered a great deal of attention. Sarsour supports the Boycott, Divestment, and Sanctions movement, a lightning rod in progressive American politics, and she has held her ground as she continues to be attacked for her pro-Palestinian stance. It is not an exaggeration to say that Sarsour has been made an example of what happens to activists who take certain political positions. In 2020, Sarsour served as a surrogate for the Bernie Sanders campaign to become the Democratic nominee for president, but when Joe Biden was nominated, he immediately distanced himself from Sarsour as dangerous to his centrist campaign. Eventually, his campaign backtracked somewhat, after recognizing the significance of Sarsour for Arab and Muslim American voters.[69] Meanwhile, vitriolic and rhetorically aggressive writing about Sarsour (as well as pieces that vigorously defended her) abounded and led to concerns for her personal safety. An indication of the severity of the online threats is that they prompted an NYPD investigation in 2017.[70]

Sarsour's involvement with US Muslim organizations, including the Council on American Islamic Relations (CAIR), the Islamic Society of North America (ISNA), and the Islamic Circle of North America (ICNA), as well as her self-identification as a Muslim woman in her words and actions and in the wearing of her headscarf, put her at the intersection of Islamophobic, pro-Israel, and pro-Zionist targeting. This targeting, combined with the denial of her "feminist credentials," illustrates the connection between pro-Israel propaganda and anti-Muslim hostility. In their respective books, Nathan Lean and Stephen Sheehi, along with the authors of the investigative report, "Fear Inc.," all offer a similar analysis of the link between the production of Islamophobic rhetoric, evangelical Zionism, and the pro-Israel Right.[71] It is somewhat of an ironic twist that those political alliances, too, could be described as a form of solidarity even if those involved would be unlikely to invoke that language. They certainly do embrace the language of oppression and marginalization, as evident in evangelical rhetoric, the fear of Muslims overrunning the United States, and the fear of the destruction of Israel by hostile Arab neighbors.

To return to Sarsour, the attacks against her from the alliance I described above are expressions of anti-Muslim hostility and anti-Palestinian bias as well as racism. Jewish women who might embrace such Far Right political positions nevertheless are (and/or feel) compelled to take affinity group positions that identify them as the victims of Sarsour's "antisemitic" stances. There are numerous examples of Jewish women writing about their decision to distance themselves from the Women's March because of Sarsour (and Mallory).

In one of these articles, Carol Gilligan, an acclaimed feminist psychologist who is also Jewish, offers an academic exposé and reflection, written for New York University's Applied Research Collective for American Jewry. She writes about the intersectional identities of the organizers of the Women's March and reflects on the peculiar position of Jewish women, including herself, whose marginalization as Jewish she sees as sacrificed to the narrative of Jewish Whiteness. Gilligan points out that not all American Jews are White—a case in point is the fact that all three of the Jewish women on the new march board are women of color—but also that even those usually assumed to be White experience discrimination and denial of Whiteness as part of antisemitism.[72] Gilligan ponders the question of "the anti-Semitism on the left, including the confusion of anti-Semitism with legitimate criticism of current Israeli politics."[73] Elsewhere, and not linked to actual Israeli policies, she writes, "It is only by ignoring Jewish victimhood that one can so easily ignore the parallels between Zionism and other claims for self-determination of oppressed people, including the Palestinians, and the danger that all movements for liberation, when fueled by a distrust of a bad other, can give way to the very modes of oppression they were initially protesting against."[74] Gilligan concludes with policy recommendations specifically for Jewish communities and organizations, including radical listening training and supporting Jewish women's leadership. Before those recommendations, she asks, "Is it too early for a united feminist political front—or, more disconcertingly, too late?"[75] The article is written as a series of reflections that include incidents, thoughts, and moments in Gilligan's life that have led to her reflecting on the Women's March as it concerns her understanding of the Jewish question and questions of solidarity, difference, and feminist movement building.

Solidarity, Movement Building, and Accountability: Closing and Opening

I arrive at a final moment of reflection: drawing together conclusions but more fruitfully, I think, formulating new questions. One of my conclusions is that movement and coalition building is complex and fraught with many challenges, and feminist movement building is no exception. If anything, feminist commitments to the analysis and transformation of oppressive racial and class hierarchies can be an invitation to reflect deeply and continuously on the distribution of power and can lead to the formulation of more nuanced and contextually rooted goals.

Solidarity can be a powerful community-building tool as long as it does not get confused for a definition of justice and as long as it is not used as a blanket to cover over important differences between different parts and members of a movement. The Women's March, significantly, began as an event, not as a movement, and the transition from one to the other might have required more self-reflection than seems to have happened among its leadership. While I associate the charismatic leadership model with patriarchal institutions (and states), the Women's March depended on its visibility and self-advertising on the prominence of the four national co-chairs as figureheads and representatives of the organization. This representational function both benefited from Mallory, Perez, and Sarsour being recognized and well-known local organizers and activists and received a boost from Sarsour's established notoriety at the center of anti-Muslim and pro-Israel media punditry. The attacks on Sarsour and Mallory over alleged antisemitism and LGBTQIA discrimination—at least Mallory not distancing herself from Farrakhan—as well as debates about other aspects of their political positions, serve as a reminder of the impossibility of the perfectly aligned political activist. It is indeed impossible to embrace all the right positions on all the important issues subsumed under social justice commitments and make every other member of a movement happy.

I do not see the conclusion that movements are perhaps more viable if they do not rely to this extent on individual leaders as an indictment of affinity (or identity) politics. Rather, with Patricia Hill Collins and Simra Bilge, I see potentially fruitful outcomes for considering identities as "strategically essential, . . . as defacto coalitions," and as transformative.[76] The first, based on Spivak's notion of strategic essentialism, allows us to recognize identities, especially group identities, as not static but stabilized intentionally for the purpose of political organizing. Such temporary stabilization does not have to be calcified into an eternal identity for a group or as the foundation for the definition of group boundaries.[77] The second recognizes that group coalitions along identity lines can help negotiate group interests in a coalition rather than at the expense of another group's interests. The third, Hill Collins and Bilge argue, comes closest to expressions of intersectionality in its potential to (trans)form individual and group identities through political struggle.

The Black Lives Matter movement, founded in 2013 by Alicia Garza, Patrisse Cullors, and Opal Tometi, three Black and queer women, has over the years of its existence and continuing relevance not depended on Garza, Cullors, and Tometi as figureheads. The "About" section of the BLM website does not even mention their names. And while all three of them have given talks and interviews and Cullors and Garza have written books,[78] the movement is so much larger than their personalities and even their intersectional identities. It may be that the main difference, however, is that BLM is focused on a singular cause that has never tried to address everything else that is wrong with the United States and the world. BLM activists and organizers have indeed expressed solidarity, for example, with Palestinians, and for that matter with the Women's March.

I began this chapter with a reflection on what solidarity as a word and as a concept has meant to me. I have also considered the different valences of solidarity around the Women's March as an event in 2017, and as an organization formed in late 2016, that continues to operate in various forms and through events. The organization has rightfully been described as a demonstration of the power of White women in American society, a power that also carries the privilege of protection from state violence, even when protesting that very state.[79] This is a privilege that women of color, and especially Black women, do not have. Muslim women activists carry some of their intersectional identities on their bodies. They are marked by racial and religious otherness and continue to take center stage in anti-Muslim hostility in many forms. My opening to further conversation is a series of questions that I myself have not been able to resolve: How can intersectional feminists who also consider religion as a resource maintain a practice of critical reflection on power dynamics, the contextual nature of formulations of justice, and the complexity of coalition building? Is solidarity the best vehicle or concept for such reflections? How can we cultivate and continuously adjust practices of feminist critique that calls allies, movement partners, and accomplices *in* rather than *out*,[80] as calling out is a practice that in my view has done significant damage to Left and progressive movements and organizations? I am reminded of Joan Scott's pronouncement that critique is "still feminism's most potent weapon" and that it "does not offer a map that leads to a guaranteed future; rather, it disturbs our settled expectations and incites us to explore, indeed to invent, alternate routes."[81]

And it is with Jennifer Nash that I step from pondering solidarity to pondering love: Black feminist conceptions of love as a unifying political principle encourage us to ask about our deep responsibility to each other by virtue of our collective inhabitation of the social world. This view, of course, entails risk. It is risky to view one's self as bound up with others and to fully accept the responsibility and potential peril that are entailed in embracing and practicing a worldview of linked fate. But this is the visionary call of Black feminist love politics—a radical embrace of connectedness.[82]

NOTES

1. See Kimberlé Crenshaw, "Mapping the Margins: Intersectionality, Identity Politics, and Violence against Women of Color, " *Stanford Law Review* 43, no. 6 (1991): 1241–99. Crenshaw is credited with coining the term "intersectionality." See also Patricia Hill Collins and Simra Bilge, *Intersectionality: Key Concepts* (Cambridge: Polity Press, 2016).

2. Hill Collins, Jennifer Nash, and Anna Carastathis are among the scholars who have explored the debates about and limits of intersectionality in significantly different ways and with different conclusions. See Hill Collins and Bilge, *Intersectionality*; Jennifer Nash, *Black Feminism Reimagined: After Intersectionality* (Durham, NC: Duke University Press, 2019); Anna Carastathis, *Intersectionality: Origins, Contestations, Horizons* (Lincoln: University of Nebraska Press, 2016).

3. Hill Collins, together with Bilge, has considered identity labels, identity politics, social movements, and the international and transnational potential of intersectionality as an analytic rather than rejecting the identity dimension and its utility altogether. See Hill Collins and Bilge, *Intersectionality*, esp. 114–35.

4. See Tomoko Masuzawa, *The Invention of World Religions* (Chicago: University of Chicago Press, 2005); Juliane Hammer, "Center Stage: Muslim Women and Islamophobia," in *Islamophobia in America*, ed. Carl Ernst (New York: Palgrave, 2013), 107–44; Juliane Hammer, "Muslim Women, Anti-Muslim Hostility, and the State in the Age of Terror," in *Muslims and Contemporary US Politics*, ed. Mohammad Khalil (Cambridge, MA: Harvard University Press, 2019), 104–26; Leila Ahmed, *Women and Gender in Islam* (New Haven, CT: Yale University Press,

1992); Charlotte Weber, "Unveiling Scheherazade: Feminist Orientalism in the International Alliance of Women, 1911–1950," *Feminist Studies* 27, no. 1 (Spring 2001): 125–57.

5. With regard to Islam as the religion in question, there are obvious connections to Perin Gürel's chapter in this volume where she explores an instance of unrealized South-South solidarity between Muslim women that is not as directly embedded in an anti-Muslim context as US Muslim women are.

6. See Juliane Hammer, *Peaceful Families: American Muslim Efforts against Domestic Violence* (Princeton, NJ: Princeton University Press, 2019); Beverly M. Weber, "Gender, Race, Religion, Faith? Rethinking Intersectionality in German Feminisms," *European Journal of Women's Studies* 22, no. 1 (2015): 22–36; Iman AbdoulKarim, "'Islam Is Black Lives Matter': The Role of Gender and Religion in Muslim Women's BLM Activism," in *Race, Religion, and Black Lives Matter: Essays on a Moment and a Movement*, ed. Christopher Cameron and Phillip Luke Sinitiere (Nashville, TN: Vanderbilt University Press, 2021).

7. While this chapter focuses on Muslim women activists in the Women's March and on their engagement with intersectional feminist politics, I also see a need for a sustained analysis of how Muslim women activists, especially Linda Sarsour, have been perceived by US Muslim communities and their leaders. There are questions to ask about supporting Sarsour as a Muslim woman representing communities but also about embracing her political positions, including LGBTQIA acceptance, that may not be acceptable to segments of those communities. In addition, there are questions about the political representation of Muslims as unified, the possibility of women as authority figures and leaders (also relevant for elected officials such as Congresswomen Rashida Tlaib and Ilhan Omar), and the anti-Muslim hostility that they experience and that might unite them more than other aspects of their identities and their work.

8. One example is Feminist Studies in Religion Inc. (FSR), which I have been involved with for several years. The organization has both included Muslim feminists and remained dominated by Christian and, to a lesser extent, Jewish scholars and their religious priorities.

9. I have written about my growing dislike for the term "Islamophobia"; see, e.g., Hammer, "Center Stage" and "Muslim Women, Anti-Muslim Hostility, and the State in the Age of Terror."

10. The public syllabus titled #IslamophobiaIsRacism, created by Su'ad Abdul Khabeer, Arshad Ali, Evelyn Alsultany, Sohail Daulatzai, Lara Deeb, Carol Fadda, Zareena Grewal, Juliane Hammer, Nadine Naber, and Junaid Rana, https://islamophobiaisracism.wordpress.com/, provides a solid overview of this literature.

11. See #IslamophobiaIsRacism syllabus. See also Junaid Rana, "The Story of Islamophobia," *Souls* 9, no. 2 (2007): 148–61; Eric Love, *Islamophobia and Racism in America* (New York: New York University Press, 2017).

12. I am committed to a contextual analysis. Thus, while I do believe comparative analysis of anti-Muslim hostility in different geographic contexts can be useful, I

caution against models that claim these are simply particular variations on a common theme. European forms of anti-Muslim hostility differ from US or Canadian ones while also differing among each other. There are of course historical connections and European roots to these formations, but that does not make them all the same.

13. See Ahmed, *Women and Gender in Islam*; Weber, "Unveiling Scheherazade."

14. Saba Mahmood, "Feminism, Democracy, and Empire: Islam and the War on Terror," in *Women's Studies on the Edge*, ed. Joan Scott (Durham, NC: Duke University Press, 2008), 81–114; Saba Mahmood and Charles Hirschkind, "Feminism, the Taliban, and Politics of Counter-Insurgency," *Anthropological Quarterly* 75 (2002): 339–54.

15. For an incisive analysis of what Megan Goodwin calls "contraceptive nationalism," see Megan Goodwin, "'They Do That to Foreign Women': Domestic Terrorism and Contraceptive Nationalism in *Not Without My Daughter*," *Muslim World* 106 (2018): 759–80; and *Abusing Religion: Literary Persecution, Sex Scandals, and American Minority Religions* (New Brunswick, NJ: Rutgers University Press, 2020), esp. 67–100.

16. Crenshaw, "Mapping the Margins."

17. Alice Walker is credited with having coined the term "womanist" in a 1979 short story and more prominently in her collection of essays from 1983, *In Search of Our Mothers' Gardens: Womanist Prose* (New York: Mariner Books, 1983). See also Delores Williams, *Sisters in the Wilderness* (Maryknoll, NY: Orbis Books, 1993); Stacey M. Floyd, ed., *Deeper Shades of Purple: Womanism in Religion and Society* (New York: New York University Press, 2006); Monica Coleman, ed., *Ain't I a Womanist, Too: Third Wave Womanist Religious Thought* (Minneapolis, MN: Fortress Press, 2013).

18. Brittney Cooper, Susana Morris, and Robin Boylorn, eds., *The Crunk Feminist Collective* (New York: Feminist Press, 2017).

19. See, e.g., the roundtable conversation, "Roundtable Discussion: Mujeristas Who We Are and What We Are About," which includes contributions from Ada Maria Isasi-Diaz, Elena Olazagasti-Segovia, Sandra Mangual-Rodriguez, Maria Antonietta Berriozábal, Daisy L. Machado, Lourdes Arguelles, and Raven-Anne Rivero, *Journal of Feminist Studies in Religion* 8, no. 1 (Spring 1992): 105–25; Ada Maria Isasi-Diaz, *La Lucha Continues: Mujerista Theology* (Maryknoll, NY: Orbis Books, 2004); Ada Maria Isasi-Diaz, *Mujerista Theology: A Theology for the 21st Century* (Maryknoll, NY: Orbis Books, 1996).

20. Fatima Seedat, "When Islam and Feminism Converge," *Muslim World* 103, no. 3 (July 2013): 404–20; Fatima Seedat, "Islam, Feminism, and Islamic Feminism: Between Inadequacy and Inevitability," *Journal of Feminist Studies in Religion* 29, no. 2 (Fall 2013): 25–45; Fatima Seedat, "Beyond the Text: Between Islam and Feminism," *Journal of Feminist Studies in Religion* 32, no. 2 (2016): 138–42.

21. Rochelle Terman, "Islamophobia, Feminism, and the Politics of Critique,"

Theory, Culture & Society 33, no. 2 (2016): 177–102 (100).

22. The poster, based on a photo of Munira Ahmed, a thirty-two-year-old Bangladeshi American from Queens, was made into the iconic image by Shepard Fairey, who produced a series of poster images of diverse women for protesters at the Trump inauguration, including a Latina and an African American woman. They were a very visible presence at the Women's March. Notably, the other two included in his "We the People" series do not wear items of clothing that are the US flag like the Muslim woman does with her hijab. In reference to anti-Muslim hostility, the poster with the Muslim woman reads, "We the People are greater than fear." See image and story at https://qz.com/887358/the-story-behind-shepard-faireys -powerful-posters-for-donald-trumps-inauguration/.

23. There is some scholarship on religious participation in the Women's March. One example is a sociological study by Beyerlein and Ryan, but it focuses on the Women's March in Chicago, not Washington, DC, which is where the march was led by the leadership team I discuss here. See Kraig Beyerlein and Peter Ryan, "Religious Resistance to Trump: Progressive Faith and the Women's March on Chicago," *Sociology of Religion: A Quarterly Review* 79, no. 2 (2018): 196–219. Beyerlein and Ryan conclude "that faith was a secondary rather than a primary motivation for progressive religious marchers. Second, clergy did not mainly drive mobilizing efforts in that laity played a key role. Last, while many progressive faith communities self-identified at the event to show the world they were there in solidarity, they eschewed strong, distinctively religious expressions during the WMC" (196).

24. Marie Berry and Erica Chenoweth, "Who Made the Women's March?," in *The Resistance: The Dawn of the Anti-Trump Opposition Movement*, ed. David S. Meyer and Sidney Tarrow (Oxford: Oxford University Press, 2018), 75–89.

25. Ibid., 76.

26. Sierra Brewer and Lauren Dundes, "Concerned, Meet Terrified: Intersectional Feminism and the Women's March," *Women's Studies International Forum* 69 (2018): 49–55.

27. Rachel Presley and Alane Presswood, "Pink, Brown, and Read All Over: Representation at the 2017 Women's March on Washington," *Cultural Studies ↔ Critical Methodologies* 18, no. 1 (2018): 61–71 (66).

28. Jessica Gantt-Shafer, Cara Wallis, and Caitlin Miles, "Intersectionality, (Dis)unity, and Processes of Becoming at the 2017 Women's March," *Women's Studies in Communication* 42, no. 2 (2019): 22–40 (223).

29. Pamela Moss and Avril Maddrell, "Emergent and Divergent Spaces in the Women's March: The Challenges of Intersectionality and Inclusion," *Gender, Place & Culture* 24, no. 5 (2017): 613–20 (614).

30. Without going down the rabbit hole of feminist theory and history, the feminist religion problem is clearly connected to the Marxist origins of at least some feminist theory and intersectionality theory as well. I am grateful to Atalia Omer for the suggestion to make that link explicit.

31. Here again there are clear connections to Perin Gürel's chapter in this volume, in which she shows that Muslim women's and Muslim feminist agency is neither singular nor disconnected from nationalist discourses or various forms of secularism, both in Muslim-majority contexts and, as in my chapter here, in the United States.

32. Deborah Frizzell, "Positions in Solidarity: Voices and Images from the US Women's Marches," *Cultural Politics* 13, no. 3 (2017): 315–25 (321).

33. Diane H. Felmlee, Justine I. Blanford, Stephen A. Matthews, Alan M. MacEachren, "The Geography of Sentiment towards the Women's March of 2017," *PLoS ONE* 15, no. 6 (2020): 1–21.

34. Presley and Presswood, "Pink, Brown, and Read All Over," 68.

35. Moss and Maddrell, "Emergent and Divergent Spaces in the Women's March," 614.

36. Ibid., 615.

37. Ibid., 619.

38. Ibid., 613.

39. Ashwini Tambe, "The Women's March on Washington: Words from an Organizer: an Interview with Mrinalini Chakraborty," *Feminist Studies* 43, no. 1 (2017): 223–29 (223).

40. Linda Sarsour, "Speech at the Women's March, January 21, 2017" (transcript), https://awpc.cattcenter.iastate.edu/2018/09/27/speech-at-the-womens-march -on-washington-jan-21-2017/.

41. Alan Feuer, "Linda Sarsour Is a Brooklyn Homegirl in a Hijab," *New York Times*, August 7, 2015, www.nytimes.com/2015/08/09/nyregion/linda-sarsour -is-a-brooklyn-homegirl-in-a-hijab.html.

42. Linda Sarsour, *We Are Not Here to Be Bystanders: A Memoir of Love and Resistance* (New York: Simon and Schuster, 2020), 157.

43. Ibid., 174.

44. Ibid., 176.

45. Ibid., 177. The Al-Hidaya Mosque, according to Sarsour, was founded by Palestinian Muslim immigrants, thereby constituting "her" community in a dual sense, as Palestinians and as Muslims.

46. Danusha Goska, "An Open Letter to Muslim Feminist Linda Sarsour," *FrontPage Magazine*, August 17, 2015, www.frontpagemag.com/fpm/259811 /open-letter-muslim-feminist-linda-sarsour-danusha-v-goska.

47. Shireen Qudosi, "Linda Sarsour's Muslim Identity Politics Epitomize Feminism's Hypocrisy," *The Federalist*, January 24, 2017, http://thefederalist.com /2017/01/24/linda-sarsours-muslim-identity-politics-epitomize-feminisms -hypocrisy. It is worth highlighting the obvious antisemitism that is paired with Qudosi's anti-Muslim hostility in this quote.

48. www.facebook.com/linda.sarsour, August 3, 2017.

49. Melissa Harris-Perry, "What Women's March Co-Chairs Tamika Mallory,

Carmen Perez, & Linda Sarsour Are Doing Next," *Elle Magazine*, January 19, 2018, www.elle.com/culture/career-politics/a15755101/power-to-the-polls-one-year-after-the-womens-march/. The passage quoted here contains references to the following other articles: Mattie Kahn, "Women's March Organizer Linda Sarsour Is Under Attack on Social Media," *Elle Magazine*, January 23, 2017, www.elle.com/culture/career-politics/news/a42375/womens-march-organizer-linda-sarsour-is-under-attack/; Alexander Nazariyan, "Linda Sarsour, Feminist Movement Leader, Too Extreme for CUNY Graduation Speech, Critics Argue," *Newsweek*, May 24, 2017, www.newsweek.com/linda-sarsour-feminist-movement-leader-too-extreme-cuny-graduation-speech-615031.

50. See FITNA Facebook page and examples such as this from summer 2020: www.facebook.com/groups/feministfitna/permalink/2727224680935933. Anti-Black racism is an ongoing issue in Muslim communities, as much as it is in the surrounding US society. Organizations such as the Muslim Anti-Racism Collaborative, founded in 2014 during Black History Month with the hashtag #BlackandMuslim, work to raise awareness and provide antiracist education in and beyond Muslim communities.

51. Sarsour, ISNA speech, 2016, www.youtube.com/watch?v=Ocswa0okscs; and 2017, www.facebook.com/watch/live/?v=10154538687786105&ref=watch_permalink.

52. Emily Crockett, "The 'Day Without a Woman' Strike, Explained," *Vox*, March 7, 2017, www.vox.com/identities/2017/3/3/14721468/international-womens-day-strike-a-day-without-a-woman-march-8; *CBS News*, January 21, 2018, "Women's March 2018: Global Demonstrations Continue into 2nd Day," www.cbsnews.com/news/womens-march-2018-global-demonstrations-continue-into-second-day/.

53. Marissa Lang, "Women's March Replaces Three Original Leaders, after anti-Semitism Accusations, with 16 Board Members," *Washington Post*, September 16, 2019, www.washingtonpost.com/dc-md-va/2019/09/16/womens-march-cutting-ties-with-three-original-board-members-accused-anti-semitism/.

54. Danielle Silva, "Three Founding Women's March Leaders Leaving Board after Anti-Semitism Accusations," *NBC News*, September 17, 2019, www.nbcnews.com/news/us-news/three-founding-women-s-march-leaders-leaving-board-after-anti-n1055351.

55. The debate about antisemitism, its definition and its link, or lack thereof, to criticism of Israel and/or Zionism, is a complex topic and one fraught with the danger of falling into the trap of being accused myself. I have long hesitated to address this issue directly in my writing, despite the fact that I come from a Palestine Studies background.

56. Farah Stockman, "One Year after Women's March, More Activism, but Less Unity," *New York Times*, January 15, 2018, www.nytimes.com/2018/01/15/us/womens-march-anniversary.html.

57. Lucia Graves, "Women's March to Take to Streets after Controversy Divides Movement," *The Guardian*, January 18, 2019, www.theguardian.com /world/2019/jan/18/womens-march-2019-controversy-antisemitism.

58. The quotation marks around "diversity" and "inclusion" denote at least a hint of sarcasm at the fact that DEI (diversity, equity, and inclusion) programs, while often using the language of intersectionality, significantly defang the sharp insights of intersectionality theory, as Jennifer Nash has shown. See Nash, *Black Feminism Reimagined*.

59. Danielle Silva, "Three Founding Women's March Leaders Leaving Board after Anti-Semitism Accusations," *NBC News*, September 17, 2019, www .nbcnews.com/news/us-news/three-founding-women-s-march-leaders-leaving -board-after-anti-n1055351.

60. Matthew Rozsa, "Tamika Mallory and Linda Sarsour Out at Women's March Following Allegations of Anti-Semitism," *Salon*, September 17, 2019, www.salon.com/2019/09/17/tamika-mallory-and-linda-sarsour-out-at-womens -march-following-allegations-of-anti-semitism/.

61. See B'Tselem, "This Is Apartheid," January 12, 2021, www.btselem.org /publications/fulltext/202101_this_is_apartheid; Human Rights Watch, "A Threshold Crossed," April 27, 2021, www.hrw.org/report/2021/04/27/thresh-old-crossed /israeli-authorities-and-crimes-apartheid-and-persecution#.

62. Tatiana Sanchez, "Bay Area Muslim Leader Booted Off Women's March Board over Israel Tweets," *San Francisco Chronicle*, September 19, 2019, www .sfchronicle.com/bayarea/article/Bay-Area-Muslim-leader-booted-off-Women-s -March-14453150.php.

63. www.stopantisemitism.org/antisemite-of-the-week/antisemite-of-the -week-zahra-billoo-the-lindasarour20-edition.

64. Liz Jackson, "The Women's March Made a Huge Mistake in Voting Out the Leader We Need," September 27, 2019, https://palestinelegal.org/news/2019 /9/27/the-womens-march-made-a-huge-mistake-in-voting-out-the-leader-we-need.

65. Sarah Lazare, "Pro-Israel Groups Smear the Movement for Black Lives for Its Solidarity with Palestine," *Alternet*, August 4, 2016, https://www.alternet.org /2016/08/pro-israel-groups-smear-movement-black-lives-its-solidarity-palestine/.

66. Gina Salamone, "Women's March Leader Tamika Mallory Defends Calling Louis Farrakhan 'the GOAT,'" *Baltimore Sun*, January 14, 2019, www .baltimoresun.com/ny-news-womens-march-leader-explains-farrakhan-goat -20190114-story.html.

67. See Tamika Mallory, "Tamika Mallory Speaks: 'Wherever My People Are, Is Where I Must Be,'" *NewsOne* (blog), March 7, 2018, https://newsone .com/3779389/tamika-mallory-saviours-day.

68. Adam Serwer, "Why Tamika Mallory Won't Condemn Farrakhan," *The Atlantic*, March 11, 2018, www.theatlantic.com/po litics/archive/2018/03 /nation-of-islam/555332/.

69. Marcy Oster, "After Disavowing Sarsour, Biden Reaffirms Vow to Work with Arab Americans," *Jerusalem Post*, August 25, 2020, www.jpost.com/american-politics/after-disavowing-sarsour-biden-reaffirms-vow-to-work-with-arab-americans-639832.

70. Sameer Rao, "Online Threats against Linda Sarsour Prompt NYPD Investigation," *Colorlines*, February 22, 2017, www.colorlines.com/articles/online-threats-against-linda-sarsour-prompt-nypd-investigation.

71. See Nathan Lean, *The Islamophobia Industry: How the Right Manufactures Fear of Muslims* (London: Pluto Press, 2012); Wajahat Ali, Eli Clifton, Matthew Duss, Lee Fang, Scott Keyes, and Faiz Shakir, "Fear Inc.: The Roots of the Islamo-phobia Network in America," 2011, www.americanprogress.org/issues/religion/reports/2011/08/26/10165/fear-inc/; Matthew Duss, Yasmine Taeb, Ken Gude, and Ken Sofer, "Fear Inc. 2.0: The Islamophobia Network's Efforts to Manufacture Hate in America," February 2015, https://cdn.americanprogress.org/wp-content/uploads/2015/02/FearInc-report2.11.pdf; Stephen Sheehi, *Islamophobia: The Ideological Campaign against Muslims* (Atlanta, GA: Clarity Press, 2011).

72. Carol Gilligan, "Discord in the Ranks: The Women's March and the Jewish Question" (Applied Research Collective for American Jewry, New York University, 2019), https://static1.squarespace.com/static/56abab9d8b38d4b28f7d183e/t/5e139db001f0792d92ea5d53/1578343857120/Carol+Gilligan_Women_Mech-2.pdf, 10.

73. Ibid., 5.

74. Ibid., 14.

75. Ibid., 20.

76. Hill Collins and Bilge, *Intersectionality*, 102.

77. See Gayatri Spivak, "Criticism, Feminism, and the Institution," Interview with Elizabeth Grosz, *Thesis Eleven*, nos. 10–11 (February 1985): 175–87. Spivak has since distanced herself from this notion, but I find it an eminently useful tool for analysis and activism. See Gayatri Spivak, "An Interview with Gayatri Spivak, by Sara Danius and Stefan Jonsson," *boundary 2* 20, no. 2 (Summer 1993): 24–50.

78. Patrisse Cullors and Asha Bandele, *When They Call You a Terrorist: A Black Lives Matter Memoir* (New York: St. Martin's Press, 2017); Alicia Garza, *The Purpose of Power: How We Come Together When We Fall Apart* (London: Oneworld, 2020).

79. Jessica Watters, "Pink Hats and Black Fists: The Role of Women in the Black Lives Matter Movement," *William & Mary Journal of Women and the Law* 24, no. 1 (2017): 199–207.

80. Willie Jackson, "Don't Be an Ally, Be an Accomplice," November 13, 2019, https://forge.medium.com/dont-be-an-ally-be-an-accomplice-437869756ab5.

81. Joan Scott, "Introduction: Feminism's Critical Edge," in *Women's Studies on the Edge*, ed. Joan Scott (Durham, NC: Duke University Press, 2007), 1–16 (7).

82. Nash, *Black Feminism Reimagined*, 117–18.

CHAPTER 3

Transgressive Geography and Litmus Test Solidarity

Atalia Omer and Ruth Carmi

ABSTRACT

While it is tempting to simply assimilate Israel into a global analysis of race, Whiteness, and settler colonialism, this assimilation itself participates in erasures that are potentially detrimental for reimagining moral and political geographies in the Middle East. This chapter probes how the case of Israel and, in particular, the enduring and increasingly emboldened legacy of the extremist racist ideology of Rabbi Meir Kahane—made in the United States and mutated in Israel—exemplifies the complex, global, and semiotic interrelation among racist ideologies, antisemitism, and Jewish self-determination. It shows how these interrelations constitute one possible modality of Jewish modernity. We juxtapose Kahanist ideology to emancipatory and transgressive moral visions. Doing so allows us to highlight how the deployment of Palestinian liberation as a normative compass and a litmus test for South-South solidarity reinforces a binary that positions Israelis as White supremacists and settler colonialists and Palestinians as colonized and oppressed. Beyond metaphorizing each protagonist in this zero-sum game, this binary also conceals the predicaments faced by Mizrahi, Ethiopian, and other non-normative and marginalized Israelis. This concealment prevents the building of South-South solidarities and alternative political and ethical possibilities in the region.

REALIST CONSTRAINTS TO IMAGINING THE WORLD OTHERWISE:
AN INTRODUCTION

If you want to find a decolonial Jewish sociological imagination that grapples with the legacies and tragedies of Jewish modernity and Jewish power, you may want to go to the people who are silenced and sit at the margins of Israeli society rather than to Jewish diasporas. In the diaspora, one is likely to hear privileged (White) Jews decry the Israeli state as the derailment of Jewish history caused by modernity. However, when we critically interrogate lives and silences at the Israeli margins, what is illuminated is the interlinking of Palestinian and Black and Brown Jewish experiences, even though ideological constructs and institutional practices have prevented translating such interlinking into an intersectional political and socioeconomic force. These experiences provide resources for destabilizing the civilizational and orientalist discursive formations underpinning Jewish power and Ashkenormativity while also making possible the recovery of memories of pluralistic cohabitation in the Middle East.[1] Indeed, Mizrahi feminist thinkers and activists had this insight and made decolonial conceptual links between Palestinians and Arab Jews and Mizrahim long ago.[2] Such insights came with recognition of concrete possibilities for forming broad Palestinian-Mizrahi coalitions and emancipatory movements. The genealogy of this decolonial thread includes Ella Shohat's employment of Edward Said's postcolonial lens and Smadar Lavie's critical application of Gloria Anzaldúa's concept of the borderlands, along with many others.[3] Their insight was that Mizrahi empowerment, if entailing oppression of another group, was no empowerment at all.[4] Israel as an expression of political Zionism came into being as a result of a confluence of factors not the least of which was the mechanism of settler colonialism, which European Jews have maneuvered since they colonized Palestine in the late nineteenth century and especially after the watershed event of the Balfour Declaration of 1917. Settler colonialism entails the dispossession and erasure of Indigenous life and culture.

While it is tempting to simply assimilate Israel into a global analysis of race, Whiteness, and settler colonialism, this assimilation itself participates in erasures that are potentially detrimental for reimagining moral and political geographies in the Middle East. This chapter probes how the case of Israel and, in particular, the enduring and progressively emboldened legacy of the extremist racist ideology of Rabbi Meir Kahane—made in the

United States and mutated in Israel—exemplifies the complex, global, semiotic interrelation among racist ideologies, antisemitism, and Jewish self-determination. It shows how these interrelations constitute one possible modality of Jewish modernity. We juxtapose Kahanist ideology to emancipatory and transgressive moral visions. Doing so allows us to highlight how the deployment of Palestinian liberation as a normative compass and a litmus test for South-South solidarity reinforces a binary that positions Israelis as White supremacists and settler colonialists and Palestinians as colonized and oppressed. Beyond metaphorizing each protagonist in this zero-sum game, this binary also conceals the predicaments faced by Mizrahi, Ethiopian, and other non-normative and marginalized Israelis. This concealment prevents the building of South-South solidarities and alternative political and ethical possibilities in the region. We return to this point after examining one of the most grotesque expressions of White Jewish supremacy in Israel.

To understand Kahane, we build on an important insight that the American Studies scholar Keith Feldman, in addition to others, has had, namely, that transgressing national boundaries is necessary when analyzing "transnational circuits of racialization, migration, and cultural exchanges."[5] Feldman exposes the interconnections between the occupation of the Palestinians and racial politics and formations in the United States. His unmasking of the global and transnational circuits of racialization carries the potential to decolonize political imaginations and "reconstitute," as Alex Lubin writes in his study of global Afro-Arab solidarities, "the geographies of modernity into . . . a geography of liberation."[6] For Lubin, this refers to the transgressive "dialectical spaces produced in the collision between nationalism and colonialism, on the one hand, and subaltern decolonial and liberation politics, on the other."[7] If modernity constructs interlocking structures of oppression and dehumanization, then transgressive geographies name the ability of marginalized communities to see these topographies with clarity. Seeing then entails recognizing a common struggle regardless of one's distinct subjectivity and location. This recognition of the global matrixes of control and oppression constitutes a potential for a transgressive geography and for drawing different liberatory pathways. Seeing beyond divisions constitutes a decolonial act by unsettling the colonial mechanisms that seek to generate illusions of unbridgeable differences, often through a mechanism of privileging some groups over others.

Before mapping transgressive geographies of liberation, we analyze the case of Kahane's legacy as an ironic and extreme illustration of coloniality and the subversion of the traditional Jewish imagination. In doing so, we expose the operative force and global circulation of "Judeo-Christian" civilizational narratives, White supremacy, and the racialization of religion through modern nationalist discourses. We then contrast the Kahanist phenomenon to the decolonized alternative: political-religious geographies articulated by Jews of Color (JOC; i.e., non-White Jews) in Israel and the United States.[8] This alternative gestures to the hidden potential of an otherwise impossible avenue for solidarity. The latter depends on a humanistic and universal interpretation of the lessons of Jewish genocide rather than Kahane's racist, ethnocentric, and exclusionary interpretation, which itself reflects modernity's political project. The persistence of the category of citizenship as well as rights discourse finally invites a robust analysis of postcolonial and decolonial approaches to nation, religion, race, and the meanings of citizenship and political belonging. Finally, we return to the story of failed or unrealized solidarity.

What Is "Jewish Power"?

Otzma Yehudit (lit., "Jewish Power") is the name of an Israeli political party established in 2004 as an offshoot of the right-wing and territorial maximalist Herut Party. It has since reconstituted itself in multiple forms but has retained the same ideology. This ideology has relied on a few basic principles, including a belief in Jewish chosenness, the divine promise of the land of Israel in its entirety to the People of Israel, the subsequent indivisibility of the land, and the implementation of the principles of the Torah in all facets of life in Israel. The party, accordingly, has focused on promoting Torah-centric legal transformation, establishing settlements, and attaining political sovereignty over its conception of the biblical landscape, including the Haram al-Sharif, or Temple Mount. It encourages and works actively for the expulsion, dispossession, and transfer (i.e., ethnic cleansing) of perceived enemies of the Israeli state (the "Arabs")[9] and the elevating of the Jewish character of the state over any universal principles and values.[10] The party is implicated in the mechanisms of dispossession of Palestinian families from occupied East Jerusalem. Its head, Itamar Ben-Gvir, for example, was directly involved in inciting Jewish vigilantism prior to and during the nonviolent Palestinian grassroots resistance in occupied East Jerusalem against the looming dispossession of the Palestinian residents of Sheikh Jarrah. The escalation around Sheikh Jarrah during the Ramadan month of 2021 resulted eventually in provoking Hamas to yet another round of "mowing the lawn" in Gaza. Meanwhile, Ben-Gvir, at the time a member of the Knesset due to Prime Minister Benjamin Netanyahu's political maneuvering, was central in inciting violent Jewish mobs against Palestinian citizens of Israel in the so-called mixed cities, such as Lydda (Lod), which are only mixed because of the ethnic cleansing of the Nakba, or the Palestinian catastrophe of 1948.

The roots of the leadership of Otzma Yehudit can be found in the legacy of the American-born Kahane and his Kach (This Is the Way) Party, established in 1971. Before redirecting his attention to Israel, under his leadership, Jewish Power emerged on the streets of New York as the Jewish Defense League (JDL) in 1968. Its aim was to resist—through violent tactics, if necessary—African American antisemitism and anti-Jewish violence. During that time, Kahane was preoccupied with the Movement for Soviet Jewry and was propelled by a foreboding sense of existential threat to Jews. This sense animated his political career in Israel. His extremism (including explicit calls for the "transfer," or ethnic cleansing, of Palestin-ians) was only relative to a political spectrum of actors who initially eschewed him, legislating the "racism law" (1987) with this explicit intention. It was an amendment to the Basic Law, which prevents parties and individuals whose purpose is to incite racism from running for seats in the Knesset. The amendment explicitly targeted what, at the time, the Israeli mainstream perceived as an outrageous departure from the good old liberal Israel enshrined in the Declaration of Independence. Later, however, the mainstream migrated in his direction, and in 2018, without shame or efforts to cover it with pretenses to democratic norms, the Jewish Nation-State Law was passed, enshrining Jewish supremacy in law. This shift was not surprising considering the inherent contradictions between democratic norms and Zionism as a Jewish supremacist political project. Indeed, Kahane was explicitly antidemocratic, which was a novelty at a time when various actors continued to grapple with the tensions between the "Jewish" and the "democratic" identities of the Jewish nation-state. Kahane did not want to pretend that a reconciliation between the two was a possibility or something desirable. Hence, as the Jewish Studies scholar Shaul Magid notes,[11] Kahane was eventually assassinated, but Kahanism has won and converged with Jewish settler land theology, or religious Zionism. If Kahanism embraces Jewish power as a core value and destiny, settler land theology infuses a sacred mission into the actions of Palestinian dispossession. Both Jewish redemption and settler colonialism are ingredients of political Zionism. The convergence (solidarity?) of religious Zionism (also enabled by Christian Zionist lobbies, especially in the United States) and Kahanism reflects and augments these motifs: the "return" to the land and the presence there depends on force, a settler colonial logic, and the collapse of the secularist distinction between physical redemption and messianic aspirations. With the collapse of the latter also comes the collapse of a commitment to democratic norms. The kind of convergences and alliances we highlight here rely on undemocratic, racialized, and racist, as well as theological, accounts of solidarity and redemption. The basis for Kahane's form of Jewish solidarity (Jewish power to protect and redeem Jewish people) is therefore grounded in an exclusionary account of Jewish blood and Jewish land.

The Kach legacy not only has refused to die, but continues, at the time of this writing, to be propelled into the foreground of Israeli politics. This is manifest in Netanyahu's offer to the political heirs of Kahane's ideology, the Otzma Yehudit Party, to form a political coalition during the April 2019 elections to the Knesset. In a subsequent election that came in short order—due to Netanyahu's ultimate inability to form a coalition—Otzma Yehudit did not pass the threshold for gaining seats in the Knesset. But in the 2021 elections—the fourth elections in the course of two years—Netanyahu struck deals with Otzma Yehudit and other racist political parties such as Religious Zionism. Accordingly, their bloc granted them six mandates in the Knesset on the eve of the violent escalation of May 2021 in occupied East Jerusalem, Gaza, and against Palestinian Israeli citizens. The ascendance of Kahanism reflects broader shifts in Israeli politics toward an explicit embrace of Jewish supremacy and a jettisoning of democratic principles as part of an Israeli political ethos.[12] While many observers depict the turn to the extreme Right as a "takeover" and a radical departure from Israeli norms,[13] others (especially Palestinians) see it as simply one more manifestation of the same core problem: the occupation and its underpinning settler colonial logic.[14]

Indeed, to understand the mainstreaming of Jewish power and its convergence with currents of messianic religious Zionism, one need only go

to the city of Hebron or its southern hills and witness how the routine acts
of violence by Jewish settlers against Palestinian residents are enabled by
the infrastructures of the occupation qua annexation and met with close to
total impunity. The image that haunts many visitors to Hebron is of Shuhada
Street, the previously bustling heart of the Palestinian city, which is now open
only to Jews. The street is an eerily quiet ghost town. The only pedestrians,
in addition to tours run by the veterans' organization Breaking the Silence,
which are intended to tell delegations the truth about the occupation by
breaking the walls of silence and deception, are settlers and soldiers who
jubilantly interact with one another. The streets are closed to Palestinians,
and they are forced to gain entrance to their apartments and houses via
other paths in the heavily segregated city that is dissected with checkpoints
and armed soldiers. The implementations of the restrictions were absurdly
justified by the aftermath of the 1994 massacre of twenty-nine Muslim wor-
shippers in the Ibrahim Mosque (the Tomb of the Patriarchs) that was carried out by a Jewish settler and Kahane supporter, Baruch Goldstein, who
is celebrated as a martyr among younger Kahanists such as Ben-Gvir. The
latter even had Goldstein's photo on display in his home. Goldstein's grave in
the Meir Kahane Memorial Park in Hebron has continued, after all these
years, to be a site of pilgrimage and veneration. What one sees in Hebron is an
ethnoreligious-centric vision for Israel that is obtained by force. Indeed, even
if Hebron represents an extreme case, it does not reflect a fringe phenomenon but rather a policy with deep roots. It is a policy designed to increase the
amount of land for settlement development and decrease the number of Palestinians on that land.[15] Indeed, the settlement project has taken its Hebron
model into the 1948 territories in a process some analysts have termed
"Hebronization" of the political geography of cities, including targeting
the Palestinian neighborhood of Sheikh Jarrah in occupied East Jerusalem.
This is what Palestinians have been referring to as the "ongoing Nakba."
It has been enabled by multiple Israeli governments because "Right" and
"Left" in Israel travel across a very narrow political spectrum.

Through its transplantation in the Israeli landscape, Jewish power has
been reconfigured in engagement with the territorial maximalists who
emphasize a security ethos and religious Zionism. The latter subverted the
traditional rabbinic opposition to the valorization of the state—including its
infrastructures and mechanisms, such as the military—because they viewed
it as idolatrous.[16] But neither a messianic ideology nor Jewish power would

have been mainstreamed if it were not for the elective affinities they shared with Euro-Zionism. By "Euro-Zionism," we refer to the political and cultural movement that emerged in Europe during the late nineteenth and early twentieth century with the aim of redeeming Jews from rising antisemitism and pogroms and create a Jewish nationalism or sense of self-determination with a home in Palestine. Accordingly, it coalesced with ideological and political European currents such as liberalism and Marxism and likewise reflected the European ills of orientalism and antisemitism, as well as, of course, settler colonial discourse. Importantly, Zionism cannot be reduced to these modern discourses as it also draws on Jewish meanings, memories, symbols, and imaginations. However, the initial and enduring patterns of contact with the Indigenous Palestinian population and the systematic discrimination and racism against Mizrahi and Ethiopian populations within Israel illuminate the complex operation of Ashkenazi hegemony and its links to Europe as a political and ideological project.

The normalization of the Jewish return to Palestine was made possible by colonial and orientalist frameworks that routinely displaced, dispossessed, and destroyed Indigenous communities through the transfer of White settler colonists from Europe. The orientalism underpinning Euro-Zionism was operative in the state-coordinated kidnapping of Yemenite and Balkan children in the 1950s and their placement with Ashkenazi families from Europe (often Holocaust survivors).[17] It was also operative in the channeling of Mizrahi children to vocational schools in the already depressed regions of Israel to which Mizrahi families were settled originally, what is known as "the periphery."[18] The analysis of how Mizrahi and Jews of Color within the Israeli landscape are connected and disconnected from Palestinian experiences illuminates the complex ways in which White supremacy and Europe—as political, ideological, and colonial projects—continue to play out tragically through the explicit consolidation, embrace, and mainstreaming of "anti-Arab" Jewish power. This is of course also interrelated with the erosion of the "democratic" aspects of the "Jewish democracy." To this degree Jewish Power's racialized architecture and blueprints remain beholden to Europe as a political and ideological project, as does Euro-Zionism more broadly.[19] Bluntly put, Jewish Power in its various manifestations, including in the form of "policing" the supposed threat of miscegenation,[20] conveys an internalized racial antisemitism.

Decolonial politics can emerge from Palestinians, non-Europeans, and other antiracist Israelis reimagining the meaning of Jewish inhabitation of the Middle East. This requires reclaiming Jewish Arabness, or more broadly non-Whiteness, as a concept that is not reducible to phenotypes. Decolonizing Israel means unsettling, as radical Mizrahi scholars and activists have,[21] the modernist and orientalist binarization of Jews and Arabs that is central to the construction of Ashkenazi Jews as White. Such a construction is essential to Israeli Islamophobia. It is a form of Islamophobia that also circulates in the broader terrain of right-wing populist nationalisms in Euro-America and informs what we call an exclusionary geography of solidarity.

ZIONIST ANTISEMITISM: AN EXCLUSIONARY GEOGRAPHY OF SOLIDARITY

The common Islamophobic trend threaded throughout the multiple instances of right-wing populism also betrays another commonality: right-wing populist political parties thrive on rearticulated forms of antisemitism and, at the same time, support Israeli policies of Palestinian occupation. This commonality betrays a perhaps surprising lack of a contradiction between Zionism and antisemitism. Israeli and Jewish politicians and lobbyists associated with Netanyahu's regime did not protest—indeed, they condoned—the so-called strongmen, from Viktor Orbán to Donald Trump, regardless of their active employment of antisemitic tropes or their inclusion of known Nazis in their cabinets.[22] Indeed, this apparent subversion of the Jewish Zionist ethos that has proclaimed Israel a safe haven for the Jews in the event of another Holocaust offers a moment of moral clarity for some critical Jews. The latter recognize that the Israeli government does not have their safety in mind when its representatives wink at those various strongmen and turn a feigned ignorant eye to their flirtation or active engagement with antisemitism. They are fine with antisemitism so long as Israel is not criticized and/or sanctioned for the ongoing occupation and its plans for annexation.[23] The cultivation and maintenance of this Zionist antisemitism also relies on anti-Muslim rhetoric, which is reinforced by the active exportation and globalization of Israeli technologies of "counterterrorism."[24] The latter are thus reliant on a deep-seated orientalism that also finds expression in various forms of sexual politics. For example, even while the realities in Israel reveal that the religionization of public morality increasingly dictates spatial segregation of the sexes and legal assaults on LGBTQIA communities, Israeli *hasbarah* (propaganda material) intentionally brands Israel as a gay paradise amid a supposedly hostile neighbor-hood for the LGBTQIA community.[25] Such pinkwashing of the occupation is, of course, reliant on Islamophobic and orientalist tropes and the presump-tion of Israel as an extension of the "west."[26]

Certainly, the mainstreaming of Kahanist anti-Arab rhetoric and open ad-vocacy of violence may be the Israeli variety of right-wing populism. How-ever, this is merely an expression of a politically ubiquitous ideological Jewish supremacy. For example, other candidates who have positioned themselves as "liberal" or "centrists" and thus as, on the surface, more palatable to liberal Zi-onists, in 2019 openly celebrated "bombing Gaza back to the stone age."[27] At the same time, such labeling overlooks the degree to which Kahane's anti-Arab advocacy and rhetoric of ethnic cleansing—which has been happening anyway, as the phrase "ongoing Nakba" captures—emerged from a fear of antisemitic annihilation that rejected the convergence of Jewish and Chris-tian interests. Shaul Magid writes about how Kahane ridiculed and exposed the Declaration of Independence and the Israeli commitment to being a "Jewish democracy" as a "schizophrenic" document and labeled secular Israelis "Jewish Hellenists" and "Hebrew speaking goyim." And still, unlike his grand-son Meir Ettinger, who leads the violent, vandal Kahanist Hilltop Youth, he never advocated violence against the state itself.[28] For Magid, as for many careful observers and analysts of Israeli politics and sociocultural and reli-gious developments, the alliance of Netanyahu and Otzma Yehudit was not a sudden shock but was rather highly consistent with the Kahanist story about antisemitism as a genetic condition inscribed in the DNA of the goyim (non-Jews) and about the return to the land of Zion as a fulfillment of biblical prophecy. With all his cynicism, as Magid points out, this is what Netanyahu talked about in his 2013 U.N. speech when he contextualized the supposed threat from Iran's nuclear capabilities within a narrative of Jewish history as a series of near-annihilations. This means living every moment as if it were 1938.[29] But the ethos of ontological insecurity and the Jewish reliance on military strength for its survival still cynically allows for alliances with, and tolerance of, Zionist antisemitism. This is because Euro-Zionism emerged from such alliances to begin with.[30]

Of course, Zionist antisemitism finds and shares an even deeper af-finity with Christian restorationist theologies that interpret the return of all Jews to Zion as a key stage in an end-time narrative. Christian Zionism, with its underlying restorationist theological accounts, has underpinned the intimate relation between anti- and philo-semitism and Zionism. Zionism is here understood as the restoration and/or "return" to Zion of the Jewish people. Why does this matter for the contemporary moment of antisemitic Zionism? It matters because it is necessary to comprehend the contemporary reemergence of antisemitism within its deeper cultural, theological, and political roots. It matters because of how anti- and philo-semitism have participated in the local contestation of nationalist discourses, whether in Poland, Hungry, France, or the United States, and the shrinking therein of democratic spaces. It matters as well because of how they intersect with or diverge from anti-Muslim narratives. Indeed, empirical evidence has shown that antisemitism correlates positively with high levels of Islamophobia in contexts where right-wing populists surge.[31] The co-occurrence of Islamophobia and antisemitism is only surprising if one succumbs to the discursive dichotomization of Muslims and Jews, with "Muslims" often being used interchangeably and incorrectly with "Arabs." Hence, examining the common modernist discursive roots of Islamophobia and antisemitism also matters. It matters because such analysis uncovers the exclusionary, militant, theopolitical, and Eurocentric solidarity against which transgressive geographies—constituted through an intersectional examination of race, gender, religion, and class—can consolidate a critique of coloniality.

Coloniality,[32] as a contemporary concept that describes social movements' praxis and theory, is often filtered through the "shorthand" of White supremacy and/or racial capitalism. It is an overarching explanatory framework that connects the disparate social justice struggles of marginalized communities and forms a transgressive geography via a humanistic construction of solidarity.[33] We illustrate this point below. For now, let us simply stress that various nationalisms filtered through political liberal discourses of citizenship undertheorize and/or myopically conceal "race" and racialized religion's participation in the construction of boundaries and thresholds of belonging and nonbelonging. The construct of the "Judeo-Christian" telegraphs an exclusionary form of solidarity built on theological, cultural, and political erasures.

The assimilation of the "Judeo" into civilization discourse erases both the Muslim and Arab "other" and Jewishness that stands outside of a Christian paradigm. Antisemitism and Islamophobia are interlinked and directly connect to our analysis of Jewish power and Jewish decoloniality. Failing to identify their links as the two others of Christian European modernity constrains the analytic scope for interpreting the discursive levels where debates about Palestine/Israel occur in ways that differentiate Jewish suffering from Muslim suffering (while of course recognizing that not all Palestinians are Muslims but that orientalism is deeply implicated in Palestinian suffering). South-South alliances often involve a Palestine litmus test that prevents unlearning modernity's legacy that assimilated Jews into Whiteness and civilizational discourses, with Zionism and Israel being the main mechanisms. This imposition of a litmus test occurs while at the same time the complexities of Christian supersessionism, histories of antisemitism, and the experiences and racialization of non-Ashkenazi Jews in Israel are erased. The argument is that such erasures prevent avenues for deepening resistance and expanding the transgressive geography of social justice struggles against the discursive formations that define their terms of marginality and suffering.

Below, we analyze how decolonial thinking has led to a critical juncture where Jews' participation in decolonial, emancipatory, antiracist politics requires their disassimilation from Jewish Whiteness, which itself is historically located and not reflective of an ontological and/or phenotypical basis. This process, however, also denotes a theocultural assimilation into a Judeo-Christian ethics, even while exposing its orientalist and racist conceits. But before turning to this point, we reflect on the "Judeo" in the "Judeo-Christian" and its religio-political ramifications by revisiting Jewish power and Kahane's criticism of Israeli Jews' embeddedness in goyish and Hellenistic discourse.

"Judeo-Christian" and "White"

Indeed, the construct "Judeo-Christianity" has a particular, located history. Critics of the term who deploy genealogical methods of demystification[34] usually dismiss the "Judeo" part as a function of Christian guilt and antisemitic supersessionism and focus instead on the orientalist and secularist construction of the grammar of western domination along with a set of values that project themselves as universal. What matters to such critics is the transmogrification of Christian cosmology into secular structures that mask their religious origins. However, a more robust reflection on the "Judeo" part of this construct matters because Israel/Zion and Palestine constitute sites of meanings with ramifications for the global semiotic landscape that go far beyond their specific geographies.[35] While Israel does not equal "Judeo," the logic of the construct Judeo-Christian assimilates the Jewish tradition into a Christian narrative in a way comparable to how the civilizational discourse of the west encompasses Israel as a "strategic partner" and a stronghold of its values. The "Judeo" became a part of the construct because (some) Jews were also concurrently constructed as White, an outcome of a confluence of other factors.

A full account of the construction of Jews as White is beyond the scope of this chapter. Much has been written about this construction and its particular location in Euro-America, and a great deal of focus has been given to American Judaism as it is the largest Jewish community outside Israel.[36] Some decolonial accounts illuminate distinctions between other marginalized communities and their patterns of exclusion through antimiscegenation laws and other mechanisms of exclusion. Such exclusionary measures enacted by White settlers, on this account, created built-in openings for Jews to assimilate into American Whiteness. Others examine Whiteness as a moral choice Jews made in their processes of integration into White America. Yet others locate this process in the decline of eugenics in the postbellum period and White flight, a period that also coincided with the "Judeo-Christian" heyday. However, regardless of the construction of Jews as White in America, antisemitism is complexly inscribed into the architecture of anti-Black racism.[37] While romantic and filiopietistic accounts of the civil rights movement in the 1960s posit (White) Jews as allies of Black Americans, activists who recognized the Whiteness of American Jews and their complicity with institutional racism in the United States have punctured such pretenses. A historian of American Judaism Marc Dollinger explains the emergence of (White) Jewish power and Black Power at this historical intersection as mutually reinforcing one another in a context increasingly defined by segregated identity politics.[38]

So what is Jewish power? We are interested in explaining this phenomenon not to relish in the pathologies of modern Judaism as symptomatic of Jewish tragedies, including internalized antisemitism and its role in constructing political Zionism. Instead, we want to focus on Jewish power to the extent that it helps highlight alternative, modern, Jewish political imaginations that emerge through a process of disassimilating from Whiteness and through a rigorous analysis of the global operation of White supremacy. Jewish power was a product of White Judaism but with a persistent refusal of the assimilative (perhaps supersessionist) logic of the "Judeo-Christian." Indeed, Jewish power in the United States generated a discourse about a continuous and immanent threat to Jewish existence, connecting both with Vladimir (Ze'ev) Jabotinsky's notion of self-defense and with the diasporic Jewish focus on survival through policing marriages and bloodlines. Accordingly, Jewish survival depends on monitoring blood for the sake of the endurance of tradition. The transplantation of Jewish power to the Israeli context signaled the conversion of blood-centric Judaism to land-centric Judaism. Evidence for this convergence abounds in the increased mainstreaming of antimiscegenation rhetoric, including the banning of love stories of Jewish-Palestinian youth from the canon of the high school literature matriculation exam.[39]

Kahane's emphasis on Jewish power and anti-Arab violence diverged from a Judeo-Christian assimilationist frame, which, to him, the Israeli Declaration of Independence and its paradoxical commitment to a liberal Jewish democracy represented. Instead, a Jewish defense against antisemitism necessitated purification and expulsion as well as more aggressive policing of Jewish "blood purity" (of Jewish Israeli girls and women). The Kahanist turn signals the enduring operation of orientalism and the presumed antonymous relation between Jews and Arabs. Such an assumption betrays Ashkenazi normativity ("Ashkenormativity"). It also conveys the racialization of Jewish identity and, at the same time, explicitly appeals to biblical warrants to establish claims to the land. In all these dimensions, the Kahanist turn continues to rely on European narratives and frameworks. Even if it rejects its inevitable antisemitism, Kahanism nevertheless employs its racial categories and the blood-centric biologization of Jewishness. At the same time, however, its ethno- and religio-centric framing disrupts any assimilation of Jews into a Judeo-Christian account of morality and civilizational identity (including its tradition of political liberalism). The cultural logic of the latter account, as we saw, flirts with supersessionist outlooks and acts of erasure.

The Kahanist legacy thus operates on multiple levels. The first is the aforementioned point about antisemitism and the need for Jewish defense, whether through vigilante groups in the streets of New York City or the entire military infrastructure in Israel and the Palestinian Territories. The alliance of Likkud and Otzma Yehudit on the eve of the April 2019 elections and the even more robust alliance with the Religious Nationalist Party in 2021 (combining three Kahanist types of political organizations), therefore, is only surprising if one does not understand the emergence of Euro-Zionism in a context saturated with orientalism and classical Christian and modern racial varieties of antisemitism. Jabotinsky, the "father" of Revisionist Zionism, from which the Likud Party of Netanyahu emerged, explicitly employed racial categories to articulate a Jewish nationalism that focused on self-defense in Europe and Palestine and a realist view that the actualization of national self-determination would require violence vis-à-vis the Indigenous communities in Palestine. Critically, however, Jabotinsky was a proponent of minority rights, and his positions also had humanistic dimensions that, in the Kahanist variety, devolved into unapologetic, ethnocentric, ideological platforms. Paradoxically, however, Jewish power relies on antisemitism and orientalism, the constitutive dimensions of Christian modernity and coloniality. Christian Zionism has been a poisonous ally of Jewish Zionism from its inception, working together to consolidate the geography and solidarity of exclusion and displacement in Palestine (and Israel).

Hence, after "self-defense," the second operative site of Kahane's legacy relatedly revolves around the "purity defense" in its antimiscegenation focus as well as in the interlinked, open advocacy for the "transfer," or ethnic cleansing, of the "Arabs." The "transfer" idea has thrived on coloniality. In particular, the mechanisms of dehumanization through racial, religious, and other normative classifications show that the convergence of blood- and land-centric visions of Jewish identity, and their respective reliance on Europe, occur through the legacies of antisemitism and orientalism and also reflect the very logic of modern nationalism. "Race," in European history, was an operative category before the consolidation of biological racial theories,[40] and it is constitutive of the construction of modern nations. Zionism as a European movement is no exception. The open advocacy of "purification" through ethnic cleansing is as much a legacy of Europe as are Kant and Hegel whose philosophies also exude radicalized outlooks. This is precisely what a decolonial lens exposes as it examines modernity through the histories of genocide, slavery, and other atrocities predicated on the valuation of certain humans over others.

In treating Kahane's views as already within the mainstream, we can identify the convergence of the (secular) political Zionist focus on the land as the core of Jewish survival/redemption with the blood-centric focus of diasporic survival through a traditional resistance to assimilation by way of intermarriage. Kahanists, by daylight, function no differently than the KKK or White nationalists do on the streets of Charlottesville, Virginia: they expose definitional dimensions of the "nation" or "the virtuous community" and its racialized patterns and histories, as well as multiple margins, silences, and exclusions. The Nazis and White nationalists who marched in the streets of Charlottesville on August 12, 2017, chanting, "Jews will not replace us," as a part of their protest against the removal of a symbol of the Confederacy and slavery did not come from nowhere. They share elective affinities with, and systemic support from, the more normative inclusive liberal political framework of the United States, even if on its surface the latter has moved toward greater expansion of the benefits of human rights. Hence, Otzma Yehudit, as the grotesque expression of Jewish power, is locked in a contorted, exclusionary, and self-destructive alliance/solidarity with the White nationalist neo-Nazi marchers in Charlottesville. Indeed, Otzma Yehudit's hilltop settlers' acts of vandalization, and open calls to "transfer" Palestinians and "bomb them back to the stone age," are directly linked to the anatomy of Zionism, with its inherent contradictions. Both story lines take us back to coloniality via White supremacy and its idiosyncratic but also globally resonant manifestations. Via this route of analysis we can identify patterns of domesticating Jews and the "Judeo" into coloniality's operative logic.

Decolonizing Jewish power in its extensive manifestations as normative Israeli discourse means identifying its participation in White supremacy. However, a decolonial outlook that nuances the assimilation of Jews into the "Judeo-Christian" civilizational discourse, even while thriving on its Eurocentricity, orientalism, and racism, opens up spaces for hermeneutical interrogation and reimagining beyond reductive discursive accounts. Such imagining requires accounting for the co-occurrence of Islamophobia and antisemitism in Euro-America. One path for an emboldened interpretive approach—one that is different from what Mariá José Méndez characterizes as "a freestanding critique of power"—is to shift from a critique of global designs and hegemony to a critique focused on historically located lived experiences that force us to think in terms of religiocultural and social messiness.[41] Reductive discursive accounts risk erasing histories and embodied experiences. This is why we have been searching for and listening to stories at the margins as sources for hermeneutical counterhegemonic and decolonial reimagining of belonging and citizenship. In the case of Israel and Jewish communities, more broadly, this reimagining entails disassimilation from Whiteness and land- and blood-centric conceptions of belonging. It also entails decentering the narratives of suffering and genocide and illuminating their intricate links with modernity's other genocides. This is not a zero-sum game of memory and pain. Rather, it is a recognition of the politically generative potential of a multidirectional memory.[42] Non-White Jews are often in a position to illuminate these interconnections and to destabilize Jewish Whiteness as it has played out within and beyond Israel.

JEWS OF COLOR AND TRANSGRESSIVE GEOGRAPHIES: BEYOND THE JUDEO-CHRISTIAN

Indeed, Otzma Yehudit's racism is just a more explicit articulation of Israeli nationalism and the shrinking democratic space within Israel over the past few decades. It also relates directly to the entrenchment of the occupation. However, the focus on Jewish power is not meant to unfold as an abstract ethical argument about the wrongness of Israel as a Jewish political project. Often the employment of discursive and decolonizing lenses presents complexities through simplified binaries that leave little room for on-the-ground reimagining of political and social belonging. In particular, the decolonial option tends to flirt with postnationalism and antinationalism in ways that do not fully account for activists' own dependency on citizenship rights and passports. Hence, we contrast the cases of Jews of Color in Israel and in the United States—with an understanding that the concept of JOC does not translate neatly into Hebrew—in order to exemplify alternative meaning-making processes that cannot be reduced to an analysis of matrixes of power or to the consolidation of an abstract and Archimedean antiracist positionality. It is the desire for a pure Archimedean point, with its litmus tests for attainment, that forecloses inclusionary and open solidarity frameworks as well as openings for learning across communities. As Hammer's chapter in this volume shows, such litmus tests also demobilized and substantially diminished the potentiality of the Women's March to materialize politically. Hammer's account also highlights the discursive and semiotic force of the transnational circulation of antisemitism and anti-Muslim hostility and the very localized effects of such circulation on the capacity of coalition work. Her analysis illuminates the weaponization of antisemitism against racialized Muslim communities in the United States and visibly pious feminist Muslim leaders such as Linda Sarsour. Shifting beyond an exposition of symbolic and cultural violence and its capacity to diminish the scope of antiracist and inclusive coalitions requires an examination that goes beyond apparent boundaries between Jews and Blacks. In other words, it requires a decolonial move that challenges the terms of the analysis.

JOC came to the fore in the United States as an important force enabling American Jews critical of Israeli policies and Zionism to disassimilate from Whiteness. It has required Jews to embody and foreground Jewishness as an identity that is multiracial, multigendered, and pluralistic in various ways. Such disengagement facilitated the cultivation of more robust solidarity with antiracism struggles than the false equivalencies that Jewish-Black solidarity during the Civil Rights movement assumed. The latter form of solidarity did not emphasize the different social locations of Jews and Black Americans as two marginalized minority groups. In failing to do so, the history of slavery was erased in this solidarity movement. JOC perspectives and leadership have proven effective in facilitating the building of alliances and cross-cultural learning about Whiteness, as well as antisemitism (including grappling with the history of Black antisemitism).[43] As Omer notes in *Days of Awe*, through a variety of organizing spaces, such as Jews for Racial and Economic Justice and the Caucus of Mizrahi, Sephardi, and Jews of Color, some segments within the American Jewish community have confronted their own implication in White supremacy and privilege. Whether through the legacy of Ashkenormativity in the United States and Israel or the participation and complicity of Jews in settler colonial projects, Islamophobia, and/ or structural racism that silences and makes non-White Jews disappear, JOC organizing and teaching about alternative embodied experiences of Blackness have paved the way for articulating Jewishness outside of nationalist discourse. Through the intersectional analysis performed by JOC, Zionism comes to be seen as inextricably reliant on and synonymous with settler colonialism and White supremacy. An intersectional approach thus facilitates an ethically coherent path for Jewish participation in a global struggle against racism, xenophobia, and many other sites of injustice. This internal grappling became evident in Jewish Voice for Peace's (JVP's)—the largest alternative American Jewish organization critical of Israeli policies—alliance and explicit support of the Movement for Black Lives' Platform and its use of the word *genocide* to refer to Palestinian experiences and bolster Black-Palestinian solidarity.[44] JVP's support of the platform and its analysis of the interconnections among the multiple sites of genocide and oppression associated with modernity—also within which Palestinians and Black

Americans have found points of solidarity and connections (especially since the turn to Black Power)—was expressed by their empowering and foregrounding of the JOC's caucus.

The embodied experiences of JOC's members facilitate a disengagement from the discourse of Jewish power as well as blood- and land-centric conceptions of Jewish history and identity. Inhabiting a space that is also defined by Blackness, JOC subvert and dispel the myopic conflation of the "Judeo-Christian" with Whiteness as well as the interlinking of the Judeo and the Christian in the service of empire. Within this critical space, the "Judeo-Christian" as a civilizational label represents the misdirection of Jews and their complicity with White supremacy (itself also authorized through the Christian Zionist imagination and internalized antisemitism) rather than an ethical resistance to fascism. This complicity assumes multiple forms, whether theopolitically, in what Marc Ellis has called "the ecumenical deal,"[45] or through an analysis of the continuous operation of White supremacy or coloniality manifesting in neoliberalism. Through this lens, a global framework of domination centrally features, and occasionally flirts with or even dog whistles, antisemitic tropes such as the aforementioned allusions to Soros and/or to Israel as a semantic replacement for "Jews," thus denoting a nefarious behind-the-scenes power mongering. Israel is characterized as a culprit, whether through arms sales, exportation of surveillance technologies, or exploitative economic practices. Such a framework also participates in the orientalist discourse that posits Israel as "a villa in the jungle" and "the only democracy in the Middle East" and Palestinians as metaphorical representations of all other Indigenous, marginalized, exploited, displaced, ethnically cleansed, and dehumanized people.[46] Through a discursive critique that decenters Zion, grapples with Jewish complicity with Whiteness and White privilege, and unsettles the modernist binarization of Jews and Arabs, non-Israeli Jewish critics of Israel and Zionism reimagine Jewishness beyond blood- and land-centric filters as multiracial, multigender, and plural otherwise.

If Jewish power signals the grotesque upshot of the tragedy of European Jewish modernity through an obsession with blood, land, and ethnoreligious-centric conceptions of solidarity, security, and existential threat, JOC activist spaces articulate postnationalist conceptions of Jewish strength and solidarity as dependent on and intersecting with other peoples' liberation. Their very embodied disruption of binaries becomes a source for a broader reimagining of Jewish diasporism.[47] This intersectional insight presents a very clear moral choice. One must choose between either (1) Whiteness (and, with it, Zionism), which allows for support of the Israeli state and its ethnocentric principles of inclusion and exclusion, or (2) participation in the broader movement against racism and White supremacy. The Zionist project, accordingly, is filtered almost entirely through an analysis of settler colonialism. This was evident during Jewish Voice for Peace's National Membership Meeting in 2017, where panels and plenaries, and the explicit framing of the program, connected the dots between White supremacy in the United States and White supremacy in Israel. Israeli Jews were present in the conversations to the degree that they became assimilated into the overarching struggle against White supremacy. There were Mizrahi and Ethiopian activists whose Brown and Black bodies were assimilated into the global and intersectional social justice landscape, even if they did not necessarily dismiss the religious meaning of Zion for the Jewish imagination. One Ethiopian activist stressed, in a panel discussion with key activists from Black Lives Matter, that her parents' and grandparents' longing for Zion, while having nothing to do with the European movement, cannot simply be assimilated into the discourse of settler colonialism. To the degree that she underscores her embeddedness in Zionism, her capacity for solidarity with BLM fails. This is where a binary and purist paradigm erodes and where the limits of solidarity emerge through the persistence of a nationalist paradigm. Perin Gürel's chapter in this volume likewise reveals an event of broken Muslim-Muslim and South-South solidarity between Iranian and Turkish women.

This insight, together with the multiple pockets of Mizrahi and Ethiopian activism and efforts to challenge Israeli Ashkenormativity and racism, shows that decolonizing means more than shifting the focus from Jewish power to Jewish powerlessness and from exclusionary ethnoreligious-centric solidarity to *other*-centric commitment. JOC and other Jewish critics of the occupation, Zionism, and Israeli policies do not claim to be powerless; rather they reclaim and revalorize diasporic Jewishness. This reclaiming takes multiple and occasionally overlapping shapes, from retrieving prophetic Judaism as most authentically Jewish to reconnecting to the insights of the socialist, atheist, Yiddish-centric, Eastern European Bund Movement and its principle of *doikayt*, or hereness. This entails a social and economic justice orientation of solidarity with one's neighbors wherever Jews exist, thus destabilizing any kind of teleological reading of Jewish history, geography, and meaning. Of course, this reclaiming of the Eastern European shtetel Judaism erases and precludes Jewish lives in Arab and Muslim contexts and the latter's sources for revalorizing their diasporic belongings. In the case of JOC, their intersectional experiences as Black and Brown persons enable the integration of Jews into antiracism spaces. This point coheres with Houria Bouteldja's appeal to Jews to join the struggle of the "wretched of the interior"—the marginalized within the global North—by unmasking the logic that has construed them as "buffer communities." Bouteldja reads Fanon through James Baldwin to articulate a concept of revolutionary love that offers a path to antiracism, decoloniza- tion, and the formation of alliances between Muslims and Jews, if the latter disengage from their complicity with White supremacy.[48] Certainly, as we show below, this is an elite undertaking not currently available to those inhabiting the Mizrahi ghettos in Israel's peripheries, whose ghettoization has been an outcome of long histories of marginalization and racializa- tion of Jews from Arab and Islamic countries within a Eurocentric Jewish supremacist ideological frame.

Indeed, White Jews who are self-reflexive about their White privilege and critical of the occupation and Zionism—as critical JOC similarly are—embrace Judaism as an ethical tradition that necessarily conflicts with Zionism understood as an ethnoreligious-centric political identity and set of practices rooted in settler colonialism, White supremacy, and exclusionary forms of solidarity. This results in metaphorizing Zion—that is, decentering it from the Jewish imagination—and rereading the Jewish tradition as more authentically about the prophetic rather than the land- and group-centric motifs.[49] Ironically, this rereading, which turns Zion into a spiritual locus and metaphor and highlights the prophetic as a source of intersectional solidarity with marginalized communities, reinstates another variety of the superses- sionist "Judeo-Christian" imagination. Even while disrupting (along with the discursive and decolonial critics) its racist and orientalist underpinnings, the hermeneutical maneuvers of the construction of the "Judeo-Christian" as an ethics still resonate. This time it comes in the form of a humanistic ethics that is often articulated through the rereading of Jewish stories, rituals, and meanings for lessons they can offer us in the present. This is done from the perspectives of the victims of Jewish power, precluding, of course, the Jewish victims who fail to sing the same decolonial tune. The Mizrahi and Ethiopian litmus test requires an explicit endorsement of Boycott, Divestment, and Sanctions (BDS), as one Ethiopian activist shared with Omer in her recounting of occasions when she has been invited to speak to non-Israeli audiences in Europe and North America. She is accepted as Black but not an Israeli Jew for whom the meaning of Zion is still very concrete and religiously and spiritually significant for her sense of political and social belonging. In other words, the BDS litmus test expects her to renounce her Jewish-Israeliness and to point to the shared links between her community's struggle and the Palestinian struggle. As we show in the third part of this chapter, South-South solidarities cannot succeed if they fail to acknowledge the different historical locations of the groups forming them.

The spiritualization or metaphorization of Zion within the postcolonial and decolonial Jewish imagination relies ironically on disassimilating Judeo-Christian ethics from Whiteness. Grappling with Jewish complicity in White supremacy and settler colonialism allows for the embrace of non-Zionist Jews by a global antiracism movement. Judaism transforms into a particularistic vernacular of a universal ethics that disembodies and rereads teleologically the Hebraic prophetic legacy. The statement of values expressed by the self-defined anti-Zionist synagogue Tzedek Chicago (established in 2015) exemplifies this point. Tzedek Chicago defines itself as embodying a Judaism of solidarity. Its community is "inspired by prophetic Judaism: our tradition's sacred imperative to take a stand against the corrupt use of power." The community also foregrounds "a Judaism beyond nationalism" as a related core value. It stresses an appreciation of "the important role of the land of Israel in Jewish tradition, liturgy and identity" while under-scoring a resistance to "the fusing of Judaism with political nationalism" and a refusal of "any ideology that insists upon exclusive Jewish entitle-ment to the land." This rejection of ethnocentric interpretations of Judaism concludes with the hope that the congregation's advocacy and activism will contribute to ending "Israel's ongoing oppression of the Palestinian people and seek a future that includes full civil and human rights for all who live in the land—Jews and non-Jews alike."[50] The quote reveals how Tzedek Chicago's employment and embrace of the prophetic tradition coalesces with the postnationalist imagination, resistance to what is deemed a perver-sion of Judaism in the form of Zionism, and an appeal to and a reliance on a universal rights discourse that itself relies (though nonreductively) on the nation-state unit. Theorizing Zion out of existence or spiritualizing and decentering its meaning vis-à-vis Jewishness has become a common motif for the movement of non-Israeli Jews critical of the occupation and, to varying degrees, Zionism, as a political-religious identity.

Tzedek Chicago objects to the modernist perversion of Judaism in the form of a political ideology based on blood- and land-centric interpretations of Judaism. But it accepts its own apparently proper space as a "congregation"—a category with a deep Christian and Protestant history also pivotal to a critical analysis of religion and modernity.

Non-, post-, and/or anti-Zionist diaspora Jews' disengagement from state-, land-, and blood-centric Jewishness reflects their privilege as persons who already possess citizenship rights and entitlements in the United States or elsewhere outside of Israel. Hence, their appeals to the prophetic or to the ethical (often telegraphed in interviews with Omer using the phrase, "My Judaism is about social justice") contrasts with the ethnocentric embodiment of Israeli Jews and reconfigures the supersessionist pretenses of the Judeo-Christian antifascist currents. As already noted, the latter has been coextensive with an anti-Muslim civilizationist orientalism of the west. Our point is not to diminish the significance of this revalorization of the diaspora through a decolonial intersectional outlook but rather to illuminate its limitations and ironic embeddedness still in the Judeo-Christian construct and its reading of the Jewish prophetic tradition through Christian categories. The American Jewish Palestine solidarity activists Omer follows, therefore, are increasingly clear on why their antiracist commitments within the United States require that they disengage from their affective loyalty (or ethno-Judeocentric solidarity) with Israelis and instead concentrate their solidarity compass on Palestinian liberation. Palestine, as noted, is metaphorically significant in anticolonial social justice struggles. It is a litmus test, with a complex semiotic force. It is pivotal for the formation of South-South coalitions and is critical for mapping transgressive and emancipatory geographies. As it has been generative of failed solidarities, the litmus test also reveals that a grassroots moral imagination is nonetheless limited by its realist horizons.

THE REALIST BOUNDARIES OF TRANSGRESSIVE GEOGRAPHIES

The Mizrahi feminist scholar Smadar Lavie has unsettled the certainty of appeals to intersectionality for articulating justice in Palestine and Israel as well as intersectionality's relation to broader emancipatory "geograph[ies] of liberation." An analysis and autoethnography of Mizrahi single mothers navigating the "bureaucratic torture" of Israel illuminates the relevance of an intersectional outlook but also shifts beyond simply articulating it as a self-evident resource for broad-based antiracism coalitions of disparate communities. Instead, the bureaucratic torture and the aspiration to assimilate into Ashkenormativity prevent poor Mizrahi women from seeing their links to Palestinian experiences and the broader Middle Eastern terrain beyond the Jewish parameters of the political project of which they are a part. This explains why, for the most part, Mizrahi demographics support belligerent policies against Palestinians.[51] Their struggle to survive prevents them from heeding Bouteldja's call to join the struggle against White supremacy. Indeed, her call to disengage from Jewish Whiteness makes little sense on the ground, even if Mizrahi communities are well aware of crimes committed against them by the hegemonic Ashkenazi majority. Further, one may wonder if the mere call to join the struggle, beyond an embrace of Palestine solidarity, simply expects people to overcome, instantly, their decades of socialization into a Euro-Zionist narrative that integrates Mizrahim into the occupation through Euro-Jewish supremacy discourse. They too are prisoners of this discourse of self-alienation from their Arabness and belonging to the region's cultural and social inheritances. They too are its beneficiaries and executioners.

The empirical reality reveals that Mizrahi communities in Israel reject visions of peace like Bouteldja's. Her vision is deeply located in her antiracist struggle as a French Algerian citizen who sees the ways in which the "Jews" function as "buffer communities" that enable the structures of White supremacy. It is thus not immediately relevant to those living outside that context. Bouteldja might be correct that the Jews of Europe have become White and thus co-opted into anti-Muslim racism. But in Israel, Mizrahi rejection of solidarity with other racialized and oppressed communities outside the national divides can be understood historically and sociologically as an outcome of processes that include their own marginalization and alienation from their connection to the region. Mizrahi communities were channeled to subsidized settlements in the territories occupied in 1967 after decades of intentional policies designed to prevent them from building intergenerational wealth and after the neglect of their social justice concerns by the Ashkenazi leadership of the peace movement.[52] The demographic data reveal that Mizrahim make up a plurality of the population[53] and that for them to change their voting patterns would be detrimental to themselves because it would end the occupation of Palestine and subsequently reconfigure cohabitation in Palestine and Israel in ways that disrupt the apartheid logic from which they currently benefit. The empirical realities of Mizrahi antipeace and anti-Arab expressions can thus be explained historically and sociologically. Such explanations deflect any kind of essentialist approach—though such orientalist approaches are, of course, ubiquitous.[54] The tragedy resides precisely in how rigid Jewish supremacist boundaries are erected to prevent Mizrahim from seeing how their predicament of marginality relates to Palestinian stories of displacement and occupation. This of course blocks the building of substantial coalitions across identitarian divides. To make such connections would allow for South-South solidarity to shine with clarity. Indeed, as Melani McAlister concludes in her contribution to this volume, ultimately, myopias, or the walls that prevent people from seeing what is in front of them, constitute the main obstacles for inclusive solidarity. These myopias also embody the colonial legacy that continues to imprison people.

Therefore, typically and as a matter of realist and pragmatic considerations, key Mizrahi feminist activists, even if they themselves practice this kind of intersectional approach, strategically bracket their concern for inclusive solidarity that would connect the antioccupation or antiapartheid struggles to Mizrahi marginalization. They do so to focus first on the survival of Mizrahi communities in their deprived neighborhoods, vocational schools, and "development towns." For them, this is a preliminary step to consciousness raising. Hence, preliminarily, the works of Black and Chicana feminisms, such as Anzaldúa's, and Arab feminists, such as Nawal El Saadawi, cannot fully express an intersectional South-South solidarity that will connect the struggle of Mizrahi feminists with antiapartheid Palestinian struggles. This also helps explain why a BDS litmus test excludes most Mizrahim and Ethiopian Jews from joining the Palestinian struggle. The need to fight for one's own survival, together with the historical and sociological processes that situate most Israeli Mizrahim on the political Right and as beneficiaries of the Israeli occupation,[55] is maybe best captured in Smadar Lavie's description of Viki Knafo's protest in *Wrapped in the Flag of Israel*. This literal and symbolic act illuminates how Knafo's protest and struggles as a Mizrahi single mother were limited not only by her resources or marginalized social location but also by her commitment to the national boundaries of the Israeli state. Indeed, the ability to see the links between the poverty of south Tel Aviv and the occupation of Palestinians is not the starting point for people who are hungry and marginalized. The failure to identify links between these struggles is detrimental to peace and justice and exposes the limits of an emancipatory solidarity discourse.

The case of Israel and Palestine, therefore, exposes the realist constraints that delimit the imagination of the horizons of antiracist solidarity. Hence, the case of Mizrahi feminists exemplifies yet another instance of what Gürel refers to in her chapter as "failed solidarity," though here it unfolds under different circumstances. However, both the examples of Iranian/ Turkish feminists and Mizrahi/Black American and Chicana feminists expose the critical role of nationalist discourse in constraining the horizons of moral and political imaginations and, concretely, religio-cultural and political mobilization. The boundaries of transgressive geography are thus constrained by the empirical and realist arguments regarding Mizrahi belligerence. These constraints can be explained contextually in the same way that Black American antisemitism can be explained in Hammer's account of Tamika Mallory's coziness with Louis Farrakhan and the Nation of Islam. The answer to such constraints is to reconfigure legal policies, promote education, engage in consciousness raising, and more generally enhance people's capacity to survive. Instead, Mizrahi belligerence that is born of racialization into Jewish supremacist nationalism ends up trumping their entry into South-South solidarity. Ironically, this reveals South-South solidarity discourse as itself persistently operative within a European framework. Reuven Abergel, one of the founding members of the Israeli Black Panthers, described, in a conversation with Omer, how organically he experienced the relations with the Palestinians in occupied East Jerusalem in the aftermath of 1967 when the physical barrier between the two parts of Jerusalem were dissolved. This was not a pre-arranged peace camp by the United States, as is standard within the peace industry in Israel, with an overrepresentation of Ashkenazi Jews therein. Instead, it was an organic reconnection to sounds, smells, foods, and languages. Abergel, who was relocated from Morocco and settled at a very young age in Musrara (a Palestinian neighborhood in Jerusalem from where Palestinians were expelled during the Nakba), had longed to reconnect to his landscape. But it took several years of political activism for him to understand the links between Mizrahi and Palestinian grievances and their histories of displacement. Making such connections, Abergel underscored, threatened the authorities, and thus they would crush any pathway for making them.[56] This crushing of the potentiality of Palestinian-Mizrahi solidarity relates back to the logic of Euro-Zionism that continues to work itself out in the sociological realities of Israeli Jews from the region of the Middle East and their self-alienation in the form of antipeace and anti-Arab/Palestinian voting patterns. While Abergel had authentic memories of being a part of the landscape, Mizrahi communities "native" to Israel were incubated in Jewish supremacy and thus themselves became its prisoners and executioners. Their noninclusion in South-South openings likewise reveals the acceptance of such realities and thus a refusal of boundary-breaking accounts of political horizons. Indeed, such boundary breaking would potentiality exemplify what Martin Savransky calls "alter-realism," which he defines as a "realism that takes the risk of asserting the reality of what is deemed improbable, implausible, marginalized, suppressed, irrelevant, even scandalous, and seeks to draw out its possible implications for the transformation of what is considered credible, reliable, and serious."[57]

To take alter-realism seriously means "to take seriously a form of truth that seeks not to represent reality but to set realities in motion" and to recognize the decolonial sociological imagination in "the realities of others for whom reality itself is in the making, for whom the cry 'another world is possible!' can never be reduced to a simple metaphor."[58] Hence, together with Boaventura de Sousa Santo's concept of the "sociology of absences," Savransky gestures to the locations of alter-realism and the horizons of the decolonial sociological imagination in the margins. The focus on alter-realism and the sociology of absences unsettles what Santiago Slabodsky calls the "hermetic reading" of Europe as a metanarrative, excluding the possibility of other story lines and transgressive dialectics.[59] When the poststructural turn in intersectional theory and praxis, accordingly, defines agency only in terms of being against oppression, it overlooks the agency of multiple actors, including women of faith.[60] Likewise, a discursive critique of Christian modernity's working itself out through enduring patterns of coloniality (including through its manifestation in Israel and Palestine), silences story lines from the margins about "another world being possible."

The potentiality of a transgressive geography of liberation presented itself with lucidity when Tom Mehager, a Mizrahi public intellectual and activist, spoke at a workshop organized by the feminist organization Zochrot.[61] The aim of this workshop was to discuss the interlinking of the two erasures of Arab Jews (Mizrahim/yot) and Palestinians at the time of the Nakba.[62] Zochrot recovers the lost geography of Palestine, which includes the stories of individual Palestinian villages that were depopulated, massacred, and thus erased from the landscape. One can download the Zochrot app, a "GPS to nowhere," as one key researcher and guide of Zochrot's tours of depoplated villages describes it,[63] to comprehend the massive scope of the displacement and destruction. As one drives along Israeli roads, the app will indicate the locations and stories of those who were erased. Users of the app need to exercise imaginative capacity to see villages where there is nothing but an identifiable pattern of cacti and, occasionally, a few ruins. Often, there are only pine trees (a non-native tree) or settlement villas with their distinctive red roofs. Zochrot, like other feminist peace organizations, is gradually ascertaining the links that connect the Mizrahi experiences of displacement and discrimination to Palestinian tragedies via a meta-analysis of White settler colonialism, here implemented by European Jews. However, Mehager, the activists in Zochrot, and other activists cannot simply re-create in reality the transgressive geography the Zochrot app imaginatively reconstructs. Indeed, Mizrahi identity did not exist before it was constructed through the matrix of Ashkenormativity and racialization. It is historically embedded and articulated in the discourse of Israeli citizenship. However, seeing the intersections and the root causes of marginality illuminates possibilities for remapping transgressive geographies through agentic meaning-making and telling alternative stories to that of White settler colonialism and "Judeo-Christianity."

ANOTHER WORLD IS POSSIBLE: REALITIES IN MOTION

We now turn to anecdotes that illuminate that "another world is possible." These are sites of reimagining Jewish meanings in and about Israel. The first story is of Noam Shuster-Eliassi, a Jewish Israeli comedian. Shuster-Eliassi was raised in Oasis of Peace (Waat al Salaam or Neve Shalom), an experimental binational community near Tel Aviv, by an Iranian Jewish mother and an Ashkenazi father. Her family comes with what she calls the "H word," or the Holocaust story, but also has memories of being from the Middle East.[64] In addition, growing up speaking Arabic at Waat a-Salaam immediately connects her to the region. This is unique in that many other Mizrahi people of her generation are estranged from the Arabic and Persian languages of their roots.

Shuster-Eliassi's remarks in her weekly satirical spot on 124 News Arabic in late February 2019 went viral in the Arab media because, in fluent Arabic, she declared her intention to marry the Saudi crown prince Mohammed bin Salman, especially considering (sarcastically) the warming relationship between the Gulf and Jerusalem. This is what she said:

> I'm thirty-two now, and I'm still not married. . . . My aunts and grand-mother are driving me crazy asking: "When are you going to get married already?" My grandmother told me, "Noam, now that you're thirty-two, you can marry anyone—Jewish, not Jewish, I don't care." But I don't want to just marry anyone, I want to aim higher. And when I do—who is it that I see? They say Bashar Assad is tall—but he's not right for me. MBS! MBS is tall! And I know that ties are warming up between Israel and Saudi. And so I want to address MBS directly: I tried starting a party named "Naama" so we can work together for peace in the Middle East. I know you don't want to be meddling in Israeli politics but please, if you could support the "Naama" party or just me, that would be really really great.

The clip went viral because it touched on the critical issue of the Saudi's participation in normalizing relations with Israel. But it also went viral because of Shuster-Eliassi's fluent Arabic. Of course, her appeal to MBS to support the fictional Naama introduced added layers of satire, recognizing that an alliance between dictators and Netanyahu's regime, which itself reflects autocratic and undemocratic commitments, is not the path toward peace in the Middle East. What is a path is for Israeli Jews to learn Arabic, to become a part of the Middle East, and to relinquish the pretenses of being European. Indeed, this is why Shuster-Eliassi often writes, "Learn Arabic!," as a preface to the many clips from Arab media recapping her "proposal" to MBS.

Shuster-Eliassi is the latest artist, this time a comedian, to reconnect Jewishness and Jewish bodies back to the Middle East. She joins the company of other Mizrahim such as the Iraqi Israeli Jewish writer Almog Bahar when he writes in his poem, "My Arabic Is Mute," that Hebrew "Speaks out in public / Prophesies the coming of gods / And bulldozer" while his "Arabic is scared / Quietly poses as Hebrew . . . And at each passing cop in the street / Draws the Identity Document / And points to the protective phrase: / 'I am a Jew, I am a Jew.'"[65] In an interview, Bahar describes the absurdities of Mizrahiness in Israel, echoing Lavie. He told his interviewer about his participation in a protest against the forced evacuation of Palestinians from the East Jerusalem neighborhood of Sheikh Jarrah and how a former student of his who was wearing a military police uniform recognized him. In a heated discussion with Bahar, the student asserted his commitment to his role as an instrument of the Israeli military and police (a variation of Bouteldja's analysis of Jews as "buffer communities"). Bahar commented that the absurdity was that this same young man is often, as in the poem, stopped by security forces because of his "Arab appearance," which the former student finds can be slightly mitigated by frequent shaving. Bahar expressed his dismay that the interests of the rich and ideologically driven Americans (who purchased the Palestinian homes, often through a complex, deceitful bureaucratic torture aimed at depopulation) are misguidedly more important to this former student than the Palestinians whose predicament is so interlaced with the Mizrahi one. The Arabic language connects the Israeli Jew to the Middle East. Embracing Arabic disrupts Europe as the main protagonist for working out the dual Muslim and Jewish questions and reveals the region in its potentiality as a transgressive geography of liberation.

Bahar's books are translated into Arabic and circulate in Cairo, Iraq, and other literary markets.[66] He is in the vanguard of artistic efforts to redefine the Israeli cultural terrain. In doing so, however, he articulates an alternative to Israel's definitional (and modernist) dichotomies: Jews versus Arabs, religious versus secular, and so forth. It is clear to Bahar that there is a direct link between Mizrahiness, the recovery of Arab Jewishness, and the resolution of the Palestinian-Israeli conflict. This involves overcoming the internal turmoil within the self-alienation of the Mizrahi soul by illuminating the link between Mizrahi Arab memory, Ashkenazi oppression, and socioeconomic domination.[67] He subsequently argues that the focus of activism needs to be on social justice issues, such as public housing in the periphery or the "development towns" of Israel.

Bahar stresses, however, a need for more than unlocking the Jewish-Arab-Palestinian links through an intersectional prism. He also reminds us of the importance of theological thinking as well. Such thinking interrogates the historical-theological Jewish-Muslim dimensions of the meanings attached to the land. Hebrew—which he reads through the lens of the Iraqi Shaul Abdallah Yosef of the late nineteenth century and the Jerusalemite Ariel Ben Tzion—is an oriental language whose revival depends on reconnecting it to Arabic and to its mystical and theological roots in the East; hence, the "return" to Eretz Yisrael meant a return to the East rather than becoming a European estrangement therein.[68] Accordingly, for Bahar, "Mizrahi literature" should not be a subcategory of Hebrew Israeli literature, but rather all Hebrew literature should become Mizrahi. Therefore, he fights exactly against the folklorization of Mizrahiness, stressing the absolute need to subvert the narrowing of Jewish culture within the Middle East.[69] Such broadening also involves recovering the depth of Hebrew itself within the Jewish tradition, including *midrash* and *piyyut*, but also cross-fertilizing it with Arabic literature and traditions. Bahar and Shuster-Eliassi both demolish the walls around the Hebrew Jewish ghetto by relinking Arabness with Jewishness and connecting it through cultural activism to the region, not as settlers, but as Indigenous peoples. They both paint a picture that is much more complex than simply undoing settler colonialism. Their new painting requires interpretations and reinterpretations of Jewish Arab meanings and forms of being in the Middle East, via both religion and language.

Another cultural activist, Orly Noy, translates Iranian literature into Hebrew and sees her translation as deeply political. Like Shuster and Bahar, she relinks the Jews to the region in nonhegemonic ways. Noy is also a member of a Palestinian-Israeli political party, Balad, that envisions Israeli citizenship as including full equality and a reckoning with historical injustices. Her translation work and blogging and journalism as well as political activism all reflect the complexity of reintegrating Jews into the region and creating alternative (transgressive) political horizons. She is also aware of the empirical realities of Mizrahi estrangement, as well as Mizrahi complicity with the occupation, but refuses to delimit her imagination to such empirical realities. In this, she sees herself as linked to the history of Mizrahi social justice struggles in Israel.[70] As another queer Mizrahi activist, Sapir Sluzker-Amran, underscores, the challenge is to create an archive or a historical memory of these struggles so that it becomes possible to challenge and disrupt the forces that have an interest in division, social, cultural, and linguistic amnesia, and selective co-optation. Hence, Sluzker-Amran spearheaded the creation of a public archive for people to record their knowledge of struggles, to create cross-references between struggles, and to expand coordination and coalitional work. Sluzker-Amran, like Lavie, also thinks that for Mizrahim, as we shift beyond an artistic vanguard and intellectual class, making connections between their marginalization, the Palestinian predicament, and imagining equitable cohabitation in the space requires attending to their struggles to survive, without any Palestine litmus test.[71]

Hence, the second anecdotal site of alter-realism relates to the Mizrahi feminist organizing of Ahoti (lit., "Sista") and its work in the impoverished neighborhoods of south Tel Aviv. Ahoti has an extensive activist history. However, we want to focus specifically on its leader, Shula Keshet, who has mobilized a solidarity movement to stand with African asylum seekers fighting against their looming deportation back to almost certain death (primarily in Eritrea and South Sudan). Keshet, a veteran feminist warrior for Mizrahi communities, called the bluff behind the government's rhetoric of fear (of "infiltration" by Africans) and saw through the Israeli government's cynical lie that the African asylum seekers needed to be deported in order to rehabilitate the depressed neighborhoods of south Tel Aviv. She knew that the Mizrahi poor would be next in the push for gentrification, and she knew that the government had intentionally channeled the refugees and asylum seekers toward the economically deprived neighborhoods and "development" towns in the "periphery." The asylum seekers were not allowed in the lavish neighborhoods of north Tel Aviv, even if volunteers from the "White" neighborhoods came to engage in occasional "do-goodism" with the asylum seekers.

For Keshet, "the equation of rehabilitation in return for deportation" is unethical and amounts to a cynical use of Mizrahi misery. She was able to see beyond the blinders of the racialized discourse Lavie identifies—that the policies targeting the asylum seekers are indeed in continuity with decades of maltreatment of the poor Mizrahi communities. The latter, sitting on undeveloped (potentially prime) real estate, are also under constant threat of removal for the sake of gentrification. Keshet also identified an atmosphere of fear being spread through propaganda and the use of various Jewish power motifs in the neighborhoods to divide Africans and the Mizrahi poor. However, Keshet has indicated that surveys in the Tel Aviv region consistently show that the highest objection to the deportation comes from the residents of the poor southern neighborhoods. This is no surprise, she says, given that "the asylum seekers are our neighbors, they are people with faces and names." The hegemonic structures and policy makers are trying to frighten people into believing that they are all rapists and drug dealers, which she recognizes as the "delegitimization of already depressed communities in order to advance the interests of market and political domination." Keshet also recognizes that the systemic neglect of the actual residents and their routine struggles for basic needs and services by various self-defined "Left" organizations working in south Tel Aviv—who focus on prostitution and migrant labor—deepened the animosity marginalized Mizrahi communities felt against "White" Israelis, an animosity that is easily manipulated by the Right through anti-African and anti-Arab racism and the othering of even weaker populations. The failure of "Left" organizations in the neighborhoods, which is related to the attendant labeling of Mizrahi communities as "racist," is a familiar story for Mizrahi feminist activists who were bracketed out of "peace" efforts led by Ashkenazi women. The latter appeared more keen to engage with Palestinian rights rather than Mizrahi social justice concerns.[72] Keshet reads the root cause of the situation with clarity: "It's the white hegemony and its racism."[73] And so she became a leading actor in the struggle against deportation, dispossession, and gentrification. By connecting the dots clearly, she was able to advocate for the common struggle of poor residents in various neighborhoods as well as the plight of asylum seekers. The massive protest she led, together with other organizers, disrupted the logic of domination and illuminated a momentary transgressive geography in the southern neighborhoods of Tel Aviv. This was an instant—a brief moment in time and space—of South-South solidarity.

The third site of reimagining that "another world is possible" is Ethiopian activism. Efrat Yerday sees the potential for Palestinian-Ethiopian solidarity, especially around the experiences of police brutality. But Yerday likewise recognizes that very few Ethiopians are willing to relinquish the privilege provided by the stratified and racialized Jewish supremacist landscape, especially considering that they are the most marginalized among the Jewish population. On the other front, Palestinian Israeli activists and politicians, such as Ayman Ouda (the leader of the former Joint List Alliance of the Arab Parties), identify the importance of interlinking the struggles of those on the margins of Israeli society for advancing a vision of a different Israel for all its citizens. In response to a 2015 protest of Ethiopians against police brutality, to which Ethiopians are routinely subjected, Ouda said, "As an Arab citizen, I know well the experience of standing in front of a police blinded by racism, to such an extent that s/he does not see me as a human being but only a different nationality of color and so I was able to imagine what the young Ethiopians felt when the police started to beat them and tear gas them."[74] Ouda clearly exercises empathy, solidarity, and an intersectional analysis in advancing a human rights and democratic approach. He marched with the Ethiopians, even though he knew quite well that some of them have become the faces of the occupation, standing at checkpoints and serving in the military police (undesirable jobs for more privileged communities). He also knew that many of the Ethiopians marching against police brutality endorsed Jewish supremacy. But this endorsement, like Mizrahi anti-Arabness, can be understood within the infrastructures of socialization. And the very act of marching in solidarity may generate a glimpse into the intersectionality of oppression. Ouda, in other words, rejects the logic in which violations of the antiracist movement space's values result in excommunication and thus failed or unrealized solidarity that could have materialized on the basis of moments and glimpses into such possibilities. The movement of the Israeli Black Panthers of the 1970s revealed such possibilities when their framers realized that their struggle and the Palestinian struggle were all directed against one ideological foe, Euro-Zionist hegemony. Ouda, along other Palestinian Israelis, chose to march with Ethiopians against police brutality and through this action resisted this ideological hold.

The Ethiopian Jewish community in Israel reveals the limits of articulating a geography of liberation defined by antiracism and a political program to overthrow White supremacy. To identify the potentiality of Palestinian-Ethiopian-Mizrahi solidarity and connect to the Black American struggle, it is necessary to cultivate an alternative Jewish Ethiopian story and account of belonging that is not an exoticized and folklorized account. Yerday writes about the struggle of Ethiopian Jews to even be identified as Jews within the racialized system of Jewish power and within the various intellectual accounts that treat Ethiopian Jewishness as inauthentic. Both Ethiopian Jewishness and the texture of the Ethiopian community have been violently disrupted in the racialized context of Israel. Children have been separated from their parents and channeled (as was also the case in Mizrahi communities) to boarding schools under the religious-Zionist educational and Shas systems. In addition, their religious authorities were dismissed and subordinated to Ashkenazi orthodoxy in order to control "religious affairs" within Israel.[75] Yerday's point about the delegitimization of the very Jewishness of Ethiopian Jews reinforces Bahar's approach that, in addition to recovering Blackness and Arabness, Mizrahim and Ethiopians need to actively reimagine their Jewishness.

Ethiopian millennials draw deep inspiration from Black American music and narratives of resistance.[76] However, this inspiration, as noted, comes without also connecting to Black American solidarity with Palestinians. What we found telling was to hear from both Palestinian hip-hop artists in Lydda (Lod) and Ethiopian social justice activists from the periphery who were both inspired by and incubated in the American rapper Tupac Shakur's music. For Yerday, the connection between Black American and Ethiopian experiences in Israel is clear in the patterns of their routine and daily subjection to criminalization, "ghettos," a de facto segregationist educational system, police brutality, and so forth. However, the experiences are also distinct. Yerday understands that contemporary anti-Black racism relates to the metamorphosis of slavery into the "new Jim Crow."[77] In her case, however, she asks: Why did my parents come here? Is it worth it? Will I ever really want to be a part of this depressing and oppressing place? She recognizes her lack of choices about how she is able to live her life as well as her lack of connection to Ethiopian culture in Ethiopia. Instead, she is rooted in the Jewish Ethiopian Israeli culture that needs to be rearticulated outside of the racialization discourse.[78] Yerday and other Ethiopian activists and artists reimagine Jewish Ethiopian Israeli meanings and produce alternative narratives. Doing so constitutes a pivotal dimension in the meaning-making process that is necessary for a robust understanding of the geography of liberation and global and local solidarities. In other words, an alternative Jewish Israeli Ethiopian story cannot simply rely on a Black critique of White supremacy. It must rearticulate itself from within its historical location in a way that prevents the erasure of Ethiopian Jews' Jewish-Israeliness.

Even if the Ethiopian-Palestinian-Mizrahi intersectional horizon is not yet becoming a "reality in motion" due to the entrenched operation of White supremacy through Jewish power, the art (as in the above examples of poetry and comedy) represents already an alter-reality with creative potentialities that illuminate moments of rare clarity. One example of this is Keshet's recognition of the cynical operation of the discourse of mainstreamed Jewish power and its intersection with neoliberalism.

These sites of alter-reality illustrate how unlocking intersectional potentialities relates to tackling racialization and White supremacy but also to alternative agentic meaning-making from the grassroots. These forms of meaning-making open up and broaden the meanings of Israel. To operate only with a rigid critique of White supremacy that equates or assimilates the Israeli case to a broader story about Europe erases the meaningful struggles and moments of clarity that people like Keshet experience in the neighborhoods of south Tel Aviv, the cultural work of reconnecting Hebrew to Arabic and the Middle East, and Ethiopians' struggle against their folklorization and employment as an adornment for the Israeli brand of pluralism. This is a necessary process (like the Mizrahi reclaiming of their cultural robustness) in channeling Ethiopian diminishment and racialization for emancipatory ends. Erasing these complexities confines the question of South-South solidarity to an elitist discourse.

What is at stake in the intersectional approach we advocate for here is not only the critique of racialization, the global scope of White supremacy, and the self-referential project of Europe that plays itself out through Jewish power in a perverse manner. Also at stake is the meaning-making process that follows this critique. Bahar, Yerday, and the numerous alternative stories on the ground also show the need for hermeneutic, artistic, and interpretive tools that go along with a critique of discourse and hegemony. By analyzing their reimagining of their identity in nonreductive ways that go beyond their predicament of oppression and reclaiming of Judaism from its Ashkenormativity and flattening within the nationalist discourse of Israel, we identify what is missing in an abstract intersectional analysis of power. The latter simply assimilates Brown and Black Jewish Israelis (as exemplified in the JVP's membership conference above) into the many victims of White supremacy, an abstraction whose flip side for American Jewish critics is a recovery of, and reliance on, a thin account of Judeo-Christian ethics. This ethics amounts to recovering the "prophetic" dimensions of Judaism without anchoring it in Zion, indeed by superseding it. This ethical antidote to land-centricity reflects Jewish critics' ethical outrage at a Zion that is not prophetic. Such a vision of Judaism is most pronouncedly represented in Otzma Yehudit. The racism of Otzma Yehudit, these critics deem, is endemic to Euro-Zionism, and thus struggling against White supremacy in the United States and Jewish power qua Israel (or Israeli policies) has become for them one and the same. Zion, in this case, is a metaphor that represents a spiritual destination of an ideal that is not embodied in any particular geographic location or political arrangement. To make Zion into a metaphor vis-à-vis the Jewish imagination is to remain beholden—despite the critique of White supremacy and settler colonialism and despite disassimilating from Jewish Whiteness by centering JOC—to the story of European modernity. The JOC in southern Tel Aviv or the periphery can only assimilate into the struggle by relinquishing the meanings of Zion/Israel that are specific to their Jewish identity formation. If Shuhada Street in Hebron embodies the unfolding plot of racialized Euro-Zionism/Judaism, Shuster-Aliassi, Bahar, Yerday, Keshet, Lavie, Noy, Mehager, Sluzker-Amran, and others are agentic alter-realist storytellers who reimagine, in their specific historical and social locations, the meanings of Jewishness in the Middle East. This is not an exercise in undoing historical crimes through erasure but rather an attempt at historically embedded survival for those who are on the ground and cannot retreat into some other diasporic ethical and physical space. For these persons, the imagination of "another world" erodes the walls of the ghetto of Jewish power and thus constitutes a fluid and constructive potential site for a transgressive geography of liberation.

CONCLUSION

Other scholars have written about how the Zionist ethos and claims for liberation misled thinkers otherwise sympathetic to decolonial struggles into supporting the Israeli settler colonial project.[79] Still others have written about the need to destabilize zero-sum conceptions of memory and suffering.[80] In this chapter, however, we move beyond an analysis of power and discourse to analyze constructive alternative modes of imagining belonging and solidarity. We argue that such an analysis is necessary even if such alternatives are prevented from becoming fully realized because of empirical and realist constraints and delimiting litmus tests. Decolonial Jewish sociological imagination, we contend, can fully disengage from the supersessionist logic of the "Judeo-Christian" as an ethical discourse with attention to embodied contestations of racialized citizenship discourses and their relations to the security ethos that authorizes the occupation of the Palestinians. Simply turning away, as diaspora Jews critical of Israel increasingly do, from such on-the-ground and historically contingent processes remains, despite decolonial pretenses, within a modernist Christian discourse. Recovering the Jewish prophetic tradition, retrieving and embracing non-White Jews as a bridge into anti-racism spaces, and theorizing Zion out of the Jewish imagination as an antidote to Jewish power and complicity with Whiteness coalesces with the Judeo-Christian paradigm and generates a reactive Jewish diasporic ethics. The challenge is to navigate the interrogation of Jewish ethics and identity outside the binary of Jewish power and reclaimed powerlessness.

Above, we identified the persistent operation of the Judeo-Christian ethos in an effort to critique ethno- and religio-centric manifestations of Judaism. Likewise, we showed the continued force of citizenship and human rights discourses in ascertaining the wrongness of the occupation of Palestinians and its metaphorical function vis-à-vis other marginalized communities affected by the enduring force of coloniality. This allows us, through a focus on marginalized communities of color in Israel, to think historically and sociologically rather than in reactionary and binary ways. This epistemology from the margins entails decolonizing from within the complex landscape of citizenship and national discourse that challenges White supremacy, Ashkenormativity, and orientalism but does not—indeed, cannot—entail relinquishing the task of grappling with the possibilities and potential alternative meanings of Middle Eastern Jewishness. Mizrahi and Ethiopian Israeli Jews are located in positions that can disrupt the semiotics of Jewish power by cross-fertilizing across the geographies of liberation and grappling with the operation of Whiteness in Israel. A critique of the mainstreaming of Jewish power that erases the experiences and political imaginations of Ethiopian and Mizrahi Israeli Jews (not to mention Palestinians) enacts silences that ultimately work against politically and socially concrete decolonial justice. When a Palestine litmus test delimits the capacity of Mizrahi struggles to connect to Arab feminisms, Chicana and Black American struggles, and other social justice activism, this erasure is further reinforced and solidarity fails to materialize where it could.

NOTES

1. "Ashkenormativity" refers to the foregrounding and domination of European (Ashkenazi) experiences and traditional practices.

2. "Mizrahim" or "Mizrahi" is a coalitional term encompassing diverse communities of Jews who trace their roots to Southwest Asia, North Africa, India, and the Balkans. Since it is a coalitional term, it erases the distinctiveness of each of these communities. The label "Mizrahim," literally meaning "Orientals," like many such terms, started as a derogatory term that was then turned into a form of political consciousness and empowerment.

3. Ella Shohat, "Sephardim in Israel: Zionism from the Standpoint of Its Jewish Victims," *Social Text*, no. 19–20 (1988): 1–35; Smadar Lavie, *Wrapped in the Flag of Israel: Mizrahi Single Mothers and Bureaucratic Torture*, rev. ed. (Lincoln: University of Nebraska Press, 2014).

4. See, e.g., Smadar Lavie, "Mizrahi Feminism and the Question of Palestine," *Journal of Middle East Women's Studies* 7, no. 2 (2011): 56–88.

5. Keith P. Feldman, *A Shadow over Palestine: The Imperial Life of Race in America* (Minneapolis: University of Minnesota Press, 2015), 12.

6. Alex Lubin, *Geographies of Liberation: The Making of an Afro-Arab Political Imaginary* (Chapel Hill: University of North Carolina Press, 2014).

7. Ibid., 7.

8. Although Jews of Color is not a concept that is employed in Hebrew, we will occasionally use the term to also encompass Mizrahim/yot.

9. Among Far Right activists, in particular, members of Otzmah Yehudit, the terminology "enemies" has become a common way to indicate Arabs. This terminology is used to avoid legal accusations of incitement to racism since it supposedly refrains from addressing a person's national-ethnic origin.

10. On the Kahanist ideology and the legal actions against Kahane and Kach, see Riki Tessler, "Religious Radicalism between Defensive Democracy, Politics and Citizenship," *State & Society* 3, no. 1 (April 2003): 585–619; Benyamin Neuberger, "Self-Defending Democracy in Israel, 1948–2008," *Social Issues in Israel* 6 (2008): 68–93 (81–84).

11. See Shaul Magid, *Meir Kahane: The Rise and Fall of an American Jewish Survivalist* (Princeton, NJ: Princeton University Press, 2021).

12. On the rise of Israel's radical Right, see Ami Pedhazur and Daphna Canetti-Nisim, "Kahane Is Dead but Kahanism Is Alive: Explaining the Support for the Extreme Right-Wing in Israel [Hebrew]," *Megamot* 44, no. 2 (February 2006): 215–46; Ami Pedhazur, *The Triumph of Israel's Radical Right* (Oxford: Oxford University Press, 2012). One of the bluntest expressions of the shift to explicit Jewish supremacy is Israel's Basic Law: Israel as the Nation-State of the Jewish People. On Israel's Nation-State Law and the process that led to its enactment, see Amal Jamal, "Constitutionalizing Sophisticated Racism: Israel's Proposed Nationality Law," *Journal of Palestine Studies* 45, no. 3 (Spring 2016): 40–51; Dov Waxman and Ilan Peleg, "The Nation-State Law and the Weakening of Israeli Democracy," *Israel Studies* 25, no. 3 (Fall 2020): 185–200; Doreen Lustig, "'We the Majority . . . ': The Israeli Nationality Basic Law," *Israel Studies* 25, no. 3 (Fall 2020): 256–66.

13. E.g., Idith Zertal and Akiva Eldar, *Lords of the Land: The War for Israel's Settlements in the Occupied Territories, 1967–2007* (New York: Nation Books, 2007).

14. E.g., Raef Zreik and Azar Dakwar, "What's in the Apartheid Analogy? Palestine/Israel Refracted," *Theory & Event* 23, no. 3 (July 2020): 664–70.

15. E.g., Ilan Pappe, *The Ethnic Cleansing of Palestine* (Oxford: Oneworld Publications, 2007).

16. On messianism and ideological processes among national Zionist settlers, see Assaf Harel, "Beyond Gush Emunim: On Contemporary Forms of Messianism

among Religiously Motivated Settlers in the West Bank," in *Normalizing Occupation: The Politics of Everyday Life in the West Bank Settlements*, ed. Marco Allegra, Ariel Handel, and Erez Maggor (Bloomington: Indiana University Press, 2017), 128–48. On obedience and nonobedience of national Zionist settlers to the state, see, in Hebrew, Helinger Moshe and Itzhak Hershkovitz, "Obedience and Non-Obedience in Religious Zionism from Gush Emunim to a Price Tag," Israel Democracy Institute (2015), www.idi.org.il/media/4039/obedience-and-civil-disobedi ence-in-religious-zionism-book.pdf. On the settlement project, see Idith Zertal and Akiva Eldar, *Lords of the Land: The War for Israel's Settlements in the Occupied Territories, 1967–2007*, trans. Vivian Eden (New York Nation Books, 2007).

17. See, e.g., Tammy Riklis and Yonit Naaman, "New Web Series Spotlights Disappeared Yemenite Children," *972 Magazine*, May 7, 2017, www.972mag.com /new-web-series-spotlights-disappeared-yemenite-children/.

18. E.g., Yossi Yonah and Yitzhak Saporta, "The Education System and the Division of Gender and Ethno-Gender Labor in Israel: A Look at the Past [Hebrew]," in *Nashim ba-darom: merhav, periferya, migdar*, ed. Henriette Dahan-Kalev, Niza Yanay, and Niza Berkovitch (Be'er Sheva: Ben Gurion University Press, 2005), 188–223; Michele Lamont, Graziella Moraes Silva, Jessica S. Welburn, Joshua Guetzkow, Nissim Mizrachi, Hanna Herzog, and Elisa Reis, *Getting Respect: Responding to Stigma and Discrimination in the United States* (Prince-ton, NJ: Princeton University Press, 2016).

19. For an analysis that highlights modernity's relation to hierarchization of Israeli society and the Eurocentricity of the Zionist movement, see Yehouda Shanhav, *The Arab Jews: A Postcolonial Reading of Nationalism, Religion, and Ethnicity* (Stanford, CA: Stanford University Press, 2006).

20. One of the most prominent organizations to "police" the threat of miscegenation in Israel is Lehava (lit., "Flame"), led by the right-wing extremist and Kahane follower Bentzi Gopstein, a member of the Jewish Power party. On the activities of the various religious right-wing organizations involved in antimiscegenation and the gender and racial aspects of these activities, see Ruth Carmi, "What If an Arab Would Hit on Your Sister: Racism and Gender in Israel," Reform Centre for Religion and State, Jerusalem (2014), https://static1.squarespace .com/static/5f8f43ad4e9b64055875ce6b/t/609270e2e8e2eb73698e1df7/1620 209892615/IRAC+racism+and+gender+report+2014.pdf

21. E.g., Lavie, "Mizrahi Feminism."

22. While many Israeli politicians unequivocally condemned the event in Charlottesville, Virginia, few made the connection between Trump's regime and the rising antisemitism in the United States. Netanyahu himself only addressed the events three days later, condemning the antisemitic attack but ignoring Trump's statements that violence occurred on "both sides." See, in Hebrew, Tal Shalev, "Israel Angry with Trump: 'There Are no Two Sides to Antisemitism and Nazism,' *Walla!News*, August 16, 2017, https://news.walla.co.il/item/3089587. On Viktor Orbán's relationship with Israel and Netanyahu, see, in Hebrew, Itamar Eichner, "Guest of Honor in

Israel: Prime Minister Praising Collaborators with the Nazis [Hebrew]," *Ynet*, July 18, 2018, www.ynet.co.il/articles/0,7340,L-5311884,00.html; Noa Landau, "Commentary: Orbán's Visit to Israel Provided an Opportunity for a Meeting between 'Two Patriotic Leaders' [Hebrew]," *Haaretz*, July 19, 2018, www.haaretz.co.il/news /politics/.premium-1.6292783. On the connection between Trump and the Far Right, see David Smith, "Q&A: What Are Trump and the White House's Links to the Far Right?," *The Guardian*, August 14, 2017, www.theguardian.com/us-news/2017/aug /14/donald-trump-steve-bannon-breitbart-news-alt-right-charlottesville.

23. See Atalia Omer, *Days of Awe: Reimagining Jewishness in Solidarity with Palestinians* (Chicago: University of Chicago Press, 2019).

24. See, e.g., Azadeh Shahshahani and Ilise Benshushan Cohen, "U.S. Police Are Being Trained by Israel—And Communities of Color Are Paying the Price," *Progressive*, October 7, 2019, https://progressive.org/dispatches/us-police -trained-by-israel-communities-of-color-paying-price-shahshahani-cohen -191007/; Alex Kane, "How Israel Became a Hub for Surveillance Technology," *The Intercept*, October 17, 2016, https://theintercept.com/2016/10/17/how-israel -became-a-hub-for-surveillance-technology/.

25. On pinkwashing, see, e.g., Sarah Schulamn, *Israel/Palestine and the Queer International* (Durham, NC: Duke University Press, 2012); Gili Hartal and Orna Sasson-Levi, "New Oriental-Gay Subjectivity and Proud Tourism in Tel Aviv," *Israeli Sociology* 35, no. 2 (December 2019): 34–58. On the various forms of gender segregation in the Israeli public sphere, see Orly Erez-Likhovski and Riki Shapira-Rosenberg, "Excluded, for God's Sake: Gender Segregation and the Exclusion of Women in the Public Sphere in Israel," Fourth Annual Report, Israel Religious Action Center, Israel Movement for Reform and Progressive Judaism (IRAC 2013–14), https://static1.squarespace.com/static/5f8f43ad4e9b64055875ce6b/t /60926ff84d4af26ab20d6294/1620209657765/excluded+for+gods+sake+4 +final.pdf; Noya Rimalt, "Gender Segregated Academic Programs for the Ultra-Orthodox: Between Access and Integration and Policies Encouraging Segregation [Hebrew]," *Law, Society and Culture* 1, (2018), https://law.haifa.ac.il/wp -content/uploads/2017/05/Ultra-Orthodox.pdf.

26. For a classical account of American orientalism, see Melani McAlister, *Epic Encounters: Culture, Media, and the U.S. Interests in the Middle East since 1945* (Berkeley: University of California Press, 2005).

27. Ali Abunimah, "Israeli Election Ad Boasts Gaza Bombed Back to 'Stone Ages,'" *The Electronic Intifada*, January 21, 2019, https://electronicintifada.net /blogs/ali-abunimah/israeli-election-ad-boasts-gaza-bombed-back-stone-ages; see also Tom Mehager, "Why Benny Ganz Is More Dangerous than the Kahanists," March 10, 2019, https://972mag.com/benny-gantz-dangerous-kahanists/140499/.

28. In 2015 Ettinger was arrested by Israel's General Security Services for formulating the "rebellion plan." The plan included intentions to establish a state of Halakhah, deliberately deteriorating ties between Jews and Palestinians, and undermining the state's stability through violent actions. Chaim Levinson, "After

Ten Months, GSS Target No. 1, Meir Ettinger, Will Be Released from Administrative Detention [Hebrew]," *Haaretz*, May 17, 2016, www.haaretz.co.il/news /politics/1.2946441.

29. Shaul Magid, "Is Meir Khahane Winning: Reflections on Bejamin Netanyahu, the Hilltop Youth, and AIPAC," *Tikkun*, March 24, 2016, www.tikkun.org /newsite/is-meir-kahane-winning-reflections-on-benjamin-netanyahu-the-hilltop -youth-and-aipac; see also Shaul Magid, "Anti-Semitism as Colonialism: Meir Kahane's 'Ethics of Violence,'" *Journal of Jewish Ethics* 1, no. 2 (2015): 202–32.

30. Christian Zionists played a significant role in consolidating a case for Jewish political Zionism. See, e.g., Paul C. Merkley, *The Politics of Christian Zionism 1891–1948* (New York: Routledge, 1998).

31. On the relationship between Islamism and antisemitism in the United States and Europe, see Arno Tausch, "Islamism and Anti-Semitism: Preliminary Evidence on Their Relationship from Cross-National Opinion Data," *SSRN Electronic Journal*, 2015, https://doi.org/10.2139/ssrn.2600825; "Table 1," FBI, https ://ucr.fbi.gov/hate-crime/2017/tables/table-1.xls; Bridget Clerkin, "Synagogue Shooting Suspect Believed to Have Acted Alone, San Diego Sheriff Says," *Reuters*, www.reuters.com/article/us-california-shooting/synagogue-shooting -suspect-believed-to-have-acted-alone-san-diego-sheriff-says-idUSKCN1S406S; Samuel Osborne, "Islamophobia and Xenophobia on the Rise in Germany, New Study Claims," *Independent*, November 8, 2018, www.independent.co.uk/news /world/europe/germany-islamophobia-xenophobia-racism-study-survey -extremism-a8622391.html.

32. E.g., Anibal Quijano, "Coloniality and Modernity/Rationality," *Cultural Studies* 21, no. 2–3 (2007): 168–78; Walter Mignolo, *The Darker Side of Western Modernity: Global Futures, Decolonial Options* (Durham, NC: Duke University Press, 2011); María Lugones, "Methodological Notes toward a Decolonial Feminism," in *Decolonizing Epistemologies: Latina/o Theology and Philosophy*, ed. Ada María Isasi-Díaz and Eduardo Mendieta (New York: Fordham University Press, 2012), 68–86.

33. E.g., Angela Y. Davis, *Freedom Is a Constant Struggle: Ferguson, Palestine, and the Foundations of a Movement* (Chicago: Haymarket Books, 2016).

34. E.g., Gil Anidjar, *Blood: A Critique of Modernity* (New York: Columbia University Press, 2014); Elizabeth Shakman Hurd, *The Politics of Secularism in International Relations* (Princeton, NJ: Princeton University Press, 2008).

35. E.g., Helga Tawil-Souri and Dina Matar, eds., *Gaza as Metaphor* (London: Hurst & Company, 2016).

36. E.g., Karen Brodkin, "How Jews Became White Folks—and May Become Nonwhite under Trump," *Forward*, December 6, 2016, http://forward.com/opinion /356166/how-jews-became-white-folks-and-may-become-nonwhite-under-trump/; Eric L. Goldstein, *The Price of Whiteness: Jews, Race, and American Identity* (Princeton, NJ: Princeton University Press, 2006).

37. See Eric K. Ward, "Skin in the Game: How Antisemitism Animates White Nationalism," June 29, 2017, Political Research Associates, www.political

research.org/2017/06/29/skin-in-the-game-how-antisemitism-animates-white
-nationalism.

38. Marc Dollinger, *Black Power, Jewish Politics: Reinventing the Alliance in the 1960s* (Waltham, MA: Brandeis University Press, 2018).

39. Or Kashti, "Israel Bans Novel on Arab-Jewish Romance from Schools for 'Threatening Jewish Identity,'" *Haaretz*, December 31, 2015, www.haaretz.com /israel-news/.premium-israel-bans-novel-depicting-arab-jewish-romance-from -schools-1.5383970.

40. See, e.g., Geraldine Heng, *The Invention of Race in the European Middle Ages* (Cambridge: Cambridge University Press, 2018); Nelson Maldonado-Torres, "Race, Religion, and Ethics in the Modern/Colonial World," *Journal of Religious Ethics* 42, no. 4 (2014): 691–771.

41. Mariá José Méndez, "'The River Told Me': Rethinking Intersectionality from the World of Berta Cáceres," *Capitalism Nature Socialism* 29, no. 1 (2018): 7–24.

42. Michael Rothberg, *Multidirectional Memory: Remembering the Holocaust in the Age of Decolonization* (Stanford, CA: Stanford University Press, 2009).

43. Jews For Racial and Economic Justice, "Understanding Antisemitism: An Offering to Our Movement: A Resource from Jews for Racial & Economic Justice," November 2017, www.jfrej.org/assets/uploads/JFREJ-Understanding-Antisemi ism-November-2017-v1-3-2.pdf.

44. Jewish Voice for Peace, "JVP Response to the Movement for Black Lives Policy Platform," August 4, 2016, https://jewishvoiceforpeace.org/jvp4bl/.

45. Marc H. Ellis, "The Mennonites and the Interfaith Ecumenical Deal," Mondoweiss, July 10, 2017, http://mondoweiss.net/2017/07/mennonites-inter faith-ecumenical/.

46. E.g., Rafeef Ziadah, "World Social Forum—Free Palestine," Socialist Resistance, January 23, 2013, https://socialistresistance.org/world-social-forum-free -palestine/4584.

47. Omer, *Days of Awe*.

48. More of this analysis can be found in Omer, *Days of Awe*. See Houria Bouteldja, *Whites, Jews, and Us: Toward a Politics of Revolutionary Love* (South Pasadena, CA: Semiotext(e), 2017).

49. See Tzedek Chicago's exposition of its orienting values: www.tzedek chicago.org/our-values.

50. Ibid.

51. Tamar Hermann et al., "A Conditional Partnership: Jews and Arabs, Israel 2017 [Hebrew]," Israel Democracy Institute, www.idi.org.il/media/9512/limited -partnership-jews-and-arabs.pdf.

52. Lavie, "Mizrahi Feminism."

53. It is difficult to obtain official data on the percentage of Mizrahim in Israel. The Central Bureau of Statistics in Israel determines Jewish ethnic origin until the second generation only based on the country of birth or the country of origin of the father. Thus, someone born in Israel to a father born in Israel and a mother born in

one of the Arab countries will be considered Israeli and not Mizrahi, even if they define themselves as Mizrahi. Nofar Moshe, "The Central Bureau of Statistics Does Not Count Mizrahim [Hebrew]," Kan11, August 4, 2017, https://www.kan .org.il/item/?itemid=21294. According to a 2016 survey by the Shaharit think tank, Mizrahim make up between 35% and 40% of Jews in Israel and Ashkenazi Jews about 25%. See "Mizrahi Survey [Hebrew]," Shaharit, 2016, https://tinyurl .com/vdpfnh7c; Alona Mirya Iluz, "Why Do Mizrahis Continue to Vote for the Likud? [Hebrew]," *Haoketz*, February 8, 2019, https://tinyurl.com/2nhwuy85.

54. Nissim Mizrahi, "Sociology in the Garden: Beyond the Liberal Grammar of Contemporary Sociology," *Israel Studies Review* 31, no. 1 (2016): 36–65; for a critical engagement with Mizrahi's argument, see Lihi Yonah, "Beyond 'Beyond the Garden and the Jungle': On the Rise of Difference Discourse in Mizrahi Theory," *Law & Social Change* 11 (2020): 77–117.

55. For an analysis of Mizrahim as beneficiaries of the Israeli occupation, see Yali Hashash, "We Are All Jews: White Trash, Mizrahim, and Multiple Marginalities within the Hegemony [Hebrew]," *Theory and Criticism* 50 (2018): 249–64.

56. Conversation with Omer during visit in January 2020.

57. Martin Savransky, "A Decolonial Imagination: Sociology, Anthropology and the Politics of Reality," *Sociology* 51, no. 1 (2017): 11–26 (22).

58. Ibid., 22.

59. Santiago Slabodsky, "Systemic Continuities and the Coloniality of the Liberal-Populist Genocidal Marriage," in a forthcoming volume of the Contending Modernities series.

60. Jakeet Singh, "Religious Agency and the Limits of Intersectionality," *Hypatia* 30, no. 4 (2015): 657–74.

61. Fore more information on the Zochrot Organization, see https://zochrot .org/en.

62. Zochrot, "Panel: Between Mizrahim and Palestinians: The Tension between Exclusion and Responsibility," April 23, 2016, www.youtube.com/watch?v =1zj5Xa1kIUo.

63. Zochrot tour in January 2019.

64. Tsafi Saar, "'It's Impossible to Reduce Me': The Most Up-and-Coming Jewish Comedian Dares You to Put Her in a Box," *Haaretz*, January 10, 2019, www.haaretz.com/israel-news/MAGAZINE-meet-the-jewish-activist-comedian -who-refuses-to-be-reduced-to-a-single-identity-1.6826888.

65. Another example is Sami Shalom Chetrit, a Mizrahi author, poet, and scholar. See Sami Shalom Chetrit, *Jews: Poems, Translation from Hebrew 1982–2013* (Somerville, MA: Červená Barva Press, 2015). See also Almog Behar, "Identity and Gender in the Poetry of Amira Hass," Almog Behar, November 26, 2013, https://almogbehar.wordpress.com/2013/11/26/identity-and-gender-in -the-poetry-of-amira-hess/; on Sigalit Banay, see Yochai Oppenheimer, "'I am an Arab Refugee': Mizrahi Political Poetry [Hebrew]," in *A Voice Calls*

Out Fiercely: Politics and Poetry in Israel, ed. Asaf Midani and Nadir Tzor (Jerusalem: Israel Political Science Association, 2012), 85–107; on Adi Keissar, an Israeli poet and founder of the cultural group Ars Poetica, see *Haaretz*, December 5, 2013, "Four Poems by the Members of Ars Poetica [Hebrew]," www.haaretz .co.il/gallery/literature/1.2181481.

66. Carmit Sapir Weiss, "'Hebrew Is a Mizrahi Language': The Poet Who Defines a Vision for a Jewish-Arab Culture [Hebrew]," *Maariv*, August 28, 2016.

67. Ibid.

68. Ibid.

69. As Yali Hashash demonstrates, an uncritical reimagination of the Mizrahi past produces a model of Mizrahi masculinity that replicates some of the premises of Israeli Whiteness and denied dark femininity. Without critical engagement, reimagining the past becomes a tool for positioning Mizrahim on an existing hierarchy rather than as a tool for social change. Interrogating the historical-theological Jewish-Muslim dimensions of the meanings attached to the land should be done to decipher the power relations in Israeli society rather than reconstruct an apolitical history of ideas and culture. As Hashash shows, Mizrahi feminism offers the tools to criticize hegemony and acknowledge Mizrahim in order to realize Mizrahi scholarship's radical potential. Yali Hashash, "The Politics of Longing for Baghdad [Hebrew]," in *Racism in Israel*, ed. Yossi Yona and Yehuda Shenhav (Jerusalem: Van Leer, 2008), 287–309; Yali Hashash, "Between Christianity and Islam: The Theological Turn in Mizrahi Discourse [Hebrew]," *Theory and Criticism* 50 (2018): 41–60.

70. Jen Marlowe, "Israel's Mizrahi Activists Are Fighting the Racist Nation-State Law," *The Nation*, May 27, 2020, www.thenation.com/article/world/israel -racism-mizrahis-palestinians/.

71. Conversations with Omer, May 2017.

72. Lavie, "Mizrahi Feminism."

73. Inas Elias, "Spoken Mizrahit Shula Keshet Knows That after the Refugees, the Mizrahis from South Tel Aviv Will Also Be Thrown Out [Hebrew]," *Haaretz*, April 16, 2018, www.haaretz.co.il/gallery/.premium-1.6007514.

74. Orna Cohen, "The Joined List: Gender Struggle and Social Change [Hebrew]," *Forum of Regional Thinking*, June 28, 2015, https://tinyurl.com/7uz fx94m.

75. E.g., Steven Kaplan. "Black and White, Blue and White and Beyond the Pale: Ethiopian Jews and the Discourse of Colour in Israel," *Jewish Culture and History* 5, no. 1 (2002): 51–68; see also Efrat Yerday, "Between Yosef Salamsa and Martin Luther King [Hebrew]," *Hamakom*, July 24, 2016.

76. See, e.g., in Hebrew, David Retner, *Hearing Black Music and Identity among Young Ethiopians in Israel* (Tel Aviv: Resling, 2015).

77. Michelle Alexander, *The New Jim Crow: Mass Incarceration in the Age of Colorblindness* (New York: New Press, 2010).

78. Yerday, "Between Yosef Salamsa and Martin Luther King."

79. Santiago Slabodsky, *Decolonial Judaism: Triumphal Failures of Barbaric Thinking* (New York: Palgrave Macmillan, 2014).

80. Rothberg, *Multidirectional Memory*; Bashir Bashir and Amos Goldman, *The Holocaust and the Nakba: A New Grammar of Trauma and History* (New York: Columbia University Press, 2018); Edward W. Said, "Invention, Memory, and Place," *Critical Inquiry* 26, no. 2 (2000): 175–92.

CHAPTER 4

"To Confound White Christians"

Thinking with Claude McKay about Race, Catholic Enchantment, and Secularism

BRENNA MOORE

ABSTRACT

Some scholars have rightly pointed out that the discourse on enchantment, disenchantment, and secularism in the study of religion now feels exhausted, outdated, and may have simply run its course. This chapter seeks to reinvigorate these topics by exploring the writings of a small community of understudied Black Catholic writers who collaborated in the United States and the Francophone worlds in the early and mid-twentieth century. Claude McKay, poet of the Harlem Renaissance and convert to Catholicism, in particular displays a concern with the "mystical" and "enchanted" dimension of religion and is critical of those who have claimed secularism as a desirable social or political ideology. McKay was part of what has been called an "Afro-Catholic moment"—a small, transnational counterculture of writers, activists, and artists for whom Catholicism was key in their efforts to forge interracial and international affiliations that could counter the rise of nationalism, European imperialism, and White bigotry. They were skeptical of the political promise of disenchantment, but they were also aware of the mainstream desires to romanticize "enchantments" along racial lines, to exoticize Black religiosity, to fetishize the Black church. Already a century ago, artists and writers like McKay worked to disrupt racialized categories that are still entrenched in our field such as White secularism versus Black religiosity. Despite the long legacy of racism and bigotry among Catholics, for this network the mystical dimension of Catholicism was perceived to offer some substance to a worldview and set of practices that could foster new kinds of solidarities across national and racial lines. Though it was a short-lived, ephemeral moment, it was an experiment in imagining and embodying alternative modes of affiliation.

In May 2020, Courtney Bender reflected on the state of the term "enchantment" in the academic study of religion. It is a "closed-loop language game," she argued, "once you say 'enchanted' among scholars of religion you know where the conversation will go. No matter where one begins, the possible moves around enchantment are all mapped out."[1] Scholars of religion have now largely accepted the idea that secular modernity is not a space simply evacuated by religion. Departing from Weber's description of modernity's disenchantment, some have argued that modernity was never empty of spirits, except perhaps in the minds of elite theorists; others saw modernity's enchantments in the persistence of magic, spirituality, and the occult.[2] Some scholars have pointed out that the perceived absence of religious particularism in the secular sphere misses the ways in which secularism is a product of theology and histories in the Christian West.[3] Some have shown, for instance, how the enchantment of Catholic, divinely ordered natural law was smuggled into secular human rights discourse and then transformed into a disenchanted universalism.[4] Moreover, the critique of orientalism has helped us see how power works in discourses of enchantment and disenchantment: the bodies that are imagined as more enchanted, spiritual, and exotic are seen as eternally and inherently religious, always and forever unsecular, irrational, inassimilable, and powerless.[5] Jane Bennett, among others, has traced how modern literary theorists and philosophers have accessed enchantment via the wondrous matters of nature, or of the grotesque, the sublime, the fantastic.[6] In describing the "fun" that comes with mapping various forms of disenchantment and enchantment, Courtney Bender notes, "This fun is interesting in the same way a James Bond film can be, where you are curious about the variations and also take comfort in the fact that there won't be many."[7] She invites readers to consider whether arguments about enchantment and disenchantment "are coming to an end." Might there be "term limits," Bender asks, on terms basic to the study of religion?

I read Bender's essay at the beginning of summer 2020 in the midst of the COVID-19 pandemic and just as the world rose up in rebellion against centuries of oppression of Black lives following the killing of George Floyd, Breonna Taylor, and so many others. Read during the most intense and significant social and political events in my lifetime, Bender's insights about the relatively worn-out conversations in the study of religion seemed so true, so refreshing to hear acknowledged. More personally, I even thought, I can't believe I spent so much of my life finding such conversations interesting. But it's tricky: as a scholar of modern religious thought, primarily in Europe, the intellectual labor of challenging secularism's alleged disenchantment and mapping the subtlety of its many enchantments is so centrally woven into my discipline that it almost creates the edifice from which all other conversations emerge. But the contours of the old conversation seem tired now, or at least unable to touch the heat of our current moment. It feels like a "closed-loop language game" because so many of those with whom we think about enchantment, secularization, and disenchantment are White, avant-garde thinkers connected to continental Europe. They are similarly minded writers with similar backgrounds—philosophers like William James, Julia Kristeva, and Charles Taylor, or even eclectic thinkers like Georges Bataille, or literary modernists like T. S. Eliot, or critical theorists like Theodore Adorno. In the events of summer 2020, Bender's insights spurred me to think of how relatively narrow this network is now and was then. But in an outsized way, it has shaped so much of the way in which religious studies has mapped secularism, disenchantment, and enchantment in the twentieth century.

At the same time, I had been researching Catholic writers and artists from the African diaspora, mostly Francophone Catholics in the 1930s and 1940s who were involved in forging what Brent Hayes Edwards has called *l'internationalisme noir* that began in interwar Paris.[8] This international network included writers like Claude McKay of the Harlem Renaissance who lived in France, his friend, the writer Paulette Nardal from Martinique, and

Richmond Barthé, the New Orleans-born painter and sculptor who had also lived in Paris. They were part of a numerically small but culturally significant international network of Black Catholic writers, artists, and activists in the 1920s through 1950s, most of whom had connections to the Francophone world and to Harlem in the United States. Many of the topics that these men and women focused on in their art and their lives were the ones still with us in 2020: police brutality, White mob violence against Black citizens, global White supremacy and war, colonialism. But I noticed—perhaps unexpectedly—that the familiar religious studies conversations about enchantment and disenchantment, secular and sacred, were present in their work too. For this small, transnational counterculture of writers, activists, and artists, a kind of perceived enchantment within Roman Catholicism was key in their efforts to forge interracial and international affiliations that could counter the rise of nationalism, European imperialism, and White bigotry. Historically, of course, Catholicism has a long legacy of animating racism throughout the world too, but for some in this network, its mystical dimension was perceived to offer some substance to a worldview and set of practices that could foster new kinds of solidarities that could cross national and racial lines.[9] Catholicism was seen as countercultural by some men and women raised in Protestant-majority cultures, and its internationalism helped them extract their experiences from the boundaries of nationalism and imagine international modes of belonging. For example, McKay converted to Catholicism in 1943 as an adult, having "discovered a little of that mystical world of the spirit" in Europe, and imagined that he saw within it the "one true International of Peace and Good Will to all men on earth."[10] As this passage illustrates, for McKay, Catholicism's mysticism, internationalism, and contrast to Protestantism attracted him to the point of conversion, but he romanticized and essentialized the tradition, refusing to see its own entanglements in racism and histories of enslavement.

A spiritual seeker and eventual convert, McKay can be counted among the artists, writers, and activists in the nineteenth and twentieth centuries who refused to believe in secularism's optimism, its promise, its innocence. Despite the shortcomings in their vision, and their blind spots, in ways that today are remarkably prescient they were early voices who pointed to the racism at the heart of even the most progressive secular projects. They were skeptical of the political promise of disenchantment, but they were also aware of the mainstream desires to romanticize "enchantments" along racial lines, to exoticize Black religiosity, to fetishize the Black church. Already a century ago, artists and writers like McKay worked to scramble categories that are still so entrenched in our field—categories of White secularism versus Black religiosity, the persistence of the imagined and deeply problematic "perpetual primitive."[11]

In this chapter I want to consider what new frames of theoretical reference open up for our understanding of secularism, enchantment, and disenchantment when we return to these forgotten experiments from Black Catholics like Claude McKay, what openings they offer, what political concerns they contain, and how they might point to a way out of tired conversations in the study of religion. They aimed to embody unexpected ways of being in the world. This is not an argument about the transgressive possibilities of Catholicism in general but about how one network reached for ready-at-hand alternatives to secularism, communism, Protestantism, and the White expectation of essentialized, static Black religion. It was a short-lived cultural and political experiment, so I pause too at the ways in which McKay's romanticizing of Catholicism—his sense that racism is the secret, hidden objective of Protestantism and secular modernity alone—limited the effectiveness of his vision and experiments.

CLAUDE MCKAY AND BLACK CATHOLIC INTERNATIONALISM

Claude McKay (1889–1948) was born in Jamaica. His grandparents were enslaved by British colonists and traced their lineage to Madagascar and West Africa.[12] McKay immigrated to the United States in 1912 and ended up in Harlem in 1914. A gifted poet, he published the first book of poetry in the Harlem Renaissance, *Harlem Shadows* (1922), and claimed the first American best-selling novel written by a Black author, *Home to Harlem* (1928). But like so many other musicians, artists, and writers in the United States from the African diaspora, he fled American racial violence and set sail across the Atlantic, eventually settling in France. He returned to the United States fifteen years later, where he remained until his death in 1948. McKay mined all of these journeys for his art, staggering in its range: many of his poems were written in the controlled form of the Shakespearean sonnet, which was a restrained, compact style he learned from his British colonial education in Jamaica and an unlikely vehicle for his radical and turbulent thoughts on

Black resistance. He published a book on dockworkers in southern France that became a key inspiration for the French *négritude* movement, wrote for *The Nation* on the 1935 rebellions against racist violence in Harlem, and published a novel exploring themes of Black internationalism, which was written in response to the Italian invasion of Ethiopia.

McKay was a new voice of Black resistance when his writings first appeared in the United States in 1918, but he was deeply influenced by European modernisms too, including the literary fascination with enchantment, mysticism, and, eventually, Catholicism. As a teenager he was mentored in Jamaica by a British bohemian folklorist who introduced him to the White European writers who led the way in igniting a widespread fascination with enchantment in the modern West: Baudelaire, Dostoyevsky, and Whitman. Together McKay and his White British friend read some primary sources of religions too: the Hebrew Bible, the New Testament, and Buddhist texts. But McKay linked this literary interest in sacred presence with a dark, pessimistic reading of "civilized" and "disenchanted" modernity. This was not because secular modernity was seen as merely dull or overly rational but because the most allegedly "civilized" societies in modernity were savagely racist. So McKay's enchanted modernism sounds different from its European, bohemian, modernist counterparts. He found the racism in the most "civilized" northern US cities like New York where he lived as an émigré far more brutal than anything he ever experienced in the allegedly "backward," unmodern, and deeply religious Jamaican countryside.

In McKay's art, the language of enchantment, spirituality, and religion functioned as a potent source for the critique of "modernity," "civilization," and even what he perceived as its ancillary morality, "Protestantism." He often used these nouns interchangeably, and for McKay they were all merely respectable words covering over the same racist violence, as he put it, of those "blind brute forces of tigerish tribalism which remain at the core of civilized society."[13] Witnessing racist violence in the United States as a Jamaican émigré, he saw something more gruesome and more psychological at work. For example, the summer of 1919, when McKay lived in Harlem, became known as "the Red Summer" when violent race riots swept across the United States. The riots were instigated in July 1919 in Chicago when a Black teenage boy swam in a Whites-only section of Lake Michigan and was stoned and drowned by a mob of White teenagers. The cops refused to arrest the instigator. Violence in the crowd escalated, and racial rebellion ensued.[14] A wave of violence swept through the country over the next thirteen days. The most gruesome story came from Ellisville, Mississippi, where a gang of White men severely wounded a Black man, John Hartfield, who was accused of raping a White woman. A local White doctor sadistically kept Hartfield alive so that he could die publicly by lynching the next day. Newspapers announced the time and place, and more than ten thousand "upstanding citizens gathered at the appointed tree, after fervently debating the 'best' way to torture him . . . they chopped off his fingers, hung, and burned him, and then shot his lifeless body with 2,000 bullets."[15] Parts of Hartfield's body were sold as souvenirs. His fingers were put in a jar of alcohol.

These macabre scenes from around the country set the stage for McKay's "If We Must Die," a poem published that year, which catapulted McKay to the height of literary stardom and changed his life. The poem's key line came at the end: "Like men we'll face the murderous, cowardly pack, Pressed to the wall, dying, but fighting back!"[16] Alongside the language of revolt, there was also a spiritual undertow in many of his early poems of resistance. In "Exhortation, Summer of 1919," McKay draws on the biblical imagery of opening tombs and the reversal of hierarchy that would signal a new awakening in the Black world: "O my brothers and my sisters, wake! Arise!" . . . "For the new birth rends the old earth and the very dead are waking / Ghosts are turned flesh, throwing off the grave's disguise, And the foolish, even children, are made wise."[17] And in McKay's 1920 poem, "The Lynching," he reads a gruesome scene of lynching Christologically, as Langston Hughes would do later in his 1931 poem, "Christ in Alabama," and James Cone would in his 2011 *The Cross and the Lynching Tree*.[18] McKay's father had been a devout Baptist and church deacon in Jamaica, and the biblical imagery in McKay's poems drew from his childhood memories and formation, along with this eclectic education in modernist poetry with spiritual undertones, like Baudelaire, and the books of Tolstoy and Dostoyevsky.

Though McKay rejected the Protestantism of his father and declared himself an agnostic as a teen, he exhibited a long interest in forms of recalcitrant resistance to modernity. His sense of the dark violence at the heart of "modern" countries like the United States deepened a desire for forms of culture and politics that would be off-modern, coming from somewhere else—something external to American dominant cultural forms. Non-Protestant religion, for McKay, was one of those key places. His sojourns in

Europe and North Africa gave him ample material for study. Initially drawn to Islam but then connecting with Catholics in France, Spain, Harlem, and Chicago, he eventually gravitated to a kind of Catholicism that seemed countercultural compared to the Protestantism of the United States.

We see traces of McKay's gradual spiritual journey in the literature he wrote in Europe. In France, McKay published his famous novel *Banjo* (1929), a fictional narrative that takes place in the dockyards and dilapidated bars of Marseilles where a motley crew of immigrant laborers from the African diaspora live on the edges of the shipping industry, eking out a living, sleeping on the beach, playing music, and having fun. The story was based on McKay's time living there, and the Black dockworkers he depicted were immigrant day laborers he came to know. But McKay did not just depict the misery or suffering of these men. He depicted these men from places like Mozambique, Haiti, Senegal, and Dakar as forging an international Black culture *in* Europe but outside the confines of its "civilized" "secular" modernity—no White people, no "modernity," no "liberals," no "progressives." It was possible to live joyfully, exuberantly, outside the White gaze. As the Haitian protagonist of *Banjo* put it, "Oh it was hell to be a man of color, intellectual and naturally human in the white world. Except for a superhuman, almost impossible. But of one thing he was resolved: civilization would not take the love of color, joy, beauty, vitality and no-bility out of his life."[19] A thread of enchantment is woven throughout *Banjo* when McKay lingers on what this vitality looks like. He sees a form of joyful creative resistance to White civilized modernity in his mystical, ecstatic descriptions of music and barroom dancing, in his depictions of the religious folktales from Senegal he heard shared around a beach bonfire, and in the prayers of the afflicted uttered at the local run-down Catholic hospital. The theoretical reflections McKay included in *Banjo* drew from diverse sources, both African and European, such as African language, Tolstoy's mysticism, and "the mysticism of Jesus." It depicted a spiritually and culturally eclectic form of resistance embodied by ordinary men from the African diaspora living in the shadows of "civilized" Europe and outside the colonial gaze.

Banjo was published in 1929 in the United States, but the French journal *Légitime defense* published an excerpt in 1932 that made a huge splash in the Francophone world. The excerpt was a monologue by McKay's protagonist, Ray, a Black Haitian writer who claims that "racial renaissance will be unlearning the education of white colonizers." Ray described an eclectic mix of materials for unlearning White supremacy: White and Black, European, Russian, African, Irish and Russian literature, especially Tolstoy, Gandhi's philosophy, Indigenous African language and folktales, local knowledge, and oral traditions from Black émigré men and women themselves. It signaled the diversity of vital solidarities of the Black world. For French readers, Black and White, according to Bridget Jones, "the radical nature of this challenge can hardly be exaggerated."[20] While McKay never accepted the claim that "civilized" France was less racist than the United States, *Banjo*'s eclectic sources, European *and* African, religious *and* secular, mystical *and* radical, enchanted *and* politically realist, signaled a new kind of solidarity.

Banjo entered into this landscape not at all as a "Catholic" text (it would still be fifteen years before McKay converted), but there was something in the sensibility that resonated deeply with the Black Catholic Francophone writers who read him, like Léopold Sédar Senghor.[21] Senghor likewise promoted a rediscovery and celebration of African beliefs and values but also imagined a new racial consciousness in which a dual Black and White cultural background could work toward a place of mutual enlightenment. Senghor was educated at a Senegalese missionary school and spent time in seminary studying for the priesthood (which he later abandoned). He got a PhD in French literature and put his talents toward the cause of African liberation and considered himself Black and Catholic. The community that McKay had befriended, first in Paris and then in Harlem, also included Black Catholic artists such as Richmond Barthé, the New Orleans–born painter and sculptor who lived in Paris at the same time as McKay and had produced sculptures of Catholic subjects like *Mary* (1945), *The Mother* (1935), *Head of Jesus* (1949), and *Crucifixion* (1948). He was awarded the James J. Hoey Award by the Catholic Interracial Council in 1945.[22] This network also included Paulette Nardal, a writer from Martinique who was studying in Paris and welcomed McKay into her salon along with White Dominican priests she had befriended.[23] Nardal's cousin, Louis T. Achille, also from Martinique and studying in Paris, was also in this network. He was educated in a Catholic missionary school in the French West Indies. He pursued graduate work in literature in Paris at the same time McKay was there and eventually came to the United States and became a professor of French at Howard University. During the summers while teaching at Howard in the 1930s, Achille would travel with a Catholic group, the Companions of St.

Francis of Assisi. He taught members of this group some African American spirituals in English and in 1931 reportedly made the first recordings of spirituals in France. He combined his artistic and intellectual interests on the subject in an article titled "Negro Spirituals" in the French journal *Esprit* in 1951.[24] Like McKay, Achille had a dark read of secular modernity and was interested in Catholicism as a religion that delivered a dramatic, extreme counter. The writers and artists like these in McKay's network were skeptical about secularism and intrigued with enchantment, but they were also just beginning to lay the foundations for the racially conscious Catholicism that would develop in subsequent decades (at least for a short term) in times and places like Paris in the 1950s and Chicago in the 1960s and 1970s.[25] These journals, networks, artists, and writers make up part of what Josef Sorett calls an "Afro-Catholic moment" in the early and mid-twentieth century.[26]

After McKay left France in 1928, he traveled to Spain, where he became more compelled by the particularities of Catholicism. He romanticized what he saw and felt he encountered a kind of alternative to the mainstream: "I loved the people of Catholic Spain. It was the first time I ever fell in love with any people, colored or white, as a whole. But Spaniards of all classes have such a fundamental understanding of the dignity of the individual and the oneness of all Humanity."[27] By this point his disdain for Protestantism as an Anglo-Saxon religion was bordering on an obsession, a straw man: "I discovered in Spain that Catholicism had made of the Spanish people the most noble and honest and humane of any in the world, while Protestantism had made of the Anglo-Saxons and their American cousins the vilest, hoggish and most predatory and hypocritical people in the world. . . . Spain taught me that progress was not with the 'Progressives.'"[28] After McKay's experience in Spain, he started to consolidate his thinking that American "Progressives," including liberal Protestants and Communists alike, simply covered over the racism at the core of their respective "modern" ideals.

It is worth pausing here to consider McKay's reflections on Spanish Catholicism. He was intrigued by a people he imagined as counter to the White racist "progressives" and liberals he fled in the United States. He was compelled by Black religious statuary in Spain, likely the Black Madonna in Montserrat, the enchantment and mysticism it evoked, and what he perceived as its otherness to Protestantism and secularism. McKay began to consolidate an imagined boundary where racism and violence are "out there"—in secularism, in progressivism, and in Protestant-majority countries like the

United States—while everything redemptive is found in a newly imagined "in here," in Catholicism and those Catholic countries he envisioned as unsullied by modern racist logic. But, of course, the historical realities grind against McKay's desires and mental mapping. Scholars like Willie James Jennings, for example, have argued persuasively that the late medieval and early modern Catholic imagination, at the beginning of the age of the Iberian conquest, was a critical starting point for the racist colonial categorization system.[29] Aristotelian and Thomistic logic deployed by Spanish and Portuguese missionaries to Africa and the New World, like the Jesuit José de Acosta, theorized White supremacy through a racial typology of Thomistic natural order. It was key to the social imaginary that created and maintained the social hierarchies that were central to the project of enslavement and colonialism. This history is braided within Catholic Spain's violent history, from *limpieza de sangre* to justify violence against Jews and Muslims in the early modern era to Primo de Rivera's right-wing Catholic dictatorship, which began in Spain 1923, but McKay looked the other way and romanticized what he saw there.

For the rest of McKay's life as a writer, he aimed to highlight people and stories that recovered Black religious histories that pushed against the logic of secularism and Protestantism because he identified these as the dominant covers for racism. He was intrigued, obsessed, fixated on histories that pushed against their logic. For example, in 1935, he was hired as a supervisor for the Federal Writers Project, a federally funded Depression-era public works effort to pay writers to do on-the-ground local histories around the country. In 1936, the New York City project gathered forty writers, mostly Black, some White, to work on the "Negro History of New York." (It is truly shocking today to consider that the federal government supported this sort of meaningful, creative work to support the unemployed during a national emergency.)[30] The New York project hired Richard Wright, Ellen Tarry, Claude McKay, Ralph Ellison, Roi Ottley, and others, and over a period of fifteen months, they documented New York's Black history from the seventeenth century to 1935. They analyzed materials mainly from those newly housed at the Schomburg Library, which had been opened in 1925 by Arturo Schomburg, a friend of McKay's.[31] The aim was to lay claim to a past that had been denied by mainstream historical narratives.[32] In this project, McKay was fascinated most of all with the forgotten and undiscovered histories of Black religion in Harlem. They were all aiming to recover histories of Black spirituality that had been written out of mainstream narratives, ones that ran counter to the story of modern American civilizational history. He especially appreciated histories that disrupted the traditional narratives of Black Protestant elites as "civilized," "modern." He learned the most from a Black Catholic journalist named Ellen Tarry, who he hired to work on his team and cover religion. Tarry was a Catholic, and with allegiances neither to communism nor to a Protestant denomination, she saw the religious landscape with a different set of eyes from those of most writers in New York. A focus on the mystical and spiritual dimension of Black history was not a story of unmitigated suffering and violence but showed Black culture as resilient, creative, and, most of all, one that resisted the structural forces of "progress," "secularization," and "disenchantment," words for McKay that merely served as covers for racist brutality that was constantly denied by White leftist activists.

McKay drew on this research about Black religious history in Harlem for his next two books, both of which put Harlem's unusual religious landscape at the very center. In McKay's *Harlem: Negro Metropolis* (1940) and *Amiable with Big Teeth* (1941), the central theme is how hard it was to map the deep and almost intractable religiosity of the people from the African diaspora in Harlem onto the political landscape of the 1930s. The religious sensibilities of Harlem's Black community fascinated, perplexed, and challenged McKay to think about Black culture and politics in unconventional ways. For example, in *Harlem: Negro Metropolis*, McKay explains how the "religion of the Negro people stirs and swells and rises riotously over the confines of the Negro church."[33] In Harlem, this religious excess is excluded by Protestantism and secular communism, McKay argues, so it goes underground to find expression in places like the "mystic shops," as he calls them, the little basement chapels presided over by priestesses who blend Christian and Orisha traditions. It also finds expression in the household shrines where people go to light candles and speak with the dead in the hope of bringing solace or good luck. The "lavish use of incense, oil, candles," he writes, in "an atmosphere of a rosary of meaningless words" may "appease the obscure yearnings of their minds, which civilized religion cannot satisfy." He confessed going to some of these "mystic chapels" with friends and enjoying them. McKay claimed that both the Marxist Harlem intellectuals and the respectable members of the Black churches saw these African shrines as an embarrassment: "Educated Negroes might delude themselves that there is no difference between Black folk's religion and white folks' religion," but this fundamentally overlooks the persistence of the religious imagination from Africa that serves as a powerful counter to disenchanted "progressive" America.[34] For McKay, the "religious instincts" were the noncompliant seeds of resistance to civilized modernity, so they were inherently appealing to him.

McKay's *Amiable with Big Teeth: A Novel of the Love Affair between the Communists and the Poor Black Sheep of Harlem* (written in 1941, published posthumously) also drew from the religion research in the Federal Writers Project. It was a fictional narrative based on historical events. *Amiable with Big Teeth* focused on tensions between religious Black and secular White activists in Harlem who were responding to the Italian invasion of Ethiopia in the mid-1930s. The White Communists in the novel are more educated, polished, and secular than their deeply religious Black counterparts in Harlem. They treat the religious Black Harlemites as children, coaxing them to pool resources in the fight against fascism in Europe instead of just focusing on Black sovereignty and Ethiopia. "The Communists," he wrote, "under the pretense of modernism and progressivism . . . kept urging Black residents to act against their own self-interest and against their religious instincts." McKay framed the problem using biblical imagery, starting with the title, which comes from chapter 53 of the Book of Isaiah. In that chapter, he compares Harlem's African American community to the biblical "sheep lured away" by whites.[35] White progressives miss the deep, almost religious tie most Harlemites have with Africa. "To the emotional masses of the American Negro church, the Ethiopia of today is the wonderful Ethiopia of the Bible," McKay writes, referring to Psalms 68:31, "Ethiopia Shall Soon Stretch Out Her Hands to God."[36]

In another vivid scene, two characters discuss the fact that one of the justifications Italians used to invade Ethiopia was the claim that Ethiopia practiced slavery. On this account, an "evolved" modern nation like Italy, even if fascist, would at least liberate Ethiopia from its backward barbarism. But in the novel, an American woman shows a man visiting from Ethiopia that forms of slavery still exist, even in New York in 1941. "I will take you to see it with your own eyes," Gloria says. "There are over half a dozen blocks in the Bronx where starving colored women sit and wait for white women to come and buy them to work at ten cents an hour. Ten hours of lugging and scrubbing down on their knees to make one dollar. We call it the Bronx Slave Market, for the Black women line up there and wait for the white mistresses just as the slaves down South waited for the masters to come and buy them."[37] McKay based this scene on a true piece of New York history that two journalists, Marvel Cooke and Ella Baker, uncovered and published in a 1930 issue of *The Crisis*.[38] In the Great Depression, Black women who were desperate for work came to a section of the Bronx to offer their labor and were always underpaid and often cheated out of payments. Even liberals, even Communists, used these services. This is the heart of McKay's critiques: there is a pervasive, hidden racist violent core at the heart of modernity—even in Protestant or secular "civilized" parts of the world, like New York City—and most White "progressives" are complicit. For McKay, "enchantment" is another form of resistance to their secular, progressive, and violent worldview. Ellen Tarry shared this sense.[39] She also had misgivings about Communist efforts to broaden race activism in Harlem and link it to other secular, international causes on the Left. Tarry remembered going to a meeting at which the Communists urged Black activists to send money to the antifascist fight in Spain: "What about Alabama?" she asked. "The crackers are still killing my people down there and nobody is lifting a finger."[40] Much like McKay, her skepticism about the racism she experienced in secular or progressive activist circles just drew her deeper into religion—into her own Catholic faith and as an accomplished journalist of religion. For example, anticipating some of the arguments scholars like Howard Thurman would make in his 1945 book, *Deep River: An Interpretation of Negro Spirituals*, Tarry published a 1940 essay on the tradition of the Black spirituals for the Catholic readership of *Interracial Review*.[41] In it, she urged her readers to incorporate this musical tradition into both Christian and Black education. She taught the spirituals to the African American children at a short-lived Catholic intentional community focused on racial justice called Friendship House. About that experience she writes, "We tried to give our young listeners a mental picture of our father's fathers and mother's mothers toiling in the fields longing for nightfall, when they could steal away to some isolated corn patch or cotton field. Knowing that worship was forbidden, they sang into a big black pot to muffle the prayers and songs. Set to music, these are the stories of our ancestors who could neither read nor write." In learning all this from Tarry, McKay wondered why he had spent so much time learning things about the Greeks, which had nothing to do with him, and although he was a "pariah in the United States," he wrote at the time, "I was still a son of Christendom."[42] McKay's turn to Catholicism was, for him, a rejection of the dominant cultural forms in the United States while still remaining connected to aspects of "home"—his roots: the biblical imagination of his father, the mystical modernism of poets like Baudelaire and Whitman, an itinerant European sojourn where he encountered material like the Black Madonna in Spain, the rebellious mystical ecstasy of Black internationalism in Marseilles, the religious eclecticism of Harlem. As Terry once told him, "With someone who has travelled the world like you, why not become a Catholic?"[43] Catholicism was a way to refuse secularism without succumbing to what he called an "imitative Protestant and Anglo-Saxon way of thinking and acting" or a "naïve acceptance of the Protestant god of Progress."[44]

Eventually, Tarry introduced McKay to a small network of Catholic activists and volunteers working on racial justice in Harlem who had gathered around the Friendship House. From new connections there, McKay went on to befriend Dorothy Day, Ammon Hennacy, and others. Here he found new Catholic audiences for his work; eleven of his poems were published in the *Catholic Worker*. In 1940 he moved to Chicago and accepted a new job teaching night classes on Black literature and history at a Catholic social justice night school. Readers can see his commitments to mysticism and enchantment in his early poems of resistance, in the transcendence he describes dancing on the barroom floors in Marseilles, in the candles and incense he admired in Harlem's basement shrines, in the longings he claimed to have discerned in Harlem's "uncivilized" religious imagination, illegible to most secular White activists. But now he was moving to something more organized: "I discovered a little of that mystical world of the spirit that eludes the dictators, the agnostics and the pure materialists," he explained at the end of his life.[45] He was baptized as a Catholic in Chicago in 1944.[46] He wrote, "Jesus Christ rejected the idea of any special, peculiar or chosen race or nation, when he charged his apostles: Go ye into all the world and preach the gospel. Not the gospel of Imperialism, Feudalism or Capitalism, or Socialism, Communism or a National Church. . . . I find in the Catholic Church that which doesn't exist in Capitalism, Socialism or Communism—the one true International of Peace and Good Will on earth to all men."[47] It was a romanticized notion of Catholicism to be sure, but linking up with cultural currents embodied by artists like Richmond Barthé and friends Ellen Tarry and Paulette Nardal, it was a ready-at-hand alternative to dominant cultural forms: White communism, White Protestantism, and the Black church. According to Cecilia Moore, it was part of a historical moment between 1930 and 1960 when "thousands of African Americans chose to enter into communion with the Roman Catholic Church." In the United States, between 1940 and 1965 their number more than doubled, from around 300,000 in 1940 to over 700,000 in 1965.[48]

In the study of religion, the cultural experiments with enchantment are often seen as a recoil from what T. J. Jackson Lears describes as "overcivilized modern existence" to more "intense forms of spiritual experience supposedly embodied in medieval and oriental cultures."[49] Scholars of religion have shown that the modern fascination with the mystical, the unmodern, and the numinous have also upheld modernity's most powerful structures: those in power fantasized about which cultures were naturally more mystical than others, trafficking in exoticizing and essentializing those seen as rational secular modernity's deeply desired and reviled "other." For example, Kathryn Lofton has written on the staying power of the "perpetual primitive" in African American religious historiography. Always perceived to embody static enchantment, in song and prayer, "the black symbolic religious figure" was rarely a "person of intellectual contradiction and complexity."[50] Black religiosity has been shuttled into a narrative that is "safe, comforting, and confined to a context whites could understand and if need be, control."[51]

When McKay wrote in *Ebony* magazine about his conversion, he said something that stands out: the more Black intellectuals know about Catholicism, the more they could "confound white Christians."[52] McKay especially loved finding sources that scrambled White categories of understanding Black religiosity: he mentioned finding a photo of what looked like a Black nephew of one of the Catholic popes; he rhapsodized on a Black Spanish Catholic poet, an artist at once Black *and* European Catholic; he appreciated the Black Madonna in Spain; he wrote that he discovered in his research that early Christian fathers like Augustine and Athanasias "were Negroid in the American sense of the word."[53] Likewise, Tarry was fascinated with the Black Peruvian saint, Martin de Porres. She wrote a book on Martin and dedicated her life to the study of other Black Catholics who had been ignored, forgotten, and/or exiled. They too had White European sources in their writing: Tarry wrote about the White nun Katherine Drexel; McKay often quoted Tolstoy, Keats, and Shakespeare. These resources resisted narratives of a White European religion that is cosmopolitan and spiritual, closer to secularism, on the one hand, and a Black religion that is only African or American, that is, irrational, outside of Europe, outside of Christian history, on the other. Their deliberate effort to confound the expectations of White Christians breaks open the way race has been mapped onto issues of enchantment, disenchantment, and secularism in the study of religion. The story of McKay and his network of Francophone Black Catholic intellectuals offers a religious history of mixed identities and affiliation outside the boundaries of nationalism. It confounds the binary of Black African enchantment and White European cosmopolitanism and secularism. Their story invites us, as Vincent Lloyd has articulated in his work on race and secularism, to remember the "unmanaged religious" in cultures where secularism holds considerable power.[54] At the same time, the religious imagination of McKay and his community also enhances conversations advanced by scholars like Christopher Cameron, whose work, *Black Freethinkers*, highlights the mainstream assumption that critiques of religion including free thought, atheism, nontraditional religious views, and agnosticism have always been "the preserve of educated or cultivated minds belonging to white people."[55] Cameron retraces a long and fascinating Black intellectual history, which includes Black thinkers from the Civil War through the Black Power movement, that critiques mainstream Christianity on the grounds of its entanglements with racist violence and experiments with forms of solidarity that draw from free thought and agnostic, atheistic, and religiously eclectic materials. The Catholicism of this international Black Francophone circuit is hardly atheistic, but it too is an alternative story of early intellectual critique of Christianity and racism and a move toward something grounded in spiritual seeking, religious wandering, yearning for more creative, less predictable models of affiliation.

Attending to the critiques, desires, and imaginations of Claude McKay and his network also gives us a different perspective on other conversations in the study of religion. Charles Taylor, for example, has argued that the process of modernity included a subtle, gradual transformation from the Christian order to an allegedly merely "moral order" that affirmed ordinary life and human flourishing. Protestant Christianity appeared "secular" because it was focused on mere "ordinary life" and shed its commitments to transcendence and the supernatural.[56] In modernity, to seek transcendence, something beyond the human, is to *rebel against* this affirmation of ordinary life alone and dare

to imagine that something matters "beyond life."[57] To pierce the immanent frame of secularism and open oneself up to enchantment is to open
"the way for the insight that more than life matters."[58] The spiritual, the
mystical, the numinous, and the sacred materials of religion offer a sense
of how we resist the mere moral order and move "beyond the self and even
beyond life." Taylor even speculates on the fascination with death and
violence as "at base a manifestation of our nature as homo religious."[59]

But for writers like McKay and Tarry, religious language and history
was certainly not a refusal of the modern affirmation of ordinary life. From
their perspective, secular modernity (even as disguised Protestantism)
never affirmed ordinary life and human flourishing, even as it claimed to,
at least not in their lives or those of anyone who looked like them. The
religious language they engaged to counter secularism was not something
that pointed merely beyond life but, in the words of Kelly Brown Douglas, a
weapon and a counternarrative to resist and fight the "tyranny of America's
Anglo-Saxon exceptionalism."[60] The moral energy then was not only bound
up with exposing the secular regime for its violence. There was no sense
that the world would relinquish xenophobic violence if it would excise
the hidden darkness within its allegedly positive ideals. The moral energy
was instead directed at seeing who was vulnerable under regimes of power
and joining with them in modes of resistance and solidarity and, just like
the opposition, drawing deeply from the well of the religious imagination to do so. McKay's writings take place in thick contexts saturated
with religion and with the politics of race. For him, these are impossible
to disentangle. In his hands, religion was more than consolation for the
disempowered, it was more than a portal out of boredom or the everyday,
it was more than the alterity for the rational other. It scrambled the categories, redrew the lines, invited us to consider the surplus of Black history
and the history of "secularism" with renewed focus and attention. It was a
language of resistance to White claims of "civilized" superiority and moral
advancement. This is the case even if, at least for McKay, he relied on an
imagined binary of the good "inside" Catholicism and the bad safely "outside" in Protestant and secular culture.

At the same time, I sensed some of Charles Taylor's insights when I read
the works of McKay and Tarry and looked through their letters, photos, and
unpublished manuscripts. There was a mystical, unusual way in which they
described the religious materials they studied. Although countering White

bigotry was key to the forms of Black Catholic solidarity they envisioned, McKay and Tarry seemed to also want to show that religion, in some way, operated at a level that did not quite fit into our concepts of the social, ethical, or political. Ellen Tarry was especially skeptical when White activists would use too much religion in political projects; to her it sounded "phony." The religious figures they wrote about were in a way liminal figures, to borrow a category of Victor Turner, in the sense that they did but did not exactly belong to the political realm. Anthea Butler turns our attention to similar concerns in her study of African American women involved in the Holiness movement in the early twentieth century. Though the women in this movement often get swept up in a narrative that treats them as precursors to the civil rights movement, she asks, "What if Holiness women were not primarily concerned with political issues, but instead with religious ones?"[61]

Moving to a conclusion, I would like to introduce briefly one final thinker who will help us think with Claude McKay and his community. In a 1984 essay, "Reflections on Exile," Edward Said reminds us that modern Western culture is in large part the work of exiles, refugees, émigrés. In the United States, academic, intellectual, and aesthetic thought is what it is today because of refugees from fascism, communism, and other regimes that oppressed and expelled dissidents.

This includes the Frankfurt school writers who Said admired, like Theodore Adorno, who was German born with Jewish ancestry and who left Germany for England in 1934 and eventually the United States, where he lived until 1948. Adorno refused attachment to his new country as well as the old one and resisted all conventional modes of belonging, including to religion and even to ideals that could too easily morph into ideology. Adorno pledged loyalty only to the acts of criticism and writing. But Said rightly warned readers not to romanticize exile, wandering, statelessness: "Exile is strangely compelling to think about but terrible to experience."[62] We associate depth, solitude, even spirituality with exile. We tend to forget, Said reminds us, that exile happens *to* someone. It is a harrowing estrangement produced by war and violence.

I wonder if, in the study of religion, we might consider another set of forgotten, obscure exiles—the writers and artists from the African diaspora, like Claude McKay, whose ancestors were forced to the Caribbean for enslavement and who spent his own life in the United States as an émigré, then in Europe as a self-proclaimed "vagabond wanderer," cut loose from modernity's traditional anchors of the nation and the nuclear family. McKay differs from someone like Adorno as a Black man living in diasporic modernity: a wandering sojourner from Jamaica, Harlem, France, Spain, Chicago, who was never as compelled by the promises of secular critique. His skepticism about secularism meant he was far more open to taking religion seriously, in his case, Catholicism, even to the point of refusing to see its blind spots. He had long spoken openly about racism and White supremacy but was never afraid to look at both European and non-European sources of truth. He was a wanderer, someone who experimented with different allegiances throughout his life. Intellectuals like McKay might offer one response to Said's 1993 sequel to his groundbreaking *Orientalism*, in which he surprisingly offers an indictment of theorists like Adorno whose works were so important to him: "Frankfurt school critical theory, despite its seminal insights into the relationships between domination, modern society, and the opportunities for redemption through art as critique, is stunningly silent on racist theory, anti-imperialist resistance, and oppositional practice in the empire."[63] Said claimed this was more than a benign neglect on their part. It was an active refusal of non-European knowledge and resistance that relied instead on the false purported universalism of Eurocentric philosophy and criticism. McKay and his community of Black Catholic thinkers offer an alternative, understudied mode of exilic thinking in the twentieth century.

They were compelled by a kind of religiosity that did not seem to fit into the dominant narratives on offer: Black Catholicism confounded White Christians. McKay converted to Catholicism as an adult and died too young, but my hunch is that he would have remained an itinerant wanderer all his life, experimenting further with different eclectic modes of belonging. This wandering nature joins McKay to scores of other Caribbean immigrants in Harlem from 1920 to the 1930s who, as Judith Weisenfeld has described, experimented with racial and religious identities beyond the dominant Black Protestant church.[64] Ellen Tarry and Claude McKay to me are, like Adorno, "unhoused and wanderers across language," crossing borders and breaking barriers of thought and experience.[65]

Before he died, McKay told one of his old friends, the White journalist and activist Max Eastman, that he was "battered and ready for the scrap heap."[66] After McKay's death in 1948, Eastman worked to preserve the memory of his late friend, describing him in an introduction to a new volume of his poetry in 1953 as "the rarest of earth's wonders, the true born lyric poet."[67] Every now and again, other voices seem to appear to rescue McKay from the scrap heap, bringing him to new readers as a wonder, a gem, popping up all over the world. In McKay's archive I found a 1990 translation and publication of his poem "If We Must Die" in Tamil. He appears regularly in new histories of Black resistance as voicing the anthem of the Harlem Renaissance.[68] In 2009, a graduate student discovered an unpublished manuscript of McKay's—which turned out to be *Amiable with Big Teeth*—that had been lost deep in the bowels of the New York Public Library.[69] The filmmaker Ava DuVernay features McKay's "If We Must Die" in *August 28: A Day in the Life of a People*, a film created for the Smithsonian's Museum of African American History and Culture. I wonder if scholars in the study of religion might follow suit. In modernity, the terms "enchantment," "disenchantment," and "secularism" are too central to our field for us to dispense with them. They *are* the study of religion. But Courtney Bender is right: they seem to have reached their term limit. A new set of voices and perspectives is needed. The story of this community suggests another way forward. In thinking with them, the conversation no longer feels quite so closed, quite so predictable, and comes closer to being able to speak to the issues that were at the center of their lives and to our own tumultuous time.

NOTES

1. Courtney Bender, "Enchantment," A Universe of Terms Series, *Immanent Frame*, May 1, 2020, https://tif.ssrc.org/2020/05/01/enchantment-disenchantment-bender/.

2. Leigh Eric Schmidt, *Hearing Things: Religion, Illusion, and the American Enlightenment* (Cambridge, MA: Harvard University Press, 2002); Alex Owen, *The Place of Enchantment: British Occultism and the Culture of the Modern* (Chicago: University of Chicago Press, 2006).

3. Talal Asad, *Formations of the Secular: Christianity, Islam, Modernity* (Stanford, CA: Stanford University Press, 2003); Davis Martin, *On Secularization: Towards a Revised General Theory* (Aldershot: Ashgate, 2005).

4. Samuel Moyn, *Christian Human Rights* (Philadelphia: University of Pennsylvania Press, 2015).

5. Richard King, *Orientalism and Religion: Postcolonial Theory, India, and "The Mystic East"* (New York: Routledge, 1999).

6. Jane Bennett, *The Enchantment of Modern Life: Attachments, Crossings, and Ethics* (Princeton, NJ: Princeton University Press, 2001).

7. Bender, "Enchantment."

8. Brent Hayes Edwards, *The Practice of Diaspora: Literature, Translation, and the Rise of Black Internationalism* (Cambridge, MA: Harvard University Press, 2003), 20.

9. There is a robust, excellent literature on Black Francophone writers and Black writers who traveled to Europe but little written about the role of Catholicism in this community. The following sources are excellent places to start: Edwards, *The Practice of Diaspora*; Tyler Stovall, *Paris Noir: African Americans in the City of Light* (Boston: Houghton Mifflin, 1996); Lara Putnam, *Radical Moves: Caribbean Migrants and the Politics of Race in the Jazz Age* (Chapel Hill: University of North Carolina Press, 2013); Philippe Dewitte, *Les mouvements nègres en France, 1919–1939* (Paris: Éditions l'Harmattan, 1985); Iheanachor Egonu, "'Les Continents' and the Francophone Pan-Negro Movement," *Phylon* 42, no. 3 (1981): 245–54; Eslanda Goode Robeson, "Black Paris," *Challenge: A Literary Quarterly* (January 1936); Jennifer Anne Boittin, *Colonial Metropolis: The Urban Grounds of Anti-Imperialism and Feminism in Interwar Paris* (Lincoln: University of Nebraska Press, 2010).

10. Claude McKay, "Mystical World of the Spirit," from "On Becoming a Roman Catholic," *Epistle*, no. 2 (Spring 1945): 43–45; "International of Peace and Good Will," from Claude McKay, "Right Turn to Catholicism," unpublished essay, box 9, folder 298, Claude McKay Collection, Yale Collection of American Literature, Beinecke Rare Book and Manuscript Library, New Haven, CT.

11. Kathyrn Lofton, "The Perpetual Primitive in African American Religious Historiography," in *The New Black Gods: African American Religions after the Great Migration*, ed. Edward E. Curtis and Danielle Brune Sigler (Bloomington: Indiana University Press, 2009), 171–91; Vincent Lloyd, "Managing Race, Managing Religion," in *Race and Secularism in America*, ed. Vincent Lloyd and Johnathan S. Kahn (New York: Columbia University Press, 2016).

12. I have written on Claude McKay elsewhere, and some of the reflections in this chapter appear in chapter 5 of *Kindred Spirits: Friendship and Resistance at the Edges of Modern Catholicism* (Chicago: University of Chicago Press, 2021). For a fuller biography of Claude McKay, see Wayne F. Cooper, *Claude McKay, Rebel Sojourner in the Harlem Renaissance: A Biography* (Baton Rouge: Louisiana State University Press, 1987); Tyrone Tillery, *Claude McKay: A Black Poet's Struggle for Identity* (Amherst: University of Massachusetts Press, 1992).

13. Claude McKay, *A Long Way from Home* (Boston: Houghton Mifflin), 44.

14. Cameron McWhirter, *Red Summer: The Summer of 1919 and the Awakening of Black America* (New York: St. Martin's Press, 2011), 191.

15. Ibid., 191.

16. Claude McKay, "If We Must Die," in *Complete Poems*, ed. William J. Maxwell (Champaign: University of Illinois Press, 2004), 178.

17. Claude McKay, "Exhortation, Summer 1919," in Maxwell, *Complete Poems*, 330.

18. Langston Hughes, "Christ in Alabama," *Contempo* 1, no. 13 (December 1, 1931): 1; James H. Cone, *The Cross and the Lynching Tree* (Maryknoll, NY: Orbis Books, 2011).

19. Claude McKay, *Banjo* (Boston: Mariner Books, 1970), 35.

20. Bridget Jones, "With 'Banjo' by My Bed: Black French Writers Reading Claude McKay," *Caribbean Quarterly* 38, no. 1 (1992): 32–39.

21. Tracy Denean Sharpley-Whiting, "Francophone Caribbean and the Harlem Renaissance," in *Encyclopedia of the Harlem Renaissance*, ed. Carly Wintz and Paul Finkelman (New York: Routledge, 2003), 407–13 (409).

22. Margaret Vendryes, *Barthé: A Life in Sculpture* (Jackson: University Press of Mississippi, 2008), 14–22.

23. Paulette Nardal and Phillipe Grollemund, *Fiertés de femme noire: Entretiens / Mémoires de Paulette Nardal* (Paris: Éditions l'Harmattan, 2019), 43.

24. Louis Achille, "Negro Spirituals," *Esprit*, Paris, no. 179 (May 1951): 707–16.

25. Elizabeth A. Foster, *African Catholic: Decolonization and the Transformation of the Church* (Cambridge, MA: Harvard University Press, 2019); Matthew J. Cressler, *Authentically Black and Truly Catholic: The Rise of Black Catholicism in the Great Migration* (New York: New York University Press, 2017).

26. Josef Sorett, *Spirit in the Dark: A Religious History of Racial Aesthetics* (Oxford: Oxford University Press, 2016). See also Cecilia Moore, "Keeping Harlem Catholic: African-American Catholics and Harlem, 1920–1960," *American Catholic Studies* 114, no. 3 (2003): 3–21 (6).

27. Claude McKay, "Right Turn to Catholicism," Claude McKay Collection, Yale Collection of American Literature, Beinecke Rare Book and Manuscript Library.

28. McKay, "On Becoming a Roman Catholic."

29. Willie James Jennings, *The Christian Imagination: Theology and the Origins of Race* (New Haven, CT: Yale University Press, 2011), esp. 65–117.

30. The Federal Writers Project (FWP) gave employment between 1935 and 1939 to about 4,500 American writers, 106 of which were Black.

31. Ellen Tarry gives a short history of the project in Ellen Tarry, "How the History Was Assembled: One Writer's Memories," in *The Negro in New York: An Informal Social History, 1626–1940*, ed. Roi Ottley and William J. Weatherby (New York: Praeger, 1967), x–xii.

32. Quoted in J. J. Butts, "New World A-Coming: African American Documentary Intertexts of the Federal Writers' Project," *African American Review* 44, no. 4 (2011): 649–66.

33. Claude McKay, *Harlem: Negro Metropolis* (San Diego, CA: Harcourt Brace Jovanovich, 1968), 44.

34. Ibid., 73.

35. Claude McKay, *Amiable with Big Teeth: A Novel of the Love Affair between the Communists and the Poor Black Sheep of Harlem* (New York: Penguin, 2017), 107.

36. Ibid., 3.

37. Ibid., 31.

38. Ella Baker and Marvel Cooke, "Bronx Slave Market," *The Crisis* 42, no. 11 (November 1, 1930): 330–32.

39. Ellen Tarry, "Native Daughter: An Indictment of White America by a Colored Woman," *Commonweal*, April 12, 1940.

40. Ellen Tarry, *The Third Door* (Tuscaloosa: University Of Alabama Press, 1991), 140.

41. Ellen Tarry, "Lest We Forget Our Heritage," *Interracial Review*, May 1940.

42. McKay, "Right Turn to Catholicism." See also the excellent article by Cecila Moore, "The Sources and Meaning of the Conversion of Claude McKay," *Journal of the Black Catholic Theological Symposium* 2 (2008): 59–80.

43. Tarry, *Third Door*.

44. Claude McKay, "Why I Became a Catholic," *Ebony* 1 (March 1946): 32.

45. McKay, "On Becoming a Roman Catholic."

46. Madhuri Deshmukh, "Claude McKay's Road to Catholicism," *Callaloo* 37, no. 1 (2014): 148–68; Josef Sorett, *Spirit in the Dark*, 79–114. Several Catholic authors took an interest in McKay's conversion; see Mary Jerdo Keating, "Claude McKay," *Catholic Interracialist*, September 1951; Ceclia Moore, "The Sources and Meaning of the Conversion of Claude McKay," *Journal of the Black Catholic Theological Symposium* 2, no. 2 (2008): 59–79.

47. McKay, "Right Turn to Catholicism."

48. Cecilia Moore, "Conversion Narratives: The Dual Experiences and Voices of African American Catholic Converts," *U.S. Catholic Historian* 28, no. 1 (Winter 2010): 27–40 (32).

49. T. J. Jackson Lears, *No Place of Grace: Antimodernism and the Transformation of American Culture, 1880–1920* (Chicago: University of Chicago Press, [1981] 1994), xv.

50. Lofton, "The Perpetual Primitive," 189.

51. Ibid., 186.

52. McKay, "Why I Became a Catholic," 32.

53. Ibid.

54. Lloyd, "Managing Race, Managing Religion," 15.

55. Christopher Cameron, *Black Freethinkers* (Chicago: Northwestern University Press, 2019), ix.

56. Charles Taylor, "On Western Secularity," in *Rethinking Secularism*, ed. Craig Calhoun, Mark Juergensmeyer, Jonathan Van Antwerpen (Oxford: Oxford University Press, 2011), 31–53 (51–52).

57. Charles Taylor, "A Catholic Modernity?," in *Dilemmas and Connections: Selected Essays* (Cambridge, MA: Harvard University Press, 2011), 167–87 (173).

58. Ibid., 176.

59. See the longer excerpt of this essay in Charles Taylor, *A Catholic Modernity? Charles Taylor's Marianist Award Lecture* (Oxford: Oxford University Press, 1999), 28.

60. Kelly Brown Douglas, *Stand Your Ground: Black Bodies and the Justice of God* (Ossening, NY: Orbis Press, 2015).

61. Anthea D. Butler, "Unrespectable Saints: Women of the Church of God in Christ," in *The Religious History of American Women: Reimagining the Past*, ed. Catherine A. Brekus (Chapel Hill: University of North Carolina Press, 2007), 161–83.

62. Edward Said, *Reflections on Exile and Other Essays* (Cambridge, MA: Harvard University Press, 2000), 173.

63. Edward Said, *Culture and Imperialism* (New York: Vintage, 1993), 278.

64. Judith Weisenfeld, *New World A-Coming: Black Religion and Racial Identity during the Great Migration* (New York: New York University Press, 2019).

65. For more on Black artists and writers as global, transatlantic theorists of modernity, see Paul Gilroy, *The Black Atlantic: Modernity and Double Consciousness* (Cambridge, MA: Harvard University Press, 1993).

66. Letter quoted in Christopher Irmscher, *Max Eastman: A Life* (New Haven, CT: Yale University Press, 2017), 305.

67. Max Eastman, ed., *Selected Poems of Claude McKay* (New York: Harcourt, Brace and World, 1953), 111.

68. McWhirter, *Red Summer*.

69. See the details of this fascinating story in Jennifer Wilson, "A Forgotten Novel Reveals a Forgotten Harlem," *The Atlantic*, March 9, 2017, www.theatlantic.com/entertainment/archive/2017/03/a-forgotten-novel-reveals-a-forgotten-harlem/518364/.

CHAPTER 5

Seeing Solidarity

Melani McAlister

ABSTRACT

This response essay reflects on the affective elements that have the potential to bind people together in solidarity, yet also have the potential to keep them bound to their differences. In recounting stories of unrealized solidarity both from the present volume and in other instances, this essay demonstrates the importance of analyzing feeling and attachment in feminist solidarity movements in particular. Doing so helps us see the importance but also the challenge of undoing the ideological blinders that keep us from seeing clearly how our fates are bound together with others.

Solidarity is not solid. If we could paint it, it would be striated and seamed, remarkably aged and ragged, but with bits of hopeful new growth—winding wildly in spirals or staggering in one direction only to switch sharply to another.

As I write this, the Jerusalem neighborhood of Sheikh Jarrah is terrorized by Jewish settlers who are brazenly evicting Palestinians from their homes. Again. And Hamas is lobbing rockets into Israel, while Israel targets and kills Palestinians in Gaza. An editorial in the *Washington Post* by Noura Erakat and Mariam Barghouti describes the situation as what it is: "the ongoing process that seeks to remove Palestinian natives and replace them with Jewish-Zionists." The anniversary of the Nakba is just around the corner, they say. With the Biden administration and/or the usual American policy approach in mind, Erakat and Barghouti end with a call: "We do not need more empty both sides-isms, we need solidarity to overcome apartheid."[1]

The expectation or longing for solidarity is a cry for justice against a universe determinedly insensitive to our demands. When we think of solidarity, maybe we think of a line of people, hooked arm in arm, facing down the police. Or a woman's refusal to cross a picket line at the factory gates. The Black Power fists of Tommie Smith and John Carlos at the 1968 Olympics. Maybe something as simple and brave as standing in front of a bulldozer aimed at destroying Palestinian homes—and paying with your life.[2] All of these are impassioned visions, offering a performance of moral clarity and a willingness to take a stand.

But solidarity is more than an ideological/intellectual statement; it is infused with feeling. Those on the political Left often dream of it, as outcome and object. Drawing on Sara Ahmed, I think of solidarity as being as much an emotion as an action, not that the two could be easily separated. As an emotion, solidarity connects, it is social, operating through exchange: "It is through emotions, or how we respond to objects and others, that surfaces or boundaries are made: the 'I' and 'we' are shaped by, and even take the shape of, contact with others."[3] Thus emotions, for Ahmed, do not arise from inside the person and move outward (like we think of love or anger) or start from outside and move in (like a wave of feeling in a crowd) but circulate, through signs, between bodies. We are impressed upon by a situation, a person, an object, and in this way we turn toward or away from it. Ahmed writes, "Affect is what sticks, or what sustains or preserves the connection between ideas, values, and objects."[4]

The contributors to this book show clearly just how difficult solidarity is, how sticky an object, freighted with expectations and histories. Objects shimmering with affect can lead us to lean in or turn away. They can orient us variously. As Omer and Lupo comment in the introduction, this book includes examples of people who, in multiple situations, are "unable to participate in an intersectional vision of emancipation that transcends national boundaries." The limits of that imagination are shaped by the hegemonic frameworks of state powers, racial hegemonies, religious divides, and modernist projects. If solidarity is our designed object, the desired good around which the book is oriented, then the disappointed hope that it will solidify is what marks the tenor of the project. We see in these chapters a kind of call for new affective objects, networks rewired to allow for larger, more expansive connections. Omer and Carmi call for marginalized Israelis to find solidarity with each other and/or Palestinians; Hammer's analysis shows how American women organizing against Trump failed to move beyond the forms of silencing of pro-Palestinian speech that shaped the Women's March of 2017; Gürel unpacks why Iranian and Turkish Muslim women could not find solidarity in the face of a global system that made Iranian women's offers of support seem toxic to a devout Turkish politician. These are instances of analyzing ideology, its imbrication in religion and ideas about religion. But they necessarily imagine what could have been otherwise. In a different vein, Brenna Moore's chapter on Black Catholic internationalism shows how solidarities can be produced and thrive, yet remain invisible to those outside. Religion here, perhaps more than anywhere else in the book, enables solidarity work; it enchants and connects, becomes that which "sustains or preserves the connection between ideas, values, and objects." But in the moral imagination of much that has been branded solidarity, this religious work is unseen, unseeable.

There was a time in the 1960s and 1970s when "Third World solidarity" was a mantra, a talisman, and sometimes a truth. Palestinians and African Americans met in North African capitals; Cubans and Black South Africans fought side by side; American antiwar protesters chanted the name of Ho Chi Minh.[5] These are not all equivalent, but they required a particular kind of moral geography, a vision of "three worlds" that was also somehow beyond what could be plotted on a map—a matter of affective attachment and/or political commitment.

Some historians have hailed that Third World solidarity as the creation of the 1955 Bandung Conference, officially the Asian-African Conference. At that meeting, African American observers joined with luminaries of a decolonizing world: Nasser of Egypt, Sukarno of Indonesia, Nehru of India, three leaders who seemed to represent the possibility of independence. The retrospective myth of Bandung is that it was the moment when "the darker peoples" of the world chose solidarity with each other and against the imperialist powers. They claimed the dark side of *The Color Curtain*, per the title of Richard Wright's book on the conference.[6] Today, not surprisingly, historians have revisited and re-visioned the heroic version of Bandung. It mattered, certainly, because it made clear that colonialism was entering its end game. But tensions among the solid citizens of the emerging Third

World were everywhere. There were competing visions (Asian-African solidarity versus a more global nonalignment, for example) and competition for leadership (e.g., Nasser vs. Nehru, Nasser vs. Nkrumah). A decade after Bandung, there would even be competing conferences, a multitude of alliances, and as many schisms.[7] The point is not that important racial, political, or anticolonial connections were not forged there. They were, and such connections are being made and remade still today. But there is something in the storytelling about that moment—a longing for a swelling rise of unity-in-diversity—that undercuts the *work* of it, the failures, the realpolitik of making a stand.

Our emotions are trained by expectations, attached to objects that we already anticipate will carry a charge. Ahmed writes, "If we arrive at objects with an expectation of how we will be affected by them, this affects how they affect us, even in the moment they fail to live up to expectations."[8] The attachment between objects, feelings, and the social horizon of expectations is what Ahmed describes as "sticky." Affect attaches to objects; it circulates through their circulation. The clenched fist becomes a sticky object, connecting—and disappointing—as it moves across borders and creates connection.

Feminists, too, have learned and forgotten the lessons of affective attachments again and again. Sisterhood is powerful, it is global, it is intersectional. These claims are at the center of fifty years of debates about how gender meets race, nation, privilege, sexuality, disability, and generation. Within the United States, Black and Brown feminists have for decades now questioned the uninterrogated privileges of White women who all too often seemed to imagine that the women on whose behalf feminism promised freedom were basically women-like-them. Betty Friedan's royal "we" of women who wanted to escape domesticity and the nuclear family, to work and find "ourselves," was piercingly ignorant of the lives of women who perhaps wanted nothing more than to stop working the second job, to be able to gather their families together from the centrifugal forces of neoliberal capitalism, racism, and war. Three generations of feminist theorists have challenged that normalizing moment. In fact, one becomes attached to its disavowal.

New attachments form. In 1985, when I was living as a student in Cairo, I went to hear a visiting American lecturer.[9] Angela Davis was in town, speaking to an audience of about fifty women and men, under the sponsorship of the Arab Women's Solidarity Association. She spoke mostly about the ways in which the state monitored the sexual and domestic lives of women on welfare in the United States. I remember wondering whether most people would find this a particularly compelling matter of concern, given the severe economic crisis faced by nearly everyone in Mubarak's Egypt and the rising power of Islamism. The audience seemed polite but perhaps a bit listless. Near the end of her lecture, however, Davis galvanized the crowd when she explained that she was in Egypt to do research for her contribution to an anthology commemorating the UN Decade of Women (1975–85). The formula for the book was a collection of essays, each written by a different feminist from around the world, focusing on the condition of women in countries other than her own. The writers were given specific topics: the Egyptian feminist Nawal El Saadawi had been assigned to write about "women and education" in England; Germaine Greer would cover "women and politics" in Cuba; and Davis had been assigned to write about "women and sex" in Egypt.

When Davis explained the purpose of her visit, there was an immediate outcry. Much of the audience was angry—furious, in fact—that Davis had agreed to focus on *sex* in relation to women in Egypt. They insisted to Davis that the fundamental framework of her project was wrong. Why were American and western feminists so focused on sexuality, the veil, and female genital surgeries? They were distorting the real struggles of Egyptian women, and of African and Arab women in general. Davis insisted that she intended to have a critical view of the topic, to connect sexual issues to the larger concerns of Egyptian women. The audience wasn't convinced; or rather, it didn't matter. By the mid-1980s, they were already sick and tired of this "interest" on the part of American women. As Davis reported in the article she eventually published, one woman at a similar meeting minced no words.

> Women in the West should know that we have a stand in relation to them concerning our issues and our problems. We reject their patronizing attitude. It is connected with inbuilt mechanisms of colonialism and a sense of superiority. Maybe some of them don't do it consciously, but it is there. They decide what problems we have, how we should face them, without even possessing the tools to know our problems.[10]

The 1980s were a moment when "Third World Women" was a signifier for feminist politics in the United States and when solidarity with that figure—that sticky object—was a matter of pride. Many feminists from many countries worked hard to construct alliances by hashing out debates at UN conferences or in small meeting halls in places like Cairo. Indeed, Davis tried hard to make her final report sensitive to the issues of cultural domination and feminist agenda setting that were so much on the minds of Egyptian women. She wrote about work, education, divorce laws, and political activism, including women's organizing against US economic and political influence in Egypt. But, obedient to both her assignment and the dictates of the larger discourse about "Muslim women" in this period, she also wrote in detail about the increasing practice of veiling and the decreasing practice of clitoridectomy. In doing so, Davis, an African American Communist, also implicitly took a stand that marked her in the eyes of Egyptian activists as American, as western, and perhaps even as imperialist.

I was reminded of this while reading Jennifer Nash's recent *Black Feminism Reimagined*, in which she argues that "black feminism" has taken a central position in women's studies and feminist politics, one that seems (to me) rather analogous to that earlier moment of the "Third World feminist." This position of the Black feminist is an ambivalent, complex one. Nash's exploration of the "felt experience" of Black feminism is grounded in a recognition that such experience exists in relation to a range of other experiences and other views about Black feminism itself: "When I describe the felt experience of black feminism, my investment is in considering how the tradition is felt by those attached to it, by black feminists themselves. It is clear that nonblack feminists also *feel* black feminism in certain ways, viewing it as a place of hope, retreat, anxiety, disgust, imagining it as both world-making and world-ending simultaneously."[11]

Nash doesn't say it quite this way, but she is exploring Black feminism as an affective object, one freighted with feeling as it moves among diverse feminist communities, who attach to it with varying, sedimented desires. Feminist solidarities often have been trapped by the accouterments of racism, imperialism, and exploitation that they aimed to oppose. But feminists (sometimes) know that. Back in the eighties, self-aware feminist letter writers signed off not with "in solidarity," but with "yours in struggle."[12] It wasn't supposed to be easy.

In my own work, I have written about how American evangelicals in recent decades became invested in their own version of solidarity—a sense of enchanted attachment to the Christians of the global South. Creating their own narratives of community-across-borders that idealized Africans and Asians as having a longed-for numinous faith, they simultaneously constructed a politics that posited solidarity with their "brothers and sisters" who were suffering for their faith in places like Sudan, Vietnam, or Iraq. The stories were sticky objects, fantasies of martyrdom that invested Brown and Black Christians abroad with the glow of sanctified suffering. Sometimes the process forged surprising and resilient connections that led some American believers to push for HIV/AIDS funding and debt relief for Africa, or an end to US torture in Iraq. But the dreams of the "persecuted Christians" movement were often dangerous; they narrated complex crises that involved ethnic tensions, struggles over resources, environmental degradation, and foreign intervention as simplistic morality tales of faith under fire.[13] Christians in the global South found reasons to attach themselves to these stories, or refused them, depending on their on-the-ground realities. But it is not so simple as acquiescence or resistance. US evangelical solidarities carry price tags, but they are also sticky with the dream of global Christian community. "Brother (or sister) in Christ" is the icon of a certain transnational solidarity—as well as the marker of all those others who fall outside its shimmering promise: Muslims, Hindus, or atheists; persecutors or secularists; citizens and neighbors but not believers. It is a powerful form of global mapping, its own version of what Lauren Berlant describes as "cruel optimism": the attachment that keeps us pushing toward something that ultimately prevents the thriving that might otherwise be possible.[14] Attachments create outsides; forms of seeing are also forms of making-invisible.

My favorite book by the brilliant and wildly prolific novelist China Miéville is *The City & the City*.[15] (Speaking of solidarity longings: I used to love to imagine what kind of politically radical family he had grown up in, this British man born in 1972 whose parents named him "China." Now I read that they were just looking through a dictionary for a beautiful name.) In Miéville's speculative fiction novel—he aptly describes his work as "weird fiction"—there is a murder that takes place in two fictional Eastern European cities: not on the border, exactly, because the two cities occupy the same space, the same streets. The citizens of the city-states of Besźel and Ul Qoma have somewhat different languages and very different religions, but they live side by side, sharing streets and parks. In order to live together but apart, they are trained not to see each other even when they are in the same space. "Unseeing" is a life-honed skill. They have to recognize the denizens that belong to the other city without actually *seeing* them. The conceit might have devolved into a simple allegory about race or religious difference, but what makes the novel work is its sustained and generous attention to what it takes to refuse to see that which is, literally, right beside you. The ideological work, the production of a certain self, and the lived reality of knowing what you cannot know: who is this person, right here on the same street, walking in a different city? (Some of the buildings on the street are in your city, some are in theirs; citizens of both cities know this and navigate it, perfectly.) Sometimes a person makes a "breach" across the divide, intentional or not; the breachers disappear to unknown ends. The brilliance of the tale is that the distinctions don't feel ideological to the members of the city-states; they don't talk about the (inferior) values of the other side, don't denigrate their fashion or their religion. The inhabitants are just built, from birth on, to perceive and live their bodies, their orientations, in a particular way. That they are the only place in the world like this—that this is in fact what makes the residents of these cities, together, like no one and nowhere else—is entirely lost on them.

I take Miéville's novel to be a sustained counterargument to what I have tried to say here. I have highlighted how much solidarity *cannot* be assumed, how it is process and movement, work and networks, inevitably sticky with feelings and failures. We should expect that all that is solid will melt into air, most of the time.[16] Miéville instead highlights what it takes to "unsee" the ties that are right in front of us—the institutions and cultural work that reshape ordinary human connections into a distorted imaginary of separateness. He doesn't suggest that we can simply undo or deprogram these selves, but the novel does provide a sense that there is some basic connected truth about our lives amid one another that we have to *learn* to "unsee." I would like to think that this is more than sentimental humanism but rather a form of asserting fundamental human (or, if you know Miéville, also more-than-human) living-in-relation. It is, perhaps, a matter of what Donna Haraway describes as "staying with the trouble": "learning to be truly present, not as a vanishing pivot between awful or edenic pasts and apocalyptic or salvific futures, but as mortal critters entwined in myriad unfinished configurations of places, times, matters, meanings."[17] Haraway, of course, would have us include animals, plants, trees, and air all in our "unfinished configurations." A deep and broad project of solidarity, a struggle, a refusal to rest in the unseen.

NOTES

1. Noura Erakat and Miriam Barghouti, "Opinion | Sheikh Jarrah Highlights the Violent Brazenness of Israel's Colonialist Project," *Washington Post*, May

10, 2021, www.washingtonpost.com/opinions/2021/05/10/israel-sheikh-jarrah
-palestinians-jerusalem-violence-evictions-settlers/.

2. Joshua Hammer, "The Death of Rachel Corrie," *Mother Jones*, September–October 2003, www.motherjones.com/politics/2003/09/death-rachel-corrie/.

3. Sara Ahmed, *The Cultural Politics of Emotion* (New York: Routledge, 2004), 10.

4. Sara Ahmed, *The Promise of Happiness* (Durham, NC: Duke University Press, 2010), 199.

5. Alex Lubin, *Geographies of Liberation: The Making of an Afro-Arab Political Imaginary* (Chapel Hill: University of North Carolina Press, 2014); Piero Gleijeses, *Conflicting Missions: Havana, Washington, and Africa, 1959–1976* (Chapel Hill: University of North Carolina Press, 2003); Judy Tzu-Chun Wu, *Radicals on the Road: Internationalism, Orientalism, and Feminism during the Vietnam Era*, illus. ed. (Ithaca, NY: Cornell University Press, 2013).

6. Richard Wright, *The Color Curtain* (Jackson: University Press of Mississippi, 1995).

7. Robert Vitalis, "The Midnight Ride of Kwame Nkrumah and Other Fables of Bandung (Ban-Doong)," *Humanity* 4, no. 2 (2013): 261–88.

8. Ahmed, *Promise of Happiness*, 28.

9. This account is taken from my essay "Suffering Sisters? American Feminists and the Problem of Female Genital Surgeries," in *Americanism: New Perspectives on the History of an Ideal*, ed. Michael Kazin and Joseph A. McCartin (Chapel Hill: University of North Carolina Press, 2006), 242–62.

10. Angela Davis, "Sex-Egypt," in *Women: A World Report*, ed. Debbie Taylor (New York: Oxford University Press, a New Internationalist Book, 1985), 328.

11. Jennifer C. Nash, *Black Feminism Reimagined: After Intersectionality* (Durham, NC: Duke University Press, 2019), 28.

12. Elly Bulkin, Minnie Bruce Pratt, and Barbara Smith, *Yours in Struggle: Three Feminist Perspectives on Anti-Semitism and Racism* (Ithaca, NY: Firebrand Books, 1984).

13. Melani McAlister, *The Kingdom of God Has No Borders: A Global History of American Evangelicalism* (New York: Oxford University Press, 2018).

14. Lauren Berlant, *Cruel Optimism* (Durham, NC: Duke University Press, 2011).

15. China Miéville, *The City & The City* (repr. New York: Del Rey, 2010).

16. Karl Marx and Friedrich Engels, *The Communist Manifesto* (1848) (Oxford: Oxford University Press, 2008). See also Marshall Berman, *All That Is Solid Melts into Air: The Experience of Modernity* (reissue New York: Penguin Books, 1988).

17. Donna J. Haraway, *Staying with the Trouble: Making Kin in the Chthulucene* (Durham, NC: Duke University Press, 2016), 1.

CONTRIBUTORS

Ruth Carmi is a PhD candidate in sociology and peace studies at the University of Notre Dame. She is interested in questions about gender, race and ethnicity, intersectionality, and law and society, especially with regard to how these questions pertain to Israel/Palestine. Previously, Carmi was a human rights lawyer in Israel, where she litigated in the High Court of Justice and represented committees in the Israeli parliament addressing resource allocation issues to the Arab minority in Israel and battled incitement to racism and violence. She has written several widely circulated reports on gender segregation and racism in Israel, which have informed recent public debates and advocacy efforts. Ruth holds a BA degree in law and psychology from the Hebrew University in Jerusalem, an LLM in international legal studies (specializing in human rights and gender) from American University Washington College of Law, and an MA in sociology from the University of Notre Dame.

Perin E. Gürel is associate professor of American studies and concurrent associate professor of gender studies at the University of Notre Dame. She is the author of *The Limits of Westernization: A Cultural History of America in Turkey* (2017). Her work has appeared in *American Quarterly, American Literary History, Diplomatic History, Journal of Transnational American Studies, Journal of the Ottoman and Turkish Studies Association, Journal of Turkish Literature,* and elsewhere. She is currently at work on her second book, tentatively titled, *America's Wife, America's Concubine: Turkey, Iran, and the Politics of Comparison.*

Juliane Hammer is associate professor of religious studies at the University of North Carolina at Chapel Hill. She specializes in the study of gender and sexuality in Muslim societies and communities, race and gender in US Muslim communities, and contemporary Muslim thought, activism, and practice and Sufism. She is the author of several books, including *Peaceful Families: American Muslim Efforts against Domestic Violence* (2019), *American Muslim Women, Religious Authority, and Activism: More than a Prayer* (2012), and *Palestinians Born in Exile: Diaspora and the Search for a Homeland* (2005). She is also coeditor of *A Jihad for Justice: The Work and Life of Amina Wadud* (with Kecia Ali and Laury Silvers, 2012), *The Cambridge Companion to American Islam* (with Omid Safi, 2013), and *Muslim Women and Gender Justice: Concepts, Sources, and Histories* (with Dina El Omari and Mouhanad Khorchide, 2020).

Joshua Lupo is the editor and writer of the *Contending Modernities Blog* and the classroom coordinator for the Madrasa Discourses program. He has published articles and reviews in *Soundings*, *Reading Religion*, *Sophia*, and *Religious Studies Review*. His current book project is titled *After Essentialism: A Critical Phenomenology for the Study of Religion.*

Melani McAlister is professor of American studies and international affairs at George Washington University. She is the author or coeditor of five books, including *The Kingdom of God Has No Borders: A Global History of American Evangelicals* (2018); *Epic Encounters: Culture, Media and US Interests in the Middle East* ([2001] 2005); and volume 4 of the forthcoming *Cambridge History of America and the World* (coedited with David Engerman and Max Friedman). She currently serves on the Board of Directors of the American Council of Learned Societies, as well as the boards of *Diplomatic History*, *Modern American History*, and *American Quarterly.*

Brenna Moore is professor of theology at Fordham University. She is the author of *Kindred Spirits: Friendship and Resistance at the Edges of Modern Catholicism* (2021), along with other works in modern Catholic intellectual and cultural history.

Atalia Omer is professor of religion, conflict, and peace studies at the Kroc Institute for International Peace Studies and at the Keough School of Global Affairs at the University of Notre Dame. She is also the Dermot T. J.

Dunphy Visiting Professor of Religion, Violence, and Peace Building at Harvard University and a senior fellow at the Religion, Conflict, and Peace Initiative at Harvard University's Religion and Public Life program. She earned her PhD in religion, ethics, and politics from the Committee on the Study of Religion at Harvard University (2008). Her research focuses on religion, violence, and peace building with a particular focus on Palestine/Israel as well as theories and methods in the study of religion. Omer was awarded an Andrew Carnegie Fellowship in 2017 to complete a manuscript titled "Decolonizing Religion and Peacebuilding." Among other publications, she is the author of *When Peace Is Not Enough: How the Israeli Peace Camp Thinks about Religion, Nationalism, and Justice* (2015) and *Days of Awe: Reimagining Jewishness in Solidarity with Palestinians* (2019) and a coeditor of *The Oxford Handbook of Religion, Conflict, and Peacebuilding* (2015). Omer is also codirector of Contending Modernities, a global research initiative.

INDEX

Abergel, Reuven, 112, 113
accountability, 52
Achille, Louis T., 141–42
Acosta, José de, 143
activism. *See* Left activism
Adorno, Theodore, 151, 152
African diaspora culture, 140–41,
  144, 145, 151–52
"Afro-Catholic moment," the, 13,
  133, 142, 147–48
agency
  defining, 113
  feminist, 3–4, 12, 14, 18, 20, 29,
    60, 82n31
  religious, 3–4, 12, 14, 22–23,
    29–30, 60, 67
  of women in Islam, 3–4, 12, 20,
    23, 52, 54, 59, 60
Ahmed, Leila, 56
Ahmed, Munira, 81n22
Ahmed, Sara, 59, 160, 162
Ahoti, 118
Akhavan-Bitaraf, Nayereh, 28
Alexander, M. Jacqui, 38
alter-realism, 113
Anderson, Benedict, 29
anti-Black racism
  antisemitism inscribed in, 99

Muslim communities addressing,
  83n50
antichoice women's organizations,
  70
anti-imperialism, 12, 18, 20, 21,
  38, 152
antimiscegenation rhetoric, 94, 99,
  100, 101, 126n20
anti-Muslim hostility, 55–58, 79n7,
  143
  anti-religious bias and, 60
  antisemitism accusations stem-
    ming from, 8, 71, 75, 76
  definition of, 55–56
  evangelical, 74–75
  as fear, 60
  gendered dimensions of, 56
  Sarsour as victim of, 65–66
  types of, 79n12
  of White feminists, 56–57
antiracism
  Catholic, 13
  decolonial, 103–4, 108
  Muslim, 83n50
  and revolutionary love, 107
  Zionism opposed to, 106
antisemitism, 8–10, 15, 82n47, 105,
  143

antisemitism *(cont.)*
  African American, 91, 104, 112
  Billoo accused of, 70–71
  and Donald Trump, 126n22
  IHRA definition of, 10
  Islamophobia and, linked, 97–98, 102
  Mallory accused of, 68, 69, 72–73, 76
  Muslims accused of, 8, 71, 75, 76
  and philosemitism, 97
  Sarsour accused of, 68–69, 72, 74, 76
  weaponization of, 8–11, 83n55, 103
  and Whiteness, 69, 75, 99–100
  Zionist, 95–98, 101
Anzaldúa, Gloria, 22, 59, 88, 111
Arab feminism, 111, 124. *See also under* Mizrahi Jews; Palestine
Arabic language, 114–16, 122
Arab Jewishness, 97, 115–17, 120, 124
Arat, Yeşim, 45n63
Arendt, Hannah, 47n91
Ashkenormativity, 94, 104, 110, 122, 124
  definition of, 124n1
  and Ethiopian Jews, 119–20
  and Kahanism, 100
  and Mizrahi Jews, 112, 114, 119
  in religious affairs, 120
Asian-African Conference, 161–62
Assed, Samia, 71–72
Atatürk, Mustafa Kemal, 24–26

Bahar, Almog, 115–17, 120, 122
Baker, Ella, 146
Balad Party, 117
Baldwin, James, 107
Balfour Declaration, 88
Balkan children, kidnapping of, 94
Bandung Conference, 161–62

Barghouti, Mariam, 159–60
Barthé, Richmond, 136, 141, 147
Basu, Amrita, 22
BDS (Boycott, Divestment, and Sanctions), 10, 72, 74, 107–8, 111
Bender, Courtney, 134, 135, 153
Ben-Gvir, Itamar, 90–91, 93
Bennett, Jane, 134
Ben Tzion, Ariel, 116
Berlant, Lauren, 165
Berry, Marie, 58–59
Beyerlein, Kraig, 81n23
Biden, Joe, 74
Bilge, Simra, 76–77, 78n3
Billoo, Zahra, 51, 53, 55
  media representations of, 62, 70–71
  Muslim feminist identification of, 58
binaries
  in antiracism work, 103
  Black vs. White religion, 148–49, 150
  Catholic vs. Protestant, 136, 137, 140, 142–43, 147, 150
  erasure caused by, 87, 89
  Israel vs. Palestine, 5–6, 9–10, 87, 89, 95, 105, 116, 124
  Jews of Color disrupting, 105–6, 124
  oppressive vs. emancipatory, 52
  of power and powerlessness, 123
Black Americans
  converting to Catholicism, 147–48
  Jews and, 91, 104, 112, 120–21
  solidarity of, with Palestinians, 104–5, 121, 124
Black Catholic writers, 11–13, 133–37, 141–49, 150–51, 152, 154n9. *See also* McKay, Claude; Tarry, Ellen

Black feminism, 18, 53–54, 57
  as an affective object, 164
  love in, 78
  and Mizrahi Jews, 111, 112
Black internationalism, 11–13,
    133, 135, 136, 138, 140–41,
    161
Black Lives Matter, 72, 73–74, 77
  and Jewish Voice for Peace,
    104–5, 106
Black Madonna, the, 142, 147, 148
Black Panthers of Israel, 112, 120
Black Power, 99
Black spirituals, 146
Bland, Bob, 58, 63, 67
  antisemitism accusations against,
    68, 69
  statement of, 73
borderlands, 88
Bouteldja, Houria, 107, 110, 116
Boylorn, Robin M., 57
Brewer, Sierra, 59
Bronx Slave Market, 145–46
B'Tselem, 71
"buffer communities," 107, 110,
    116
Bund Movement, 106
Butler, Anthea, 151

"calling in," 67, 78
Cameron, Christopher, 149
Carastathis, Anna, 78n2
Carlos, John, 160
Carmi, Ruth, 5–6, 9, 11, 12, 161
Catholicism, 11–13
  Black Americans converting to,
    147–48
  and Black Catholics in history,
    148–49
  McKay's conversion to, 140,
    141, 142, 147, 148, 152
  mystical dimension of, 134, 136,
    148

  nationalism resisted by, 133–34,
    136
  racial difference in, 13, 134
  racism in, 143
  romanticization of, 136, 137,
    142, 147, 148, 152
  in Spain, 142–43
  as the true international, 136, 147
charismatic activist leadership, 76,
    77
Charlottesville, Virginia, demon-
    stration, 102, 126n22
Chehabi, Houchang, 25
Chenoweth, Erica, 58–59
Chicana feminism, 111, 112, 124
Christianity
  antisemitism and, 98
  Black critiques of, 149
  and Christian Zionism, 74–75,
    92, 96–97, 101, 128n30
  and colonialism, 54, 55
  in the global South, 164–65
  Jewish tradition assimilated into,
    99, 123
  persecution fantasies in, 165
  queer feminist, 57
  and social justice, 8
  See also Catholicism; "Judeo-
    Christian" narratives;
    Protestantism
citizenship, category of, 90, 97,
    109, 124
City & the City, The (Miéville),
    165–66
"clash of civilizations," 2, 88
class, 54–55, 73, 76, 97
clitoridectomy, 163, 164
coalition building, 62, 117
Coleman, Isobel, 23
colonialism
  American, and Whiteness, 99
  and the Bandung Conference,
    161–62

colonialism *(cont.)*
  Christianity and, 54, 55, 92,
    97–99, 101, 105, 113, 143
  and the colonial gaze, 140
  framework of, solidarity in, 6
  vs. liberation, 89
  and religions, hierarchy of, 54
  and religious essentialism, 4
  settler, in Israel, 5–6, 88–89,
    92–94, 99, 104–8, 114,
    122–23
  White feminist complicity with,
    56
coloniality
  definition of, 97
  ethnic cleansing and, 101, 102
  neoliberalism and, 105
Combahee River Collective, 21
comparative feminist studies, 24
Cone, James, 139
Cooke, Marvel, 146
Cooper, Brittney C., 57
Corrie, Rachel, 160
counterculture, Catholic, 11–13,
    133–34, 136, 140–43, 147–51,
    152
"counterterrorism," Israeli, 95
Crenshaw, Kimberlé, 21, 53, 78n1
critique
  "calling in," 67, 78
  vs. deconstruction, 52
  responsible, 58, 78
  of Women's March, 51, 52–53,
    58–62, 65–70, 72–75
  of Zionism, 51–52, 53, 69,
    70–71, 95, 103–9, 122–24
"cruel optimism," 165
Crunk Feminist Collective, 57
Cullors, Patrisse, 77

David Horowitz Freedom Center, 65
Davis, Angela, 162–64

decolonization
  Bandung Conference and,
    161–62
  epistemologies of, 22
  in Israel, 94–95, 97–98, 102,
    106–7, 124
  of political imaginations, 89,
    103, 122–23, 124
  transnationalism as, 38
Demirel, Süleyman, 27, 32
democracy
  Islam and women's rights in, 18
  laïcism as necessary to, 33–34
  See also liberalism
diasporic Jewishness, 106, 123
dīn (Islamic belief and practice),
    23, 36
disenchantment, 134–35, 144, 145.
    See also modernity; secularism
"diversity, equity, and inclusion"
    programs, 70, 84n58
divisions, seeing beyond, 89, 111
doikayt (hereness), 106
Dollinger, Marc, 99
Douglas, Kelly Brown, 150
Dundes, Lauren, 59
DuVernay, Ava, 153

Eastman, Max, 152
Ecevit, Bülent, 27, 28, 30, 32
Edwards, Brent Hayes, 135
Egypt, 162–64
Ellis, Marc, 105
emotions, 159, 160
  and affective loyalty, 109
  of African diaspora, 145
  and intersectionality, 59–60
  and mythologizing, 161–62
  as "sticky," 162, 164–65
enchantment
  in American evangelicalism,
    164–65

and Black resistance, 140, 146, 147–48
and enchanted religiosity, 11–12, 133
exhaustion of, as concept, 133, 134–35, 153
race mapped onto, 149
romanticization of, 134, 136–37
epistemology from the margins, 124
Erakat, Noura, 159–60
Erdoğan, Recep Tayyip, 32
Eshkevari, Hassan Yousefi, 31
essentialism, strategic, 76–77, 85n77
Ethiopia, Italian invasion of, 138, 145
Ethiopian Jews, 5, 11, 87, 89, 122, 124
and African American culture, 121
Israeli discrimination against, 94, 119–20, 121, 122
Palestinian solidarity with, 119–20
police violence against, 10, 119–20
privileges of, 119
religious authority of, 120
Zionism of, 106, 119–20
Ettinger, Meir, 96, 127n28
Euro-Jewish supremacy, 5, 94, 96, 105–8, 110, 112–13, 119–24, 125n12
European Court of Human Rights (ECHR), 4, 19, 23–24, 33–35, 37
European Union (EU), 32–33, 36–37
Europe as metanarrative, 113, 116. See also coloniality
Euro-Zionism. See Zionism
evangelicalism, 74–75, 164–65

Evren, Kenan, 26
exiles, 151–52

Fairey, Shepard, 60, 81n22
false consciousness, religion as, 8, 12
Fanon, Frantz, 107
Farrakhan, Louis, 8, 72, 76, 112
Fazilet, 28, 32, 33
"Fear Inc.," 74
Federalist, The, 65–66
Federal Writers Project, 143–44, 145, 155n30
Feldman, Keith, 89
Felmlee, Diane H., 61, 62–63
feminism
anti-religious bias in, 14, 55, 60, 81n30
and attachment, 159, 164
colonial and racist entanglements of, 57, 163–64
definitions of, 20
inclusivity of, 69–70
intersectional, 15, 69–70, 76, 162
Mizrahi, 5–6, 88, 109–14, 118–19, 131n69
sex and, 163–64
transnational, vs. intersectionality, 20
feminist agency, 3–4, 12, 14, 18, 20, 29, 60, 82n31
Feminist Studies in Religion Inc. (FSR), 79n8
Fernandes, Leela, 59
Feuer, Alan, 64
fiqh (Islamic jurisprudence), 22
FITNA: Feminist Islamic Trouble Makers of North America, 67
fitne (sedition), 32
Floyd, George, 67, 135
foils, 17, 19, 38–39
Foucault, Michel, 32

Frankfurt school, 151, 152
Friendship House, 146, 147
Frizzell, Deborah, 61
Front Page Magazine, 65

Gantt-Shafer, Jessica, 59–60
Garza, Alicia, 77
gender hierarchies, 13
geographies
    exclusionist, 95–98
    of liberation, 89–90, 114–23,
        124, 161
    semiotics transcending, 98–99
    transgressive, 97, 98, 103–9, 161
    transgressive, boundaries of,
        109–14
Gilligan, Carol, 75
Goldstein, Baruch, 93
Gopstein, Bentzi, 126n20
Goska, Danusha, 65
Graves, Lucia, 70
Great Depression, 143, 146
Greer, Germaine, 163
Grewal, Inderpal, 37–38
Gül, Abdullah, 32
Gürel, Perin, 3–6, 12, 15, 79n5,
    82n31, 106, 112, 161

Hamas, 159
Hammer, Juliane, 7–11, 12, 13,
    103, 111, 161
Haraway, Donna, 166
Harlem
    Caribbean immigrants to, 152
    communism in, 144, 145
    and the Federal Writers Project,
        143–44
    rebellions of 1935, 138
    religion and, in McKay's writing,
        144–46, 147
Harlem Renaissance, 13, 133,
    135–36, 137

Harris-Perry, Melissa, 66
Hartfield, John, 139
Hashash, Yali, 131n69
headscarves. *See* veiling
Hebrew language, 115, 116–17, 122
Hebron, 93, 123
Herut Party, 90
Hidaya, Al-, Mosque, 64–65, 82n45
hijab. *See* veiling
Hill Collins, Patricia, 53, 76–77,
    78n2, 78n3
Hilltop Youth, 96, 102
Holiness movement, 151
homonationalism, 18
Hughes, Langston, 139
human rights, 4
    imperialism and, 24, 36–37, 38,
        39
    language, 31, 35–36, 46n72
    religion and, 3, 19, 24, 33–37,
        134
Human Rights Watch, 71

Ibrahim Mosque massacre, 93
identities
    as coalitions, 76–77
    and intersectionality, 78n3
    reimagining, 114–23
    transforming, 77
ideologies of modernity. *See* mo-
    dernity; secularism
immigration status, 57
imperialism
    and human rights rhetoric, 24,
        36–37, 38, 39
    White thinkers' neglect of, 152
International Holocaust Remem-
    brance Alliance (IHRA), 10
intersectionality, 7, 22
    and critique, 52
    and DEI programs, 84n58
    in feminism, 15, 69–70, 76, 162

and geographies of liberation,
109–14
Jews of Color and, 104, 105–6,
107
liberal appropriation of, 53–54
origins of, 21
poststructural turn in, 113
religion challenging, 8, 13, 14,
51, 52, 54–55, 77–78, 113
and the study of religions, 54
vs. transnational feminism, 20
of the Women's March, 51–53,
59–60, 77–78
Iran, Muslim women in, 3, 17–18,
36, 161
blame assigned to, 35
hijab style of, 32
Kavakçı supported by, 28–30,
31–32, 35–36, 39
and laws concerning clothing,
25–26, 27
rights of, expanded, 26–27
Iranian National Front, 26
Islam
in colonial hierarchy of religions,
54
democracy, women's rights, and,
18
dīn in, 23
EU discomfort with, 33
fiqh in, 22, 23
intersectionality and, 8, 51–53
justice in, 22–23, 35, 54–55
patriarchy within, 58
rejection of feminism in, 45n63
and women's agency, 3–4, 12,
20, 23, 52, 54, 59, 60
and the Women's March, 8, 51
See also Muslim women; Nation
of Islam
Islamic Society of North America,
67

Islamic State (IS), 65
Islamophobia, 55–56
antisemitism and, linked, 97–98,
102
Israeli, 95
See also anti-Muslim hostility
#IslamophobiaIsRacism, 79n10
Israel, 5–6, 15
affective loyalty to, 109
African asylum seekers in,
118–19
alternative possibilities for,
114–23
and antimiscegenation rhetoric,
94, 99, 100, 101–2, 126n20
antisemitism accusations and, 68,
69, 70–71, 74, 105
apartheid system of, 71, 111,
159–60
Basic Law of, 125n12
children kidnapped by, 94, 120
decolonial politics of, 94–95, 97,
103
ethnic cleansing of, 90, 91,
92–93, 101
as extension of the "west," 96
gentrification in, 118–19
and the Jewish Nation-State Law,
91
Kahanism and, 87, 88–90, 91–92,
93, 96, 100–102
liberalism and, 5–6, 91, 94, 96,
100
marginalized Jews in, 5, 6, 87, 94
Mizrahi demographic of, 129n53
and the "rebellion plan," 127n28
settler colonialism in, 5–6,
88–89, 92–94, 99, 104–8, 114,
122–23
sexual politics in, 95–96
theological thinking on, 116–17
as "villa in the jungle," 105

Israel *(cont.)*
    See also Ethiopian Jews; Mizrahi
        Jews; Zionism

Jabotinsky, Vladimir (Ze'ev), 100,
    101
Jackson, Liz, 71
Jennings, Willie James, 143
Jewish feminists, 57, 75
Jewish genocide, 90
Jewishness, pluralistic, 104, 105
Jewish power, 90–95, 96
    and blood purity, 100, 126n20
    decolonizing, 102–3
    Jews of Color challenging, 105–6
    Whiteness and, 99, 102–3, 112,
        121, 122–23
    See also Zionism
Jewish Voice for Peace (JVP), 104,
    106, 122
Jews
    and Arab Jewishness, 97, 115–
        17, 120, 124
    as "buffer communities," 107,
        110, 116
    and the ethos of insecurity, 96,
        100, 103, 106
    European, and Israel, 88, 94
    marginalized, 5, 6, 87, 89, 90,
        103, 109–23
    self-defense of, 100
    self-determination of, 89, 94, 101
    and Whiteness, 75, 94–95, 98,
        99–100, 104
    See also Ashkenormativity; Ethi-
        opian Jews; Mizrahi Jews
Jews of Color (JOC), 90, 94,
    103–9, 125n8
    and disassimilation from White-
        ness, 104, 122–23
    Jewish power challenged by,
        105–6

Mizrahi Jews as, 125n8
    and post-nationalist Jewishness,
        105–6, 107
    White supremacy and, 90, 104–7,
        110–11, 121–22, 124
    See also Ethiopian Jews; Mizrahi
        Jews
Jones, Bridget, 141
"Judeo-Christian" narratives, 90,
    102, 107–8
    alternatives to, 114, 122–24
    anti-Zionist Jews and, 109
    as exclusionary solidarity,
        97–100
    subversion of, 105, 107, 108
justice, solidarity and, 76, 106–7

Kach (This Is the Way) Party, 91
KA.DER, 29
Kahane, Meir, 87, 88–89
    and blood purity, 100, 101–2
    colonialist legacy of, 90, 91–92,
        96
    "Hellenism" critiqued by, 96, 98,
        100
    Jewish Defense League and, 91
Kahanism and Kahanists, 87,
    88–90, 91–92, 93, 96, 100–102
Kaplan, Caren, 37–38
Kavakçi, Merve, 3, 28–32, 39
    ECHR lawsuit of, 33–37
    stripped of citizenship, 47n91
Keshet, Shula, 118–19, 121, 122
Khamenei, Ali, 29
Khatami, Mohammad, 27
Khomeini, Ruhollah, 26
Knafo, Viki, 111

Lang, Marissa, 68
Lavie, Smadar, 88, 109, 111, 116,
    117
Lean, Nathan, 74

Lears, T. J. Jackson, 148
Left activism
  antisemitism and, 75
  and "calling in," 78
  group identities and, 77
  in Israel, 119
  racism in, 144, 146
  and "solidarity" language, 52,
    160
  tensions inherent to, 76
Lehava, 126n20
liberalism
  as boundary to solidarity, 3, 19
  intersectionality appropriated by,
    53–54
  Islamic feminisms and, 23–24
  Israel and, 5–6, 91, 94, 96, 100
  rhetoric of, constraining women,
    18
  and rights discourse, 90
  White supremacy and, 102
liberation
  geographies of, 89–90, 114–23,
    124, 161
  intersectionality and, 109–14
  of Palestine, 87, 89, 109
  Zionism as, 75
Likkud Party, 100–101
l'internationalisme noir, 135–36
Lloyd, Vincent, 149
Lofton, Kathryn, 148
Lorde, Audre, 18, 20, 21, 59
love, 78, 107
Lubin, Alex, 89
Lupo, Joshua, 14, 160
lynching, 139, 146

Maddrell, Avril, 60, 61–62
Magid, Shaul, 91–92, 96
Mahmood, Saba, 34, 56–57
Mallory, Tamika, 8, 10, 58, 60, 63,
  67

antisemitism accusations against,
  68, 69, 72–73, 76
Nation of Islam and, 8, 10,
  72–73, 76, 112
March2Justice, 64–65
March On, 70
Martin de Porres, 148
martyrdom, fantasies of, 165
Marxist criticism, 8, 12, 81n30
"master's house," the, 6, 18, 20, 31,
  37–39
McAlister, Melani, 4, 6, 11, 111
McCain, Meghan, 72–73
McKay, Claude, 133, 135, 136
  Catholic conversion of, 140, 141,
    142, 147, 148, 152
  Catholicism romanticized by,
    136, 137, 142, 147, 148, 152
  as exile, 151–52
  Francophone reception of, 140–41
  international influences on, 138,
    140–41, 142, 146–47, 148–49,
    151–52
  legacy of, 152–53
  racism experienced by, 138–39
  spiritual themes of, 139, 140,
    141, 144–47, 150
  works, 137–38, 139, 140, 144–
    46, 147, 153
  —*Amiable with Big Teeth*, 144,
    145–46, 153
  —*Banjo*, 140–41
  —*Harlem: Negro Metropolis*,
    144–45
  —"If We Must Die," 153
McLaren, Margaret A., 37
Mehager, Tom, 113–14
Méndez, Mariá José, 102
Mernissi, Fatima, 21
Middle East
  Jewish connections to, 114–17,
    124

Middle East *(cont.)*
  pluralistic history of, 88
  See also Israel; Palestine
Miéville, China, 165–66
Miles, Caitlin, 59–60
Mizrahi Jews, 11, 124
  anti-Arab, 120
  and Arabic language, 114–17
  attention to struggles of, 117–20
  "bureaucratic torture of," 109–10
  construction of identity of, 114
  definition of, 124n2
  as demographic, 129n53
  feminist organizing of, 118–19
  Israeli discrimination against, 94,
    110, 118–19
  Israeli Jews as, 117
  lack of solidarity of, with Pales-
    tinians, 5–6, 88, 95, 106, 110–
    11, 112–14, 116
  and Mizrahi feminism, 5–6, 88,
    109–14, 118–19, 131n69
  self-alienation of, 5, 110, 112–13,
    116
modernity, 13–14
  and enchantment, 134–35,
    148–53
  and Jewish Whiteness, 98
  violence of, 138, 139–40, 142, 150
Moghadam, Valentine, 45n63
Mohanty, Chandra Talpade, 21, 24,
  38
Moore, Brenna, 11–13, 161
Moore, Cecilia, 147–48
Morris, Susana M., 57
Moss, Pamela, 60, 61–62
Mueller, Kayla, 65
Mujerista feminism, 57
Muslim feminists, 82n31
  in a "double bind," 58, 66–67
  feminism reshaped by, 57–58
  suspicion of, 55

Muslim women
  activists, Muslim reception of,
    79n7
  agency of, 12, 20, 23, 52, 54, 59
  American women writing about,
    163–64
  broken solidarities between,
    17–18
  fiqh appealed to by, 22, 23
  liberal rhetoric used by, 18
  as objects vs. agents, 59
  orientalist views of, 23, 36–37
  public piety of, liberalism and,
    19–20, 34–35, 37
  "saving," 36–37, 56–57, 60
  See also Iran, Muslim women in;
    Turkey, Muslim women in

Nakba, the, 91, 93, 96, 113–14,
  159–60
Narayan, Uma, 22
Nardal, Paulette, 135, 141, 147
Nash, Jennifer C., 20, 78, 78n2,
  84n58, 164
Nasser, Gamal Abdel, 161
nationalism, 15
  antisemitism in, 97, 102
  Catholicism resisting, 133–34,
    136
  in Iran and Turkey, 24–25
  Islamophobia in, 95
  Judaism beyond, 108–9
  origins of, 7
  religion, race, and, 3, 97, 101–2,
    114
  See also Zionism
Nation of Islam, 8, 10, 72, 73, 112
nation-states
  as barriers to solidarity, 3–4, 9,
    13, 17–18, 29–30, 110–12
  and human-rights protections,
    47n91

instability of, 29–30
and post- or antinationalism, 103,
    108–9
problematizing, 22
religion used by, 24–25
transgressing boundaries of, 89
See also transnational feminism;
    transnationalism
Nehru, Jawaharlal, 161
neoliberalism, 105, 121
Netanyahu, Benjamin, 92, 95, 96,
    115, 126n22
New York City, 143–46
9/11, 18–19, 23
North-South solidarity, 3–4
Noy, Orly, 117

Occupy Wall Street, 61
Olson, Robert, 31–32
Omer, Atalia, 5–6, 9, 11, 12, 14,
    104, 160, 161
Organization of Islamic University
    Students, 36
orientalism, 3, 6, 23, 56, 88, 94,
    109, 124
    blood purity and, 100
    enchantment and, 134
    Palestinian suffering and, 98
    sexual politics and, 95–96
    Zionism and, 94, 95–96, 98, 101,
        105
Otzma Yehudit (Jewish Power),
    90–95
    anti-miscegenation rhetoric of,
        126n20
    Netanyahu's alliance with, 92,
        96, 100–101
    racism of, 92, 102, 103, 122,
        125n9
Ouda, Ayman, 119–20

Palestine, 52, 53, 62

bias against, 75
Black American solidarity with,
    104–5, 121, 124
dispossession of, 88, 90–91,
    92–93, 94, 102, 119, 159–60
as "enemy," 90, 125n9
Indigeneity of, 94
Kahanism and, 91–92, 102
liberation of, 87, 89, 109
as litmus test, 9–10, 89, 98, 107,
    109, 111, 118, 124
and the Palestinian genocide, 104
and police violence against Pal-
    estinians, 119–20
as symbol, 5, 15, 105, 109, 124
See also Sarsour, Linda
Perez, Carmen, 58, 60, 63, 64, 67, 76
"perpetual primitive," the, 137,
    148
pinkwashing, 9, 18, 95–96
police brutality, 10
political imagination, decolonizing,
    89, 122–23, 124
postcolonial feminism, 21, 38
postcolonialism, 88
poststructural feminism, 21
power
    critiques of, 102
    in discourses of enchantment,
        134
    distribution, 67, 77
    loci of, 38–39
    vs. powerlessness, 123
    religious critiques of, 150
    scales of, 24
Presley, Rachel, 59, 61
Presswood, Alane, 59, 61
Primo de Rivera, Miguel, 143
prophetic Judaism, 106, 107,
    108–9, 122
Protestantism
    Black, 144, 152

Protestantism *(cont.)*
  and "ordinary life," 149, 150
  racism and, 136, 137, 138, 139,
    142, 143, 147
Pruzan-Jørgensen, Julie Elisabeth, 23
public order, 34, 35
"purity tests," 6

Qudosi, Shireen, 65–66, 82n47
queer feminism, 57

race
  gender intersecting with, 12–13,
    53
  hierarchies of, 67
  nationalism, religion, and, 3, 97,
    101–2, 114
  White thinkers neglecting, 152
race riots, 138–39
racialization
  of African asylum seekers,
    118–19
  Christianity's role in, 55, 136
  in Israel, 120–21
  of Muslims, 55–56, 83n50
  in progressive secularism, 136,
    142, 144, 146
  and racialized subjects, 17, 19
  of religion, 8, 55–56, 90, 97–100,
    107, 120, 134
  revealing the circuits of, 89
  of secularism vs. religiosity, 134
  solidarity through analysis of, 11,
    12
racism
  in progressive secularism, 136,
    142–43, 144, 145–46
  Protestant, 136, 137, 138, 139,
    142, 143, 147
Rafsanjani, Faezeh Hashemi, 29,
  31, 32, 35, 36, 39, 45n63

Rahnavard, Zahra, 29, 30, 31, 35,
  45n63
"rebellion plan," the, 127n28
reform in Iran vs. Turkey, 30–31
relativism, 38
religion
  Black, 136, 137, 143–46, 148
  Black syncretic, 144
  emancipatory features of, 8, 147–
    48, 150
  as embodied, 14
  as false consciousness, 8, 11
  feminist suspicion of, 14, 55, 60,
    81n30
  freedom of, 34
  in Harlem, 144–46, 147
  hierarchy of, 54
  and human rights, 3, 19, 24,
    33–37, 134
  intersectional analysis of, 2
  liberalism and, 19–20
  modern constructions of, 10
  modernist legacies of, 4
  in nationalist discourse, 2, 4, 35
  nation-states using, 24–25
  and orientalism, 134
  politics and, 150–51
  race, nationalism, and, 3, 97,
    101–2, 114
  racialization of, 8, 55–56, 90,
    97–100, 107, 120, 134
  reclaiming marginalized voices
    in, 153
  solidarity enabled by, 161
  White categorization of, 69, 134,
    136–37, 148, 150–51
religious agency, 3–4, 12, 14,
  22–23, 29–30, 60, 67
religious feminists, 55. *See also*
  Jewish feminists; Mizrahi
  Jews; Muslim feminists

Religious Nationalist Party,
100–101
reproductive rights, 62
Reza Shah Pahlavi, 24, 25, 26, 27
rhetoric
human rights, imperialism and,
36–37, 38, 39
intersectionality reduced to,
53–54
liberal, women constrained by, 18
universalist, 31
Rorty, Richard, 19
Ryan, Peter, 81n23

Saadawi, Nawal El, 21, 111, 163
Sahin v. *Turkey*, 33
Said, Edward, 56, 88, 151, 152
Sanders, Bernie, 74
Santos, Boaventura de Sousa, 113
Sarsour, Linda, 8, 10, 51, 52–53,
60, 79n7
activist experience of, 64
antisemitism accusations against,
68–69, 72, 74, 76
Al-Hidaya Mosque and, 64–65,
82n45
intersectionality of, 63–64
media representations of, 62,
65–66
memoir of, 53, 64–65, 68
Muslim feminist identification of,
58, 62, 63–64
response of, to criticism, 66
self-representations of, 51, 53,
55, 58, 63–65
threats against, 74
Savransky, Martin, 113
Schomburg, Arturo, 143
Scott, Joan, 78
secularism
as barrier to solidarity, 13

and denial of piety, 3–4
vs. enchanted religiosity, 11–13,
133–38, 142–43, 144–47,
148–53
of feminism, assumed, 22–23
optimism of, 136
as product of the Christian west,
134
racism and, 136, 142–43, 144,
145–46
reform movements tending
toward, 23, 31, 34
and the "unmanaged religious,"
149
Sedghi, Hamideh, 45n63
Seedat, Fatima, 57–58
seeing beyond divisions, 89, 111
Senghor, Léopold Sédar, 141
Serwer, Adam, 73
sex, 163–64
Sheehi, Stephen, 74
Sheikh Jarrah, 91, 93, 116, 159
Shemsai, Nasibeh, 37
Shohat, Ella, 88
Shook, Teresa, 63
Shuster-Eliassi, Noam, 114–15, 117
Six-Day War, 112
Slabodsky, Santiago, 113
Sluzker-Amran, Sapir, 117–18
Smith, Tommie, 160
sociology of absences, 113
solidarity
affective elements of, 159, 160
and affinity groups, 73–74, 76
Black transnational, 11–13, 133,
136, 140–41
boundaries to, 4, 106, 110–12
vs. coalition building, 62
concept of, as ethically neutral,
14
and critique, 51, 61–62, 73–74

solidarity *(cont.)*
  definition of, 52, 60–61
  emancipatory, 3–4, 5, 7–9, 12,
    15, 114–23
  ephemeral, 12, 134
  evangelical, 164–65
  exclusionist geography of,
    95–98, 106, 160–61
  fragmented, 4, 5–6, 7–8, 12, 52
  Judaism of, 108–9
  and justice, 76, 106–7
  nation-states as barriers to, 3–4,
    9, 13, 17–18, 29–30, 110–12
  protest linked to, 61
  refused, 31–32, 166
  regardless of subjectivity, 89
  religion enabling, 161
  religious discourse affecting,
    2–3, 8–9, 60
  of "siblings in Christ," 164–65
  unimaginable, 6, 12, 160–61
  unrealized, 4, 5, 7, 9, 12, 159,
    160–61
  See also South-South solidarity
Sorett, Josef, 13, 142
South-South solidarity
  European framework of, 112, 121
  failures of, 3, 5–6, 11, 87–89, 98,
    106, 108–9, 111–13
  in the Middle East, 87, 88–89,
    98, 108, 109, 110–13, 119–22
Spivak, Gayatri Chakravorty, 76,
  85n77
"state feminism," 25
strategic essentialism, 76–77,
  85n77
structural critique, 20, 29, 39
Sukarno, 161

Tajali, Mona, 46n72
Tarry, Ellen, 144, 146, 147, 148,
  150–51, 152

Taylor, Charles, 149–50
Terman, Rochelle, 38, 58
"Third World solidarity," 161–62
"Third World Women," 21–22, 38,
  163–64
Thurman, Howard, 146
Tohidi, Nayereh, 31
Tolstoy, Leo, 140, 141
Tometi, Opal, 77
transnational feminism, 37–39
  as critique of broken solidarities,
    20–24
  definition of, 19
  vs. intersectionality, 20
  and LGBTQI identities, 22
  the local and the global in, 22,
    24, 38–39
  in Muslim contexts, 22–24
  origins of, 21
  post-9/11, 18–19
  western imperialism and, 20, 38
transnationalism
  from above vs. from below, 22
  Christian, 133–34, 164–65
  foreclosing, 18, 32, 103
  and relativism, 38
Trump, Donald, 7, 66, 126n22
Turkey
  coup in, 26
  and the EU, 32–33
  human rights reforms in, 33
  laïcism in, 18–19, 26–28, 29, 30,
    32, 33–34, 39
  protests against the veil ban in,
    27
  "sedition" in, 32
  veil banned in, 4, 23–24, 25–26,
    27–29, 33, 39
Turkey, Muslim women in, 3,
  17–18, 161
  laïcism punishing, 34
  and *laïcist* feminists, 27, 29–30

male politicians and, 32
Turner, Victor, 151
Tzedek Chicago, 108–9

'ulamā (religious scholars), 25
UN Decade of Women, 163–64
United States
    Civil Rights movement, 31, 99,
        104
    Jews of Color in, 104
    Muslims racialized in, 56
    Muslim women victimized in, 57
    racism of, 138–39, 143
unity, tensions masked by, 62
universalist rhetoric, 31, 32, 35, 36,
    134
"unseeing," 165–66

Vahid-Dastjerdi, Marzieh, 28
Vajrathon, Mallica, 21
Vassell, Saheed, 68
veiling, 3, 164
    as "authentic," 27
    bans on, 4, 23–24, 25–26
    Muslim women's identity and,
        23, 57
    and western imperialism, 22
    in Women's March posters, 58
violence, 20, 38, 54, 150, 151
    anti-Black, 136, 137–39
    campaigns against, 54, 73
    Jewish settler, 93, 96, 100–101
    of modernity, 138, 139–40, 142,
        150
    against Muslim women, 57
    police, against Ethiopian Jews,
        10, 119–20
    police, against Palestinians,
        119–20
    Protestantism associated with,
        142–43, 149
    White women protected from, 77

virtuosity, 13

Walker, Alice, 80n17
Wallis, Cara, 59–60
"war on terror," 18–19, 38, 57
We Are Not Here to Be Bystanders
    (Sarsour), 53, 64–65, 68
Weber, Charlotte, 56
Weber, Max, 134
Weisenfeld, Judith, 152
"west," the
    as ideological culprit, 3–4, 6
    Israel as extension of, 96
    as refugee culture, 151–52
    secularism as product of, 134
    universalizing tendencies of, 98
White Christian nationalism, 7–11,
    12, 102, 126n22
White feminism
    and anti-Muslim hostility, 56–57,
        60
    colonialist complicity of, 56
    correctives to, 20–21
    exclusivity of, 162
    hegemonic vision of, 3
    non-White women in, 21–22, 23
    sisterhood model of, 4, 15,
        20–22
    and the Women's March, 7–11,
        59, 69, 77
Whiteness
    American colonialism and, 99
    antisemitism and, 69, 75, 99–100
    Jewish disassimilation from, 98,
        99–100, 102–3, 110, 124
    Jews and, 75, 94–95, 98, 99–100,
        104
    and "Judeo-Christian tradition,"
        99, 108
    and the White gaze, 140
White supremacy, 10, 67, 89, 90,
    94, 107

American Jews and, 104, 105, 106
global operation of, 99–100
and marginalized Jews, 90, 104–7, 110–11, 121–22, 124
Thomistic thinking and, 143
Zionism and, 94, 99–100, 102, 104–8, 110, 120, 121–24
womanism, 22, 57, 80n17
women
  bodies of, policed, 7
  expanding opportunities of, 29, 45n63
  as symbols of modernity, 25
  See also Muslim women
Women's March, 7–11, 13, 51, 52–53, 161
  accused of antisemitism, 8, 10–11, 51–52, 68–69, 75–76
  Black women's responses to, 59
  criticism of, 51, 52–53, 58–62, 65–70, 72–75
  entry points into, 59–60
  as event vs. movement, 76, 77
  first leadership team of, 68–69
  internal criticism of, 66–67
  intersectionality of, 51–53, 59–60, 77–78
  Jewish women distancing from, 75
  new leadership team of, 69–72
  and Occupy Wall Street, 61
  organizing, 59, 63–68
  posters, 58, 60, 81n22
  racial tensions in, 70
  religion and, 59–60, 81n23
  scholarship on, 58–62, 81n23
  "tributary streams" of, 59, 63
  Twitter discussions of, 61
  White feminism and, 7–11, 59, 69, 77

World Conference on Women (1995), 22
Wright, Richard, 161
Wruble, Vanessa, 73

Yemenite children, kidnapping of, 94
Yerday, Efrat, 119, 120–21, 122, 123
Yosef, Shaul Abdallah, 116

Zionism, 9–10, 103
  antisemitism and, 95–98
  Christian, 74–75, 92, 96–97, 101, 128n30
  critiques of, 51–52, 53, 69, 70–71, 95, 103–9, 122–24
  and ethos of insecurity, 96, 100, 101, 103
  Euro-Zionism, 94, 96, 101, 110, 113, 121–22
  Jewish ethics opposed to, 107
  as liberatory, 75
  and the longing for Zion, 106
  and metaphorizing Zion, 107–9, 122–23
  and orientalism, 94, 95–96, 98, 101, 105
  racism and, 94, 101–2
  settler colonialism and, 5–6, 88–89, 92–94, 99, 104–8, 114, 122–23
  socialization in, 110, 112, 113, 120
  and White supremacy, 94, 99–100, 102, 104–8, 110, 120, 121–24
Zochrot, 113–14

ATALIA OMER

is professor of religion, conflict, and peace studies
at the University of Notre Dame. She is the author of *Days of Awe:
Reimagining Jewishness in Solidarity with Palestinians* and *When
Peace is Not Enough: How the Israeli Peace Camp Thinks about
Religion, Nationalism, and Justice.*

JOSHUA LUPO

is an editor and writer for Contending Modernities at the Kroc Institute
for International Peace Studies, University of Notre Dame.

CPSIA information can be obtained
at www.ICGtesting.com
Printed in the USA
LVHW080305271222
735766LV00011B/591

9 780268 203863